Take Heart
Daily Devotions to Deepen Your Faith

DAVID POWLISON

RUTH CASTLE, EDITOR

New
Growth
Press

newgrowthpress.com

New Growth Press, Greensboro, NC 27401
newgrowthpress.com
Copyright © 2022 by Nancy Powlison

Unless otherwise indicated, Scripture quotations are taken from the ESV® Bible (The Holy Bible, English Standard Version®). ESV® Text Edition: 2016. Copyright © 2001 by Crossway, a publishing ministry of Good News Publishers. Used by permission. All rights reserved.

Scripture quotations marked NIV are taken from THE HOLY BIBLE, NEW INTER-NATIONAL VERSION®, NIV® Copyright © 1973, 1978, 1984, 2011 by Biblica, Inc.® Used by permission. All rights reserved worldwide.

Scripture quotations marked NASB are taken from New American Standard Bible®, Copyright © 1960, 1971, 1977, 1995, 2020 by The Lockman Foundation. All rights reserved.

Excerpts taken from *God's Grace in Your Suffering* Copyright © 2018 are used by permission of Crossway, a publishing ministry of Good News Publishers, Wheaton, IL 60187, www.crossway.org.

Excerpts taken from *Seeing with New Eyes* ISBN 9780875526089 are used by permission of P&R Publishing, Phillipsburg, NJ 08865, www.prpbooks.com.

Cover Design: Faceout Books, faceoutstudio.com
Interior Design and Typesetting: Gretchen Logterman

ISBN: 978-1-64507-273-7 (Print)
ISBN: 978-1-64507-274-4 (eBook)

Library of Congress Cataloging-in-Publication Data on file
LCCN 2022007649

Printed in India

30 29 28 27 26 25 24 23   2 3 4 5 6

Introduction

What a wonderful irony that I have the privilege of writing the introduction to this daily devotional. Little did David know that he would be publishing books posthumously! And little did I know that after all my grumbling and complaining about David pulling all-nighters for writing deadlines, this little book would shine redeeming light into my heart. God knows how I laugh now with Abraham's wife at the birth of this "impossible Isaac," the brainchild of Barbara Juliani and New Growth Press. It has been a long labor of love for Ruth Castle and Barbara J (as David used to call his longtime editor and friend) who listened to sermons, lectures, conference talks and interviews, combed through books and articles, and added prayers and favorite hymns, as they compiled 366 days of devotions. Now you can sit beside David with your coffee in hand, as I was privileged to do for forty-three years of our life together. And you can jump with him, as I did, into the living water of God's Word, finding strength and courage in weakness and friendship and faith for the journey.

By the end of his life, David felt as at home in the Word of God as he did in the Pacific waters of his childhood. Three months before his homegoing, we flew out to say goodbye to his family in Hawaii. One spectacular day we kayaked out to the off-shore islands near his home. Huge breaking surf wrapped the rocks that day, as we hiked around one of the islands to the lagoon on the other side to jump in. Due to the large break, it became too dicey for me and some of the others to continue, so we settled ourselves in the balcony of high rocks and watched the glory splash below. Our son Peter, his cousin CJ, and David continued to the lagoon. But when they reached it, the two strong, athletic young men raised their eyebrows and decided to sit out, while David prepared to jump in. His teenage surfing-self kicked in, reading the wave action with an eagle eye, timing his moves until he was perfectly poised, waiting and waiting again until finally he took heart and flight into the foaming turquoise swirl below—trusting God to bear him up.

For David, jumping into God's Word had a similar challenge and adventure to it. To know the living God—diving into his myriad nuanced Personality, stepping carefully into controversial passages and unpacking them with wisdom, waiting and waiting for insight before jumping to premature conclusions, trusting God to bear him up. David "took heart" in an ocean of suffering over the last twenty years of his life. Through open heart surgery, five cancer surgeries, sleep apnea, and chronic fatigue, he knew great weakness. But out of his weakness came sermons, books, blogs, lectures, conferences, curriculum, and journal articles. Through these devotional readings, you can join him as he works out his friendship with God. As the Beatitudes begin by recognizing weakness, so this devotional begins. And each devotional has one or two sentences italicized to encourage you throughout your day to "take heart."

In the following journal entry, David faces his weakness, unbelief, discouragement, and negativity over the seeming impossibility of finishing his doctoral thesis. With 2 Corinthians 4:17–18 in mind, he moves from despondent weakness to victorious doxology.

Journal 1995

Nan and I spoke about understanding ourselves and each other last night. If I harbor resentment at the PhD process—is it residual sloth from the 60's, pride that does not want to work on schedule, or am I afraid of the judgment of superiors and peers, the fear of responsibility and success or failure at being shown up as a fraud?? What of it?

All this is light affliction and mild darkness, and secondary confusion.

Maybe I'll never figure it out.

BUT in You, O God of glory, are riches of splendor—the disk of Andromeda, 100,000 light years to cross her billions of suns, the God whose raiment is incomprehensible light . . . I love You. My Savior who loved, who taught, who suffered, who died, who lives and lives and lives in the power of indestructible Life. You are truly what a human being is. Good beyond incalculable goodness, You bring life out of death, mercy instead of judgment. You have entered our lives, become one of us, the man Jesus, YAWEH in the flesh, in whom is found wonder upon wonder and all true. You have loved with exceeding long-suffering and overflowing generosity a wandering, confused, and distractible race; and You have placed Your life in substitution to make propitiation for us for whom sin is as breathing and heartbeat. You are merciful and Your beauty is radiant. I love You.

Resolved:
To do the dissertation for Love, Learning, Growth, Integrity, Joy, Partnership, and Excellence.

Post Tenebras Lux
"After the darkness, Light"

It is my deepest hope that as you dive into the light of God's Word with David, you take heart and go deep.

May God bear you up.

Nan Powlison
February 2022

January 1

As for me, I am poor and needy,
but the Lord takes thought for me.
You are my help and my deliverer;
do not delay, O my God! —Psalm 40:17

"Weakness" is a comprehensive description of our human condition. We are perishable. We are mortal. We face a multitude of afflictions in our lives. And we are sinful, bent from the heart toward pride, self-righteousness, fear of man, and a multitude of desires and fears that beset us. The mercies of God meet us in this comprehensive condition of weakness.

To admit weakness is so countercultural to people who want to say, "We are STRONG!" and "You can do it!" On the contrary, *we are fundamentally weak. That weakness is a most unusual door into all the ways God enables us to be strong.*

Being unafraid to be publicly weak was true of King David. The end of Psalm 40 has always resonated deeply with me. This psalm contains a great deal of fruitful ministry and joyful worship, yet David summarizes himself this way: "As for me, I am poor and needy, but the Lord takes thought for me." David's strength grew out of his comprehensive sense of weakness, and his confidence in God's strength.

My deepest hope for you is that in both your personal life and your ministry to others, you would be unafraid to be publicly weak as the doorway to the strength of God himself.

January 2

"But seek first the kingdom of God and his righteousness, and all these things will be added to you." —Matthew 6:33

God is very concerned that we seek him, his kingdom, and his righteousness. We are to pursue him and be oriented to him because we trust he's going to take care of the other things.

What are you pursuing? What are you after? What are you obsessing about? *The answers to those questions will correlate with what you're worrying about, because if you're pursuing with your whole heart the wrong things, you're going to worry about them. Only God can be pursued wholeheartedly without worry or anxiety.*

The biggest question cuts the deepest: What do you love? We're simply turning the first Great Commandment on its head and letting it serve as a mirror into which we look. We're called to love him with all that we are. What are you loving? Who are you loving? Are you loving pleasure, money, or control? Are you loving being liked? These questions cut deep, and your answers affect everything you feel and think, how you treat people, and the way you come into a conversation.

God speaks, and those who have ears to hear, hear that question. Which voices are you tuning into?

January 3

For God, who said, "Let light shine out of darkness," has shone in our hearts to give the light of the knowledge of the glory of God in the face of Jesus Christ. —2 Corinthians 4:6

People change when the Holy Spirit brings the love of God to their hearts through the gospel. Whoever receives the Spirit of adoption as God's child learns to cry out, "Abba, Father." People change when they see that they are responsible for what they believe about God. People change when truth becomes clearer and brighter than previous life experience. We change when our ears hear and our eyes see what God tells us about himself (Psalm 103:10–13; Isaiah 49:13–16).

God is in the business of changing people's minds; he is not hindered by distortions. He can reveal himself, "[shining] in our hearts to give us the light of the knowledge of the glory of God in the face of Christ" (2 Corinthians 4:6). Life experience is not supreme; neither are the lies that people believe. God is supreme, and he alone trumps what we bring to the table.

Your life experiences do not have to dictate your view of reality. On the contrary; disappointing people and experiences can make you long to know the real King, Shepherd, Master, Savior, and God! Ask the Lord to make himself known to you today.

January 4

Jesus said to her, "I am the resurrection and the life. Whoever believes in me, though he die, yet shall he live, and everyone who lives and believes in me shall never die. Do you believe this?" —John 11:25-26

How do you know that the promises God makes to you are true? How do you know that the living God gives true, substantial hope? Because Jesus defeated death. As a willing and sinless substitute, he died in our place on the cross. And God raised him to life and joy. He is alive. Peter explains it this way: "Praise be to the God and Father of our Lord Jesus Christ! In his great mercy he has given us new birth into a living hope through the resurrection of Jesus Christ from the dead, and into an inheritance that can never perish, spoil or fade—kept in heaven for you" (1 Peter 1:3–4). Your Father in heaven has great mercy. He makes us alive. He gives us realistic joy and hope.

Jesus is alive! His resurrection is his guarantee that you can live in real hope. *Your hope is not based on a pipe dream that changed circumstances, passing of time, a new set of friends, or even giving up will somehow cure how you feel. He gives living hope based on the physical reality of the resurrection of Jesus Christ.* Because the resurrection happened and Jesus is alive, well, and at work, your story can end in life.

January 5

Even though I walk through the valley of the shadow of death,
I will fear no evil,
for you are with me;
your rod and your staff,
they comfort me. —Psalm 23:4

What will give you the most pleasure in life? What pleasure will not dim through all the changes in your life? The pleasure of knowing God and being known by him. You step into that pleasure by coming to Jesus for mercy and grace. You grow in your relationship with him by making that call for mercy a daily, lifelong habit. *Your own inability to deal with your habitual sins is God's mercy to you, because it forces you to go to God for the help you need.* As you go to God, use his Word to guide your relationship.

Psalm 23 has been my prayer for many years. Praying through it is one way to experience the pleasure of a growing relationship with God. Start by reading it out loud.

Notice how the psalmist takes hold of suffering. He looks the shadow of death right in the eye: "I will fear no evil" (v. 4). He knows the Lord is with him. Notice how he switches from talking about God in the third person ("he") to the second person ("you") in an amazing expression of intimacy with God. The last two lines say that goodness and lovingkindness are literally chasing him! "I am being pursued by your goodness and mercy all my life, and then I will live with you forever." This is the supreme pleasure.

January 6

"A new commandment I give to you, that you love one another: just as I have loved you, you also are to love one another. By this all people will know that you are my disciples, if you have love for one another."
—John 13:34–35

The Bible gives us two pictures of loving relationships. The leading theme, the richer theme, involves the people you truly enjoy—your beloved brother, sister, wife, the child you hold in your arms, and dear friends. In heaven you will see face-to-face the One you love, the supreme Person. But heaven is also a place full of other relationships you enjoy. These people love you without pretense, competition, or manipulation.

But side by side with that call to joyous intimacy is a call to get out of your comfort zone. The harder call of the Bible is to love enemies, strangers, people who are different from you, and those who are needy, sinful, and broken.

This call comes for two reasons. First, it tests whether you are turning the innocent pleasures of intimacy into a stained pleasure. Are you and the people you enjoy turning into a clique? Second, the call tests whether we are willing to widen the circle of intimacy so that enemies become friends, strangers become like family, and someone you don't know becomes like a dear sister. The goal is always the simple, joyous relationship with others—the mutual affection and give-and-take. *God calls you to widen the circle of your friendships, and to avoid making a god out of those who bring you the greatest pleasure. Doing these two things will fill your life with the pleasure of relationships with others.*

January 7

The Lord is near. Do not be anxious about anything, but in every
situation, by prayer and petition, with thanksgiving, present your
requests to God. And the peace of God, which transcends all
understanding, will guard your hearts and your minds in Christ Jesus.
—Philippians 4:5-7 NIV

The Lord has something to say about what you are going through every single day. Scripture has been designed by God himself to connect to the reality of human experience. But how do you make those connections? Start with the pithy, straightforward passages of Scripture. Philippians 4:6, for example, says, "Do not be anxious about anything, but in everything by prayer and supplication with thanksgiving let your requests be made known to God." What promise could ever anchor you, so that you can make such a response? One of them is tucked in the little verse right before Philippians 4:6. Verse 5 says, "the Lord is near." Anxiety is the experience that you're all alone in a world that's too big for you. You feel anxious because you can't control your circumstances. But if the Lord is near, everything changes. You aren't alone, and the one who is in control, to order and provide, he's near and he cares for you and he is involved.

Starting with these basic promises reminds you in the midst of your day that the Lord is with you. *Simple promises, taken to heart, get you and God on the same page with each other.*

January 8

"Pray then like this: 'Our Father in heaven, hallowed be your name. Your kingdom come, your will be done, on earth as it is in heaven. Give us this day our daily bread, and forgive us our debts, as we also have forgiven our debtors. And lead us not into temptation, but deliver us from evil.'"
—Matthew 6:9-13

Broadly speaking, there are three emphases of biblical prayer: circumstantial prayers, wisdom prayers, and kingdom prayers.

Sometimes we ask God to *change our circumstances*: heal the sick, give daily bread, protect from suffering and evil, make our leaders just, convert friends and family, make our work prosper, provide me with a spouse, quiet this storm, send rain, give us a child.

Sometimes we ask God to *change us*: deepen my faith, teach us to love each other, forgive sins, make me wise, make us know you better, help me to sanctify you in my heart, don't let me dishonor you, help us understand Scripture, teach me to encourage others.

Sometimes we ask God to *change everything by revealing himself* more fully, magnifying his glory and rule. Your kingdom come, your will be done on earth as it is in heaven, be exalted above the heavens, let your glory be over all of the earth, come Lord Jesus.

In the Lord's Prayer you see examples of all three, tightly interwoven. The Lord's kingdom involves the destruction of our sins and sufferings. His reign causes a flourishing of love's wisdom and a wealth of situational blessing. *Prayers for God to change me and my circumstances are requests that he reveal his glory and mercy on the stage of this world.*

January 9

His divine power has granted to us all things that pertain to life and
godliness, through the knowledge of him who called us to his own glory
and excellence, by which he has granted to us his precious and very
great promises, so that through them you may become partakers of the
divine nature, having escaped from the corruption that is in the world
because of sinful desire. —2 Peter 1:3–4

The Spirit and the Word recognize that we are a tangled web, individually and together. We are dark even to ourselves, hard to understand, slow to change. Every one of us has stubborn inconsistencies and blind spots. Jeremiah says that our hearts are deceitful and wonders who could possibly understand it (Jeremiah 17:9). *The only one who does thoroughly understand us is God. Sometimes he helps us to change rapidly. But he usually intervenes slowly—to transform how a person thinks, loves, fears, wants, and trusts on a scale of years and decades, over a lifetime.*

The reorientation of our hearts is a slow road. We will only be made wholly right when we see Jesus face-to-face. Someone's behaviors matter and the deep waters of the inner person also matter. Complexities do not erase simplicities, and vice versa. The ability to attend to both is much to be desired, and calls for humility, patience, and an abiding awareness of need for greater wisdom and skill.

People tend to evade personal responsibility by blame-shifting and self-justification. The courage to face hard things grows slowly in people who suffer greatly. From many angles, our Father states and restates his love for us in Christ. People need to hear that because it is by promises that we change (2 Peter 1:4). God sympathetically describes and illumines the varied challenges of tough circumstances. He invites our faith. Because he is merciful and patient, we learn to relate our needs and joys honestly to him.

January 10

If your law had not been my delight,
I would have perished in my affliction.
I will never forget your precepts,
for by them you have given me life. —Psalm 119:92-93

Psalm 119 is personal prayer. It's talking to God, not teaching about God. We hear what a man says out loud in God's presence: his joyous pleasure, vocal need, open adoration, blunt requests, candid assertions, deep struggles, and fiercely good intentions. The various words for the Word appear once in each verse, but I-you words appear about four times per verse. That's a 4:1 ratio and emphasis.

So Psalm 119 is actually not about the topic of getting Scripture into your life. Instead, it is the honest words that erupt when what God says gets into you. It's not an exhortation to Bible study; it's an outcry of faith. Psalm 119 is the thoughtful outcry that rises when real life meets real God.

So this is what we hear in Psalm 119. A person who has listened opens his heart to the Person who has spoken.

How did the psalmist learn to be so outspoken to God? He listened to what God said in the rest of the Bible and lived it. *The Lord says who he is, and is who he says. The Lord says what he does, and does what he says. Faith listens, experiences what is true, and talks back in simple sentences.*

We tend to be busy, noisy, distractible people in a busy, noisy, distracting world. This psalm teaches us to say, "I need time to listen and think if I'm ever to converse with God."

January 11

And he answered, "You shall love the Lord your God with all your heart and with all your soul and with all your strength and with all your mind, and your neighbor as yourself." —Luke 10:27

Jesus summarized the Bible's goal in this way: Love God with your whole heart. Love your neighbor as yourself. God's law is a picture of how a human being becomes truly human (Galatians 5:6; 1 Timothy 1:5).

It's the way life is meant to be. The God of the universe calls us to love him with utter devotion. When I forget my Shepherd, I orient my life around another god and love some good gift more than the Giver. God, who made people in his image, calls us to love each other with the same fierce concern that we look out for our own interests. When I forget, I get frustrated and hostile, or fearful and withdrawn. When I remember, I get fiercely caring. Will I love my self-interest and become wholly indifferent to the interests of my neighbors whose cars surround me? I am commanded to the sanity of love, and it lays my heart bare.

The law of love is a mirror showing us who we are. It is also a lamp, lighting the way to where we ought to be.

January 12

Rock of ages cleft for me
Let me hide myself in Thee
Rock of ages, cleft for me
Let me hide myself in Thee
Let the water and the blood
From thy riven side which flowed
Oh, be of sin the double cure
Cleanse me from its guilt and power
—Augustus Toplady, "Rock of Ages"

Every facet of the grace of God is tailored to make us new when we are angry, critical, fearful, and proud. In place of living deformed lives, we find the "double cure" for sin's guilt and power—those who seek Jesus find true forgiveness. In Jesus, those who ask receive the Spirit from our generous Father. We will be reformed into the image of the Son who lived and died for us that we might live for him.

What must you do? Angry people must turn and seek God. James 4:6–10 captures this relational reality called repentant faith. We turn in need to the Person willing and able to help. The Lord offers a radically "vertical" solution for the radically vertical problem of the heart. It is striking how God-centered this solution is. Submit to God and resist the devil. Draw near to God. The proud devil flees as God draws near to you. Cleanse your hands from those outward expressions of sin: the chaos and every evil practice, the quarrels and conflicts, the speaking against one another. Purify your heart from those inward defections: the double-minded desires that might profess God but serve my gods. Grieve. Humble yourself in the presence of the Lord.

Notice how *present* God is. Notice how *relational* the solution is. We seek and find Someone moves toward us. Someone who will be gracious. Someone whose power freely helps us. To really solve the heart of conflict you must seek God's mercy. *Our conflicts are fueled by usurping God's place. The grace of Jesus Christ forgives and reinstates God's rule in our hearts.*

January 13

The LORD passed before him and proclaimed, "The LORD, the LORD, a God
merciful and gracious, slow to anger, and abounding in steadfast love
and faithfulness, keeping steadfast love for thousands, forgiving iniquity
and transgression and sin, but who will by no means clear the guilty,
visiting the iniquity of the fathers on the children and the children's
children, to the third and the fourth generation."
—Exodus 34:6-7

God consistently reveals who he is in the inconceivably wonderful dance of mercy and justice. Perhaps the most vivid
expression of the moral richness of his mercies appears when he
showed himself to Moses on Mount Sinai. He approaches us
with mercy upon mercy, inviting our faith.

People who go wrong are invited into his life-giving goodness. But he is not indifferent to unacknowledged and unrepen-
tant wrong. This can perplex us. Is God patient, or is he impatient? Does God forgive, or is he unforgiving? Does he show love,
or does he not show love? He shows the constructive displeasure
of mercy and that creates a conflict with our sins. His mercy is
not niceness. His mercy is not blanket acceptance of any and all.
*Mercy to us costs him—the blood of the Lamb. And mercy comes to
us at the cost of our sins and pride.* His kindness is an open invitation to turn to him in repentance and faith, to come to him
in our need for mercies freely offered, and our trust in mercies
freely given. Go to God this day. Ask for mercy for Jesus's sake
and you will receive grace and help in your time of need.

January 14

"If I tell the truth, why do you not believe me? Whoever is of God hears the words of God." —John 8:46–47

In his life, death, and resurrection, Jesus triumphed over the powers of darkness. He knew the ugly reality of the world, the flesh, and the devil better than any human before or since. *In the midst of his real enemies, he trusted in his heavenly Father to bring light out of darkness. He continually called those he encountered to that same living, active dependence on his heavenly Father.*

Jesus recognizes that the Evil One plays a consequential role in forming the characteristics of human defection and misery. But he continually speaks to the human heart. In John 8 when Jesus describes the devil, he is speaking to the people in front of him (John 8:44–47). The devil is significant, but he is directly posing questions about life or death to his listeners. These are the same questions we are to ask of ourselves and others:

- Who is fathering you?
- Whose words are catching your ear?
- Whose desires are you following?
- Who do you say I am?

January 15

When my anxious thoughts multiply within me,
Your comfort delights my soul. —Psalm 94:19 NASB

Because there's trouble in this world, we have good reasons to be anxious. In the midst of trouble our hearts forget God, and we get attached to other masters—to all kinds of desires, needs, and beliefs. We get anxious for bad reasons, and we overreact even to the good reasons we have to be anxious. Living in a world where there is trouble, with hearts that quickly stray, means we will always be tempted to lose sight of God. When we lose sight of God, we try to control our world on our own, and become filled with worry.

But don't despair: God, in his Word, gives you better and imperishable reasons for responding to the troubles of life in faith. His comfort can and will delight your soul when you turn to him. You can learn to remember God instead of forgetting him. God wants us to know him so intimately and trust him so completely that our desire to fix our troubles in our own way will no longer consume us. As we grow in our love for God, we will experience the right kind of concern in the midst of our troubles.

January 16

Incline your ear, O Lord, for I am poor and needy. —Psalm 86:1

Faith always expresses itself in practical love for other people. As you go to God and express your need and your joy, your faith will branch out into loving concern for the people in your life (Galatians 5:6). Loving others may seem like an insurmountable wall to climb when you are in the midst of your own struggle physically, emotionally, and spiritually. But you will start to live even in the way you struggle. For example, *loving those around you in the midst of your weakness can be as simple as sharing your weakness and need with someone else.* Men sometimes have a harder time than women being honest about weakness and expressing it to others. But unloving reticence, the pretense of having it together, is not just a male tendency. The truth is that most people don't really like needing help. The Bible is candid about our weakness. David wrote many psalms out of his sense of weakness and need. Jesus asked his disciples to watch and pray with him in his dire need. Paul often shared his personal need with the church—pressures that almost overwhelmed him, his thorn in the flesh, and the sorrows God has spared him.

January 17

What then shall we say to these things? If God is for us, who can be against us? He who did not spare his own Son but gave him up for us all, how will he not also with him graciously give us all things? Who shall bring any charge against God's elect? It is God who justifies. Who is to condemn? Christ Jesus is the one who died—more than that, who was raised—who is at the right hand of God, who indeed is interceding for us. —Romans 8:31-34

God's past grace to sinners demonstrates that he is for us. How do you know God is for you? He did not spare his own Son. This good news is not simply for giving birth to Christian life and experience. What Jesus once did continues to reshape what we do. For example, 2 Corinthians 5:14–15 identifies past grace as the power at work in transforming our present Christian life: "The love of Christ controls us, having concluded this, that one died for all, therefore all died; and He died for all, so that they who live might no longer live for themselves, but for Him who died and rose again on their behalf" [NASB].

Do you want to face yourself, change, and learn to live a new life? *Past grace gives you the ability to fearlessly see yourself in the mirror of God's gaze and gives you a reason to become different.* You don't have to avoid looking or candy-coat your failures. You don't have to wallow in them either. Past grace never lets you forget that God the merciful Father is for you. Past grace keeps inviting you to trust him. It gives you confidence that today's sins will be freely forgiven too. It assures you that God will help you change now and will someday finish what he has begun.

January 18

I will instruct you and teach you in the way you should go;
I will counsel you with my eye upon you.
Be not like a horse or a mule, without understanding,
which must be curbed with bit and bridle,
or it will not stay near you. —Psalm 32:8–9

We live in a day when airing one's opinion matters more than listening intently. But Christ wants listeners. He wants whole hearts. How does he gain this audience? He tells us to listen and then tells us about himself. He communicates this rational, solid, bluntly historical message. Such hearing elicits intense emotion: profound and appropriate shame, utter gratitude, melting sorrow. Such intent, receptive listening compels action.

Are you listening?

Incessant talkers—such people not only are a problem, they have a problem. A pungent Proverb notes, "Where words are many, sin is not absent" (10:19 NIV1984). Another comments ironically, "Even a fool, when he keeps silent, is considered wise" (17:28). A talker who never stops to listen is in trouble.

The Bible says repeatedly that we grow and change only by listening, not by talking. With good reason Jesus says, "He who has ears to hear, let him hear." With good reason David utters God's call for us to hear pointedly personal counsel: "I will instruct you and teach you in the way which you should go; I will counsel you with my eye upon you." Failure to listen defines one as a mulish beast (Psalm 32:8–9). Willingness to listen is itself a significant aspect of repentance and renewal.

January 19

Blessed be the God and Father of our Lord Jesus Christ, the Father of mercies and God of all comfort, who comforts us in all our affliction, so that we may be able to comfort those who are in any affliction, with the comfort with which we ourselves are comforted by God.
—2 Corinthians 1:3-4

You have a story to tell of how God has worked in you, and it's personal. It also reaches out to other people. As you process your life, you have something to give away to others. I need your story, and you need mine. This is the "one-anothering" the Bible speaks about. You need other people to help the Bible come to life. There is this dynamic that runs throughout all of Scripture, enabling you to give away what you are receiving.

When you look through the book of 2 Corinthians, you see that Paul is tremendously encouraged not only by God, but also by people. *Paul received comfort so that he could comfort, strengthen, encourage, guide, lead, challenge, and support others, and that's the way it's meant to be for every one of us.* When the Bible comes to life for me, I'm being equipped with something worth sharing with others.

Every Christian has three elemental callings: to pray for one another, to give practically, and to speak words of wisdom and encouragement to each other. This demands that you are connected both to God and to what's really going on with each other, that you may give grace to one another.

January 20

For the wages of sin is death, but the free gift of God is eternal life in
Christ Jesus our Lord. —Romans 6:23

For those who know Jesus, death doesn't have the last say, it has the next-to-last say. *The last word for the Christian is the resurrection. The last word is life. The last word is mercy. The last word is that God will take us to be with him forever.* God's free gift of eternal life stands in stark contrast to "the wages of sin is death" (Romans 6:23). Jesus stands in contrast to the killer, the murderer, the slayer. He, the only innocent person who ever lived, faced death not for his own sins, but for the sins of his people (John 3:16). Jesus faced death for you.

On the cross he faced death in all of its dimensions. He was killed by asphyxiation and torture, but this was only the physical cause of his death. As he died he bore the wages of sin, suffered the malice of the evil one, and experienced the holy wrath of God. He, the innocent one, willingly died for the guilty.

When he freely gave up his life, death was slain by God and Jesus rose to new life. God's grace destroyed the destroyer and death was thrown into hell. Because of Jesus life has the last say. Because of Jesus you don't have to experience death as he did. He has already paid for your sins. You will die physically, but rise to life eternal (John 3:16).

January 21

Be strong and take heart,
all you who hope in the LORD. —Psalm 31:24 NIV

D avid's life, like yours, is full of troubles and discouragement. Yet because God is with him, he has hope. He says, "You heard my cry for mercy when I called to you for help" (Psalm 31:22 NIV). And he ends Psalm 31 with this call: "Be strong and take heart, all you who hope in the LORD" (v. 24 NIV). David is able to endure with courage because God is with him.

God is calling you to persevere in your suffering, but not by simply gritting your teeth. Persevering through suffering is only possible when you put your hope in the living God. *He promises to come near to you, to be present with you, and to let you experience his goodness right in the middle of your pain and difficulty.* Jesus was able to persevere through the greatest time of suffering that any human has ever endured. He did this "for the joy set before him" of doing his Father's will and of bringing salvation to his people (Hebrews 12:2 NIV). As you fix your eyes on Jesus, the author and perfecter of your faith, you will be able to persevere through this time of suffering and find joy in living for God.

January 22

The aim of our charge is love that issues from a pure heart and a good conscience and a sincere faith. —1 Timothy 1:5

Everything about a human being operates either for God or against him. Every desire and belief is either true or skewed. Every hope or fear is either realistic or illusory. Every attitude of our hearts and every interaction with others comes weighted, either serving the kingdom of God or enslaved to the kingdom of self.

Wisdom also refreshes our understanding of what a human being ought to be like. *Here is the true definition of human flourishing: love from a pure heart, a good conscience, and a sincere faith (1 Timothy 1:5).* A "pure heart" means that you are reorienting to the living God. You are resisting the madness in your heart's instinctual desires and fears. A "good conscience" means you are learning to evaluate all things as they truly are. You are reorienting to God's own evaluation of himself and you, other people and circumstances, right and wrong, true and false, worthy and worthless. A "sincere faith" means you are placing your fundamental confidence in the mercies of Jesus Christ. You are reorienting away from confidence in yourself, others, money, achievements, and the 10,000 other false gods.

Human beings are dependent on the God who made and sustains, who assesses every careless word and impulse, who has come in person to save us from ourselves. This reality has wide-ranging, systematic implications for accurately understanding every human being, and for addressing each person's deepest problems. It was radical, and it's still radical. Christ alone illumines what is most deeply wrong and begins the most wonderful making right.

January 23

Blessed be the God and Father of our Lord Jesus Christ, the Father of
mercies and God of all comfort, who comforts us in all our affliction, so
that we may be able to comfort those who are in any affliction, with the
comfort with which we ourselves are comforted by God.
—2 Corinthians 1:3–4

May God be praised for the in-person immediacy of his mercies, and for how his comforts cascade from him to us, from us to each other. In 2 Corinthians 1:3–4, Paul talks about what afflicts us, what it means to be comforted, and how God comforts us.

First, "all our affliction" and "any affliction" point to human troubles without specifying any details. Affliction (*thlipsis*) is a catch-all. So 2 Corinthians 1:4 invites you to read into it whatever presses you or distresses you, tests you or troubles you, hurts you or burdens you. Whatever tests and trials come our way, we can locate ourselves, each other, and what we each face within 2 Corinthians 1:4.

Second, what does it mean to be comforted in your troubles? God's comfort is not a passive experience and it does not remove painful struggle. God's comfort is unusual. He doesn't make life easy. He doesn't take struggle and hardship away. He even adds the pain of caring. *But our Father's comfort actively strengthens you in the midst of weakness, pain, and need—so you can take heart and take action.* "The Father of mercies and God of all comfort" heartens us when we feel disheartened. He encourages us so we become able to encourage others. To be truly comforted deepens your faith, anchors your hope, nourishes your love, and elicits your joy.

January 24

For this is the will of God, your sanctification. —1 Thessalonians 4:3a

What is God's will for you?

Where should I go to school? What job should I pursue? Who will I marry? What church do my spouse and I commit to? Where will my family put down roots? These might seem like they are the biggest life decisions, the places we most need direct guidance. These questions are important, and the decisions have consequences. There may be better or worse reasons to choose one commitment over another, and we do need wisdom. Yet such items are not on God's written list of what he wills for us. He never promises to give us "handwriting on the wall" guidance.

I vividly remember what a wise professor said to a group of us seminarians as we entered our last year of pastoral studies. "It may be relatively indifferent whether you eventually become a pastor in Kalamazoo or a missionary in Timbuktu. . . . But it may be a matter of life or death whether or not you decide to cross the street, if you spot an old friend from whom you've been estranged walking on the other side. God *really* cares what you do next."

God urgently calls us to seek peace in the midst of strife, as my professor pointed out. If you remain angry, judgmental, and avoidant, you will certainly perish. God opposes the proud but gives grace to the humble, enabling us to become peaceable and constructive.

God's will is your sanctification.

January 25

As a father shows compassion to his children,
so the Lord shows compassion to those who fear him. —Psalm 103:13

Our Lord is trustworthy. He is protective. He is generous. He nurtures. He hears our cry for help. He corrects wisely. He freely forgives when we turn. He is highly communicative—both self-disclosing of himself and quick to hear us. He pursues. He is patient. He knows us—he really, truly, always "gets us." And he gets down to our level. Like a truly good father, he has compassion on his children, and never forgets our limitations (Psalm 103:13–14). His instruction is always good, his correction always for our welfare. Even a nursing mother can forget her nursing child and act heartlessly, but God never forgets his compassion for his children (Isaiah 49:15).

So he gives us every reason to trust, even though we struggle amidst all the limitations, betrayals, and sins that contradict trust. You see this matured trust in the Psalms. It is wholly childlike, and yet fully adult. It is entirely aware of every dark thing in life, and yet it voices both the unhappy cry of need and the happy heart of contentment or joy. It has a simplicity that comprehends the complexities.

How does such trust grow in us? I have learned to take specific Scripture to heart. God is not vaguely omnipresent. He is immediately, personally, specifically, and relevantly on scene. He is paying attention, caring, helping. He has something to say that makes a difference. I know he is true because he has shown himself again and again.

January 26

But he answered, "It is written,
'Man shall not live by bread alone,
but by every word that comes from the mouth of God.'" —Matthew 4:4

We do not live by bread alone but by every word from the mouth of God. That's not just a noble-sounding religious sentiment. It's true in the details of life lived. So slow down and notice what's going on with you. It will help you see that Scripture is relevant because it is exactly keyed to your daily struggles.

- Feel dull and distant? Psalm 119's cries come alive.

- Feel the knife-edge of someone's malice toward you? Psalm 10 has been there and walks with you.

- Feel your insignificance in the eyes of other people? Jesus's approach in Luke 18:15–17 speaks warmly.

- Feel the sting of your sins? Romans 8:31–34 and Psalm 51 show you the way of repentance.

- Feel your lack of wisdom when walking into a very difficult interaction? James 1:5 and 3:17–18 come alive.

- Feel anxiety because many hard things are coming at you all at once? In hard conditions, Jeremiah 17:7–8 sparkles with hope.

- Feel the approach of death? Psalm 23 is right there beside you.

- Feel the threat of your own religious doubts? Jesus comes true to life as you watch Matthew, Mark, Luke, or John proclaim their faith. "You are the Christ, the Son of the Living God. I believe, help my unbelief."

As you become aware of your need, you awaken to where God intersects your life. Speak up about exactly the help you need.

January 27

But he said to me, "My grace is sufficient for you, for my power is made
perfect in weakness." Therefore I will boast all the more gladly of my
weaknesses, so that the power of Christ may rest upon me.
—2 Corinthians 12:9

When Scripture connects in a new, fresh way to your life, it is the mark of a living relationship with the God of the Bible. *The God who speaks wishes to speak intimately to you.* Who you are and what you are facing and where you struggle maps on to what God reveals in the Bible.

Take a look at your life: the good things about you, the bad things that you struggle with in your heart, and the hard things you face. They open existential doors to the mercies of God. As you know yourself more accurately, you'll see how your life and Scripture intersect.

There's something you need today that only God can give you—some bread from heaven. This is also true of those you know, love, and do life with—there is something specific they need that only God can give them. You and I need something from the living God that will make a difference in our lives.

Take 2 Corinthians 12:9, for example. Every single one of us could come at the thorn in the flesh passage and the promise of God in a somewhat different way. We would think of different details, different weaknesses, afflictions, heartaches, and struggles. It's not just book knowledge that we come away with after interacting with God about this passage. It's real, lived knowledge, and we end up with joy, love for God, and love for other people.

January 28

Be angry and do not sin; do not let the sun go down on your anger,
and give no opportunity to the devil. . . . Be kind to one another,
tenderhearted, forgiving one another, as God in Christ forgave you.
—Ephesians 4:26–27, 32

Spiritual warfare is not just about ourselves and our relationship with God. It's about the people around us. Who benefits when we stand against the world, the flesh, and the devil? Yes, God is glorified when we stand. Yes, we are blessed when we stand. But other people also benefit. When we live as children of light, the light of the glory of God shines in our dark world. Standing against evil is not a separate topic from the one-anothering passages in Ephesians 4 and 5. *We stand against evil and shine light into darkness as we live out Paul's call to "Be kind to one another, tenderhearted, forgiving one another, as God in Christ forgave you" (Ephesians 4:32).*

We each do our part, so we are not negating the individual, but we are doing our parts together as one body. When Paul says in Ephesians 4:27 not to give the devil a foothold, he is referring to divisions within the body of Christ. Ephesians is about union and communion with Christ and union and communion with each other in Christ. Spiritual warfare is against the forces that would divide and break our fellowship with Christ and with one another.

January 29

D o *you* have a serious problem with anger?

Yes.

How do you react to this statement?

Turn this sentence over in your mind: "I do have a serious problem with anger." What comes to mind? Do you agree or disagree? Are you not quite sure? How is that statement true? Partly true? Partly false? Do you think it's not true at all? Collect your thoughts into words and specific examples.

I can confidently write that *you* have a serious problem with anger because *I* do, because *we all* do.

Here is the sweet paradox in how God works. He blesses those who admit that they need help: "Blessed are the poor in spirit" (Matthew 5:3). Sanity has a deep awareness, *I need help. I can't do life right on my own. Someone outside of me must intervene. The sanity of honest humility finds mercy, life, peace, and strength.* By contrast, saying we don't need help keeps us stuck on that hamster wheel of making excuses and blaming others. The end result isn't life and peace; it's self-righteousness, self-justification, alienation, and bitterness.

January 30

You desire and do not have, so you murder. You covet and cannot obtain, so you fight and quarrel. You do not have, because you do not ask. You ask and do not receive, because you ask wrongly, to spend it on your passions. —James 4:2-3

Anger goes bad because of a demand. A simple desire (and the simple pain that comes when we do not get what we want) becomes magnified into something I must have. The wrong in my desires is often not what I want, but that I want it too much. My desires become my needs. I must be loved. I demand your respect. I need you to treat me the way I want. I command that you cut me slack. I insist that you be understanding. I demand that you be affectionate. "What I want is right; therefore I am right to be angry at you." Even if what you want is a good thing (e.g., your boyfriend to come on time and to have the thoughtfulness to phone if he's delayed), you want it so much that it devours you. Simple desires mutate into demands that must be met or else!

There's something high and mighty about anger, when distilled to its basic elements. Anger goes wrong when you get godlike. When anger goes right, there's always something higher, some higher purpose or person who puts a cap on anger, who sets a limit on bitterness, who gives reasons not to whine and complain. The most high God, his higher law, his loving mercies, and his higher purposes transform anger. *Something miraculous happens when I no longer say, "My kingdom come, my will be done on earth." My motives no longer operate in the God-usurping mode. The mercy that humbles us begins to master us, and my universe returns to reality.*

January 31

For the righteous falls seven times and rises again. —Proverbs 24:16

When your heart becomes fearful, and you wonder how God could ever love you, remember. Jesus took your sins upon himself. The innocent was slain in place of the guilty. When God considers your failings, he remembers his mercy.

When you feel discouraged and weak and that you have no strength to fight all that is proud, unruly, and forgetful inside you, remember. The Holy Spirit hates evil, loves good, and he will not quit working on the inside. He will complete the good work he began in you.

When you feel overwhelmed by all the heartache, unfairness, disappointment, callousness, and betrayal that you experience, remember. The Lord will destroy every cause of pain, stumbling, and tears. Because God loves those he has befriended, he will defend them from every enemy: death, sin, Satan, and unfriendly people.

When you are tempted to pack it in and give up, plunging back into the darkness, remember. The Lord is a holy fire and he disciplines those he loves that we might share his holiness. "The righteous falls seven times and rises again" (Proverbs 24:16). He will not let you go fatally astray.

February 1

"Are not five sparrows sold for two pennies? And not one of them
is forgotten before God. Why, even the hairs of your head are all
numbered. Fear not; you are of more value than many sparrows."
—Luke 12:6–7

"The Lord is near" (Philippians 4:5 NIV). If you think about your bad anxiety reactions—the unhealthy worry, fretting, and churning—you will notice that you have always forgotten that the Lord is near. When you worry and obsess, you are living as if just you and your struggles are going one-on-one. *If you remember, in even the worst circumstances, that the Lord is near, then you will have a rock on which your heart can rest.* You have a hope that is bigger than any threat, even death. You draw near to the Lord who is close.

After all, this Lord created the whole universe and controls every moment of your life. He counts the hairs on your head and notices each one that falls. You are living in his world. And this Lord is not only the all-powerful Creator of the world, but he has also experienced firsthand the anxiety-producing fragility of life.

This Lord is near you. He is raised from the dead. He will raise you with him. When you know this is true, then you have hope bigger than any loss. What you have been given in this Lord and what you will be given on the day you see his face is greater, weighs more, and has more lasting power than anything you might lose here on earth.

When you know that Jesus is near, the worried, obsessed, sinful anxiety dissipates. The caring, concerned, trusting sort of anxiety grows, and you grow in faith and love.

February 2

But I call to God,
and the Lord will save me.
Evening and morning and at noon
I utter my complaint and moan,
and he hears my voice. —Psalm 55:16–17

In the psalms, relationship with God is happening out loud. More than 95 percent of the Psalms express or invite audible words. Most are spoken directly to God. Quite often psalms speak to other people, inviting them to join in. And sometimes a psalm even speaks of the "voice" of the inanimate creation.

Prayer is a verbal interaction. In the mere handful of psalms that have no obvious verbal cue, a psalm might speak about human destinies in relation to God (e.g., Psalm 1), or God himself might be the one speaking (e.g., Psalm 110). Our audible response is then the most natural thing in the world.

In the verbal actions of the psalms—rejoicing in who God is, asking for needed help, and expressing heartfelt thanks (1 Thessalonians 5:16–18)—we are talking to someone. *It's fair to say that having a "quiet time" is a misnomer. It's more of an out loud, "noisy time"! When you talk aloud you express the reality that you are talking with someone else, not simply talking to yourself inside your own head.*

"Silent prayers" are not wrong, but they are the exception. Even in Scripture's silent prayers, the essentially verbal nature of prayer is still operative. Prayer expresses blunt, head-on, heartfelt need, gladness, and gratitude.

You and I can do the same sort of thing. Our relationship with God is not meant to become so interiorized that we lose the words of direct speech. Close the door, take a walk, get in the car—and speak up.

February 3

For we are his workmanship, created in Christ Jesus for good works,
which God prepared beforehand, that we should walk in them.
—Ephesians 2:10

Our Father works personally and purposefully in each one of his children. Each of us is handmade, one-at-a-time, one-of-a-kind. You and I evidence Christ's workmanship and craftsmanship. We are not mass-produced. We are not clones or spare, interchangeable parts. We are individual components in one infinitely intricate living body of Christ, every component playing its part.

You have been made alive by the Holy Spirit with particular purposes. He places you on location. You live here and now—not anywhere, anytime. You are on call for particular people—not anyone and everyone. The sorrows you face, the happiness you find, these universal experiences take a personal shape. Your life story, your temperament and temptations, the things you know, your abilities and limitations, your experiences and perceptions, the way you think, and feel, and choose . . . every detail happens in specifics. Nothing happens in general. *God's redemption repurposes you, gathering up every experience and characteristic into his purpose for you.*

So each day, in each situation, you have the opportunity to do and say constructive things that no other human being could do or say. In the loving hands of God, your life is custom-designed and custom-built. And we will all fit together in the end. Every hand will do its work. Every voice will sing its part.

This is your *calling.*

February 4

Even though I walk through the valley of the shadow of death,
I will fear no evil,
for you are with me. —Psalm 23:4

Our reactions to grievous wrongs are muddy, not tidy. Reactions rarely appear like primary colors, sharply separated from each other. They come in hues, shades, mixtures, and combinations. Sometimes you might get a "pure" color—for a moment. But most often, you will live out some mishmash of "all of the above."

It is extremely significant that the Bible, and Jesus, and the mercies of God directly engage all of the above. The loving kindnesses of God are exactly keyed to what is grievously wrong. When life goes easy, Christian faith either seems irrelevant or it just adds a nice frosting of spirituality and community to round out the personal résumé. But when life goes very hard (and life always ends up very hard), the true God sparkles. But making the connection isn't always easy. How on earth does "You are with me" (Psalm 23:4) connect with "Right now I am walking through a dark valley. I feel vulnerable. Shadows of death threaten me. I am besieged with evils." How does "You are with me" get traction, so that I am changed and become unafraid?

Making the connection and going forward is never an easy process. But God does meet us in our need. He enters our plight in person. He shares in our troubles. *Suffering is the crucible in which Christ shows himself. Suffering is the crucible where faith awakens. Suffering is the crucible where love becomes wise. We learn faith and love when life goes wrong.*

February 5

Love is patient and kind; love does not envy or boast; it is not arrogant or rude. It does not insist on its own way; it is not irritable or resentful; it does not rejoice at wrongdoing, but rejoices with the truth. Love bears all things, believes all things, hopes all things, endures all things.
—1 Corinthians 13:4–7

We all know that "love is patient; love is kind." Those first two words characterizing love in 1 Corinthians 13:4 can be expressed in a single phrase: love is in it for good.

Love is in it for good: patient. God is patience. He is committed for as long as it takes, whatever is going on, however arduous the process. Patience is not passive. Our Father, Savior, and indwelling Spirit work with purposeful patience. He bears with his children intentionally, through all time, in order to accomplish something. In his great patience, he will complete what he has begun, to his glory and to our joy.

Love is in it for good: kind. God is kindness. He freely gives every good gift, doing and saying what is helpful. Kindness is not sentimental. *Our God works a fiercely realistic kindness. He is always holy and constructive, always merciful and firm, always generous and probing. He knows what we are; he gives more grace.* He gives what we need. In his great kindness, he will complete what he has begun, to our glory and to his joy.

God is love; therefore he is in it for good. And of course, since every promise of God is "Yes" in the Son of God, this Jesus is in it for good.

February 6

So then you are no longer strangers and aliens, but you are fellow
citizens with the saints and members of the household of God.
—Ephesians 2:19

You are one of the Lord's "saints." In popular usage, the word
"saint" has been debased to describe extraordinary, individual spiritual achievements. But in the Bible—where God defines
sainthood—the word describes ordinary people who belong to
a most extraordinary Savior and Lord. Our Redeemer achieves
all of the extraordinary things. At our best (and too often we are
at our worst, or bumping along in the middle!), "we have done
only that which we ought to have done" (Luke 17:10 NASB). God
calls you a saint to point out who owns you, not to honor you
for going above and beyond the call of duty. It's not the Medal of
Honor. It's your enlistment papers and dog tag. When God has
written his name on you, suffering qualitatively changes. Pain,
loss, and weakness are no longer the end of the world and the
death of your hopes.

Because God calls you "his chosen ones, holy and beloved"
(Colossians 3:12), you will dwell in his house forever. This frees
you to bend your life energies toward growing more childlike
toward him and more helpful toward others. Your hopes will
come true in ways far beyond your wildest dreams. You have
been given an inheritance that is imperishable. To be a Christian
is to walk on a path that is like the light of dawn, which shines
brighter and brighter until full day.

February 7

For the word of God is living and active, sharper than any two-edged
sword, piercing to the division of soul and of spirit, of joints and of
marrow, and discerning the thoughts and intentions of the heart. And no
creature is hidden from his sight, but all are naked and exposed to the
eyes of him to whom we must give account. —Hebrews 4:12–13

Hebrews 4:12–13 could be paraphrased like this: *the Word of God discerns your reality map, and it discerns the set of purposes and intentions that you pursue.* It describes both how you see the world and what you are about as you head into the world, those intentions and thoughts that fundamentally control who you are. One of the purposes of Scripture is to show what's in our hearts. Verse 13 says all of us are open and laid bare before the eyes of him with whom we have to give account. This means God sees those things that makes you tick. Verse 12 says that part of the intention of Scripture is to search us out so that to some degree we start to understand ourselves and others. You might call this the mirror of reality.

This provides an interesting contrast to Jeremiah 17:9, which comes at the heart like this, "The heart is deceitful above all things, and desperately sick; who can understand it?" Who can understand himself? Why do we do what we do? In one sense, we don't know. The human heart is deceitful beyond all finding out. And at the same time, Scripture, under the power of the Spirit, is designed to help us begin to describe how we are coming at the world and the thoughts and intentions that rule what we do.

February 8

As for me, I am poor and needy,
but the Lord takes thought for me.
You are my help and my deliverer;
do not delay, O my God! —Psalm 40:17

The Psalms are the place to land when you face various hardships and struggles. The Psalms go first through David but primarily through Jesus Christ, who was supremely opposed and surrounded by evils and evildoers. As we read the Psalms, they become templates or patterns for our experience. The Psalms speak in generalities. In the historical parts of Scripture the story is the main point, in the Psalms, the story is left at the door.

The details of what exactly happened to the psalmist are intentionally left out of the Psalms. Instead you are given many different templates of relationship with God in many different contexts. You are invited to personalize each template with your particular situation—your troubles, hardships, fears, guilt, sorrows, and joys. *The Psalms just beg to be made personal, because they are real prayers, written by real people going through all the ups and downs of life just like us.* But praying the Psalms doesn't end with pouring our hearts out to God. They reveal who God is and remind us of his promises. Consider how our God of promise is vividly revealed in Psalm 40: "You will not restrain your mercy from me; your steadfast love and your faithfulness will ever preserve me! . . . Be pleased, O Lord to deliver me! O Lord, make haste to help me! . . . I am poor and needy, but the Lord takes thought for me. You are my help and my deliverer" (vv. 11, 13, 17). Our needs are met by God's promises to think of us, help us, and deliver us.

February 9

Watch over your heart with all diligence,
For from it flow the springs of life. —Proverbs 4:23 NASB

The way you interpret hard things is hugely revelatory of the human heart. The Bible does not present people in a vacuum. Hardships hit, and you find out things about yourself, and others find out things about you too. Are you a grumbler and complainer? Do you run through your escape mechanisms and little pleasures and attempts to make yourself feel better? Do you get gripped by fear and anxiety? Without the pressure, you would never see where your struggle is.

The human heart in its fundamental quality is the wellspring of the kind of life that we live. In whatever circumstance we are put under, we bear fruit of one sort or another. But when Jesus makes his home in your heart, the fruit we produce begins to change.

Your environment—your context, your situation, your milieu—is the living God. We live in God's world. We breathe God's air. Our heart beats by his sustenance. He searches every thought, every careless word is evaluated by him. As we think about any aspect of life, God is purposefully in it. He is in the situation, and he is up to something good in the lives of those who are his children. There is a bigger purpose going on in the narrative of your life, my life, all lives, all human history, at large levels and small. *Christ's voice rightly orients our hearts to God's purposes—to value what's meaningful, to reject what's false, and to remember that we live in God's world with Jesus at work in us for good.*

February 10

No temptation has overtaken you that is not common to man. God is
faithful, and he will not let you be tempted beyond your ability, but with
the temptation he will also provide the way of escape, that you may be
able to endure it. —1 Corinthians 10:13

The Bible makes this point: There is no struggle you face that
is not common to all people. That levels the playing field. We
each face the same temptations—everyday life brings frustration
and disappointment, and we react with irritation and complaining. We are more alike than different. Whether my problems
appear large or small, I have the same kind of struggle as everyone else. Our differences are matters of degree. Obviously, not
all of us are consumed by explosive or implosive hostility. But all
of us are tempted to grumble. That is the tiny cone and seedling
from which giant redwoods grow. Major sins are only minor sins
grown up. Complaining has the same DNA as violent rage.

So it makes sense that the life-altering solution to minor
complaining has the same DNA as the solution to major bitterness or explosive temper. The discussion in 1 Corinthians 10
helps us see how we are all in the same boat. *But the apostle Paul,
speaking for Jesus ("apostle" simply means someone's messenger),
doesn't leave us there. He leads us by the hand onto solid ground. He
goes on to say, "God is faithful and he will not let you to be tempted
beyond your ability, but with the temptation he will also provide the
way of escape, that you may be able to endure it."* When you and
I encounter frustrating circumstances, we are tempted to spiral
into a negative attitude. But here is a way out and a way forward.

February 11

Who is wise and understanding among you? By his good conduct let
him show his works in the meekness of wisdom. . . . But the wisdom
from above is first pure, then peaceable, gentle, open to reason, full
of mercy and good fruits, impartial and sincere. And a harvest of
righteousness is sown in peace by those who make peace.
—James 3:13, 17–18

The essence of living faith is something different than any particular experience. Seek the true God who speaks truth and offers true help. *Faith takes God at his word and acts on it.* There is nothing as unexperiential, unmystical, and unsentimental as faith. But robust, straightforward, simple faith is powerful. Relate your life to God in Christ, and he will rearrange your life. Take God at his word. To get to the heart of conflict you must seek God. And if you seek, you will find. And you'll change, because living faith can never prove fruitless: "the seed whose fruit is righteousness is sown in peace by those who make peace" (James 3:18 NASB).

On the day we see Christ, all who are in him will be like him. From that day on there will be no more causes of stumbling, no more "quarrels and conflicts." The process of getting to the heart of conflict will one day be finished. Simple and pure devotion will replace double-mindedness forever.

James 3:13 and 3:17–18 describe good conduct and the wisdom from above as peaceable and constructive. What particular aspect of this do you most need to cultivate in your relationships right now? What will it look like for you to do this?

February 12

Praying at all times in the Spirit, with all prayer and supplication. To that end, keep alert with all perseverance, making supplication for all the saints.
—Ephesians 6:18

Because prayer is a vital part of how we fight against the powers of darkness, Paul ends his discussion of spiritual warfare in Ephesians in prayer. His prayers are wondrously normal. *These "warfare prayers" do not speak of or to Satan, but instead address our deepest need for Christ's presence and help.* Paul's core intercession is very simple: "May God strengthen you to know him." No binding and loosing, no authoritative pronouncements and proclamations, no naming and claiming. He tells us to keep on "praying at all times in the Spirit, with all prayer and supplication" and to pray for "all the saints" (v. 18), and then goes on to ask for prayer for himself (v. 19).

Here are some ideas on how to pray at all times for every saint:

- Pray for your friends and family. The people you are most connected to need the Lord to directly impart his strength for them to be able to walk in faith and love. Pray that the Spirit would clothe them with Christ. Pray that their eyes would be open to their need for Christ.

- Take the truth that has most struck you as you've been reading and pray for the Spirit to make this truth alive in your life. Now pray that it would also be alive in your pastor's life. Leadership is a very hard calling, and your leaders need much grace.

- Ask others to pray for you. Paul knew he needed God to give him the words to say and the boldness to say it. What do you specifically need that only the Lord can give?

February 13

"Do not be afraid of them,
for I am with you to deliver you,
declares the Lᴏʀᴅ." —Jeremiah 1:8

"When he has brought out all his own, he goes before them, and the
sheep follow him, for they know his voice." —John 10:4

A nxiety, like anger, is often seen as a purely psychological, emotional problem. But anxiety also hinders us from
caring about other people and reaching out of our own world
toward others. Because we are afraid, the lies we believe isolate us
from others. We are in a spiritual war in that very action, because
withdrawal is loveless and faithless.

How do you talk to someone gripped by fear? You speak
truth to them. The central promise of the Bible to fearful people
is that "I am with you." *Do not fear is a command that doesn't
come with a warning (like the Ten Commandments); it comes with
a promise of God's help and presence.* This is a gift that we can ask
for. We don't have to listen to the lies of the evil one. We can
identify those lies and turn to God for help in our time of need.
We can learn to hear the voice of the Good Shepherd and go
in and out with him (John 10:4, 9). Once again we are back
to the #1 goal—growing in a living dependency on our Good
Shepherd.

---

* See, for example, Deuteronomy 31:6–8; Jeremiah 1:8; Matthew 14:27;
Philippians 4:4–7.

February 14

Prove me, O Lᴏʀᴅ, and try me;
test my heart and my mind. —Psalm 26:2

Anger occurs not only in your body, emotions, thoughts, and actions. It comes from your deepest motives. Underlying desires and beliefs are at work—always. Motives run far deeper than our conscious thoughts. We often feel, think, act, and react without being aware of our motives. But they are the organizing center of who you are, and what you live for. The smallest incident of irritation or the merest lingering bitterness reveals vast truths about you—if you're willing to look.

To tease out the motives underlying anger, ask "What are my expectations?" That simple question helps you stop and think. And the answer often comes in layers, not all at once. *Self-knowledge is both a simple gift and a hard-won achievement.* You might be aware of your expectations at one level, but gradually come to understand more profound levels. It's hard to see our motives. It's even harder to see them for what they are. Part of the problem comes because anger feels so "righteous"—and bad anger is so self-righteous. "I'm so right, because you are so wrong." That same passionate desire to think well of ourselves, to assert and defend ourselves continually, gets in the way of seeing and facing our motives.

When anger goes astray, it says something about how we are going astray inside, about who is the center of the universe. But when God's larger purposes are in control, the poisonous evil of anger is neutralized. Anger becomes a servant of goodness. The anger becomes just, and the purposes become merciful to all who will turn and trust and become conformed to his image. He changes our motives.

February 15

I have stored up your word in my heart,
that I might not sin against you.

Your word is a lamp to my feet
and a light to my path. —Psalm 119:11, 105

How does Scripture get personal? How does the God of the Bible actually connect to you? What's happening when you take it personally? What's going on when his words map onto your life? They fit your life. They touch your life. They take hold of your life. They speak into your life. And how does that happen?

God himself makes his words relevant. He awakens you. He gives you ears to hear and a heart to be open, and the desire to consider and take to heart the things you hear. The more you actually know yourself as you truly are, the more relevant Scripture is. As your self-knowledge deepens, Scripture will just explode off the page, because this book is about you at the deepest level, discussing things that you may not yet know about yourself.

Where are you feeling troubled? What pressures are you under—what's coming at you? Where is your conscience troubled? These are doors to the relevance of what our God says. There are things that are tailored by God himself everywhere in Scripture that speak into our need.

Scripture becomes relevant as you stop and think about God's words. As you stop and think, your troubles and God's mercies connect and start to get into conversation. Who you are and who he is starts to intersect, so that what you need and how he meets you come together.

February 16

Trust in the LORD with all your heart,
and do not lean on your own understanding.
In all your ways acknowledge him,
and he will make straight your paths. —Proverbs 3:5–6

Your troubles do not rest on your shoulders. You are living in a really big, confusing world where there is trouble, but you are in relationship with an even bigger God who is in charge of his world. He has a purpose for you in every situation where there is trouble: God is calling you to be constructive in a very small corner of his world. There is an ecology motto: "Think globally, act locally." Apply this motto to your day-to-day life. *Think globally by remembering every day that God is in charge of the world, and he is watching over his sheep. And then act locally by asking God each day to show you what small, constructive thing he is calling you to do.*

Remember, your step of obedience will always be smaller than the problem. In every area of your life where there is trouble, God is calling you to a small step of faith and love. He is not calling you to solve what is wrong. Your call to love will never be as big as what is wrong. Go through your entire list of worries. Notice that what God is calling you to do is always less than the bad things that might happen. Just knowing that will bring peace and sanity back into your life.

February 17

For the word of God is living and active, sharper than any two-edged
sword, piercing to the division of soul and of spirit, of joints and of
marrow, and discerning the thoughts and intentions of the heart.
—Hebrews 4:12

We live in a society where the words "I feel" have become
the coin of the communication realm. What people feel
has become the basis of much decision-making and much popular
counsel. "I feel" creates a potent and fuzzy cloud of legitimacy
around a dozen dubious statements. It's tough to argue with feelings. But drag all those feelings into the light of day. Take a closer
look at them. What do you find when you unpack the meanings
within the feelings?

"Feelings" are often used to communicate four very different
things: experience, emotions, thinking, and desires. It loads implicit
authority into our impulses, inclinations, wants, desires, yearnings,
intentions, will, plans, choices, expectations, cravings, and fears.

How do you use the words, "I feel"? Do feelings typically reveal
authoritative perceptions, emotions, opinions, and impulses which
can be taken as givens? Or do they reveal facets of human life meant
to be evaluated biblically? Do they typically reveal the real me, who
is meant to be actualized and asserted? Or do they reveal the human
drift from God and toward self, the flesh, autonomy, and subjec-
tivity? A biblical understanding of feelings lets us look behind the
often-deceptive language of daily life.

*In modern feeling language we could say that the Bible exposes
and judges the "feel that's" and "feel likes" which determine how people in darkness live. And what a wonderful alternative we have been
given: the truth of our Lord and Savior Jesus Christ to bring both
mercy and power to change!*

February 18

Take care, brothers, lest there be in any of you an evil, unbelieving
heart, leading you to fall away from the living God. But exhort one
another every day, as long as it is called "today," that none of you may
be hardened by the deceitfulness of sin. For we have come to share in
Christ, if indeed we hold our original confidence firm to the end.
—Hebrews 3:12-14

What do you ask people to pray for? What do others ask you to pray for? It's as though we each look at life through a video camera and ask for changes in everything except the person filming. The cameraman is never in view. In other words, the "counseling" or "wisdom" needs of the person are rarely talked about. We will pray with parents for their straying teenager to straighten out; we rarely pray for the parents not to be fearful, bitter, passive, or controlling. We will pray for a person to get a job; we rarely pray that he would grow in faith as he learns not to fret about money. We pray for the conversion of someone's loved ones; we rarely pray that the believer would grow more loving and honest in the way she treats those loved ones.

As people learn to pray in a different way, they start to have reasons to counsel each other more meaningfully. They get in touch with the real battles. They increasingly enter into the primary lifelong calling to "be a disciple," a learner. *A lifelong learner knows a profound need to give and receive counsel—every day (Hebrews 3:12–14)—in order to grow up into the image of Jesus.* As people become disciples, they increasingly understand their need for counsel. A church learning to pray rightly is a church taking a bold step toward becoming a community of mutual counsel.

February 19

Blessed is the one whose transgression is forgiven,
whose sin is covered.
Blessed is the man against whom the Lord counts no iniquity,
and in whose spirit there is no deceit. —Psalm 32:1–2

Someone who knows his sinfulness, but also knows God's mercy, can be called righteous by the grace and mercy of God. You, too, can experience what David experienced. But to do so, you must seek this Lord. In Psalm 32, David describes how he felt after his sin was exposed, when he hadn't yet confessed his sins to God. His vitality drains away; he feels hopeless and lifeless. If that is you, then do what David did—go to God with your sins and failures. *Your Savior is who he says he is: merciful. He does what he says he does; he forgives.*

Here is a wonderful description of seeking God in the midst of guilt: David says, "I acknowledged my sin to you and did not cover up my iniquity. I said, 'I will confess my transgressions to the Lord.' And you forgave the guilt of my sin" (Psalm 32:5 NIV). Notice that David is turning to God about his failures. He is not turning inward. He is not turning to those around him. He doesn't live in shame anymore. He is forgiven. He can hold up his head and write about it in the Bible, recording his sins for all time. This is because he knows that God is with him.

And then David gives the key to having God with him: "Therefore let everyone who is godly pray to You" (Psalm 32:6 NASB). He knows that asking for help brings him into God's presence where he is safe from trouble—even the trouble he brought upon himself.

February 20

Jesus said to them, "I am the bread of life; whoever comes to me shall not hunger, and whoever belives in me shall never thirst." —John 6:35

All good gifts, beginning with life itself, come from God. You will never be independent. The Lord sustains our lives physically. And every word from the mouth of God gives life. And, supremely, Jesus Christ is the bread of life. *Faith knows and embraces this core identity: "I am his dependent."*

Our dependency as created beings is compounded, complicated, and intensified by sins and by sufferings. To know ourselves truly is to know our need for help. Faith knows and embraces this core identity: "I am *poor and weak.*"

The Lord is merciful to the wayward. He redeems the intrinsically sinful, forgetful, and blind. Faith knows and embraces this core identity: "I am *sinful*—and I am *forgiven.*"

God is our Father. He adopts us in Christ and re-creates us with a childlike heart by the power of the Spirit. We need parenting every day. We need tender care, patient instruction, and constructive discipline. Faith knows and embraces this core identity: "I am God's *child.*"

The Lord is our refuge. Our lives are beset by a variety of troubles, threats, and disappointments. We aren't strong enough to stand up to what we face. God's presence is the only safe place. Faith knows and embraces this core identity: "I am a *refugee.*"

The Lord is our shepherd. He laid down his life for the sheep. He watches over our going out and coming in. We need looking after and continual oversight. Faith knows and embraces this core identity: "I am a *sheep* in his flock."

February 21

I have learned in whatever situation I am to be content. I know how
to be brought low, and I know how to abound. In any and every
circumstance, I have learned the secret of facing plenty and hunger,
abundance and need. I can do all things through him who
strengthens me. —Philippians 4:11–13

Our loving Father pointedly wills that we learn to live with no complaining about the present, no regrets about the past, and no worrying about the future. This is a high, hard calling! We fail. But our failures, honestly acknowledged, open a wide door into mercies new every morning. And Christ freely commits to teaching us the secret of contentment amid a world filled with stressors. Most of us are in the remedial class, but any progress in the direction of such significant wisdom is worth more than silver, gold, and jewels. "Nothing you desire can compare," as Proverbs 3:14–15 puts it.

Christ is forgiving, and Christ is working to make your life beautiful. When you see him face-to-face, you will be like the Savior we have trusted.

First Thessalonians 5:16–18 says: "Rejoice always, pray without ceasing, give thanks in all circumstances, for this is the will of God in Christ Jesus for you." *Candid joy, frank need, and open gratitude are three voices of faith—and faith is God's will for you.*

February 22

The Father of mercies and God of all comfort who comforts us in all our affliction, so that we may be able to comfort those who are in any affliction. —2 Corinthians 1:3-4

I t's common for people to view sanctification as a moral self-improvement project, getting rid of your bad habits and developing good habits. Under Christ's mentoring, we do "improve," of course. But it's not exactly in the ways we might expect. It's easy to think that God's goal is to make you better, happier, and more self-confident than you are now. The Lord's desired outcome is not simply a better you living your best life now, someone who has found a sense of inner peace and gotten your act together. *His goal for you is to embody love by taking to heart the troubles and struggles of others. He does it by first taking to heart your troubles and struggles.*

When you find the hope and encouragement of Christ in your troubles, his goal is not simply to make you feel better. He has a much deeper purpose. You are receiving a dynamic gift that you can bring to other people in whatever troubles and unhappiness they experience. Their welfare and yours are knit together. This means that their afflictions become yours.

Sanctification is not really interested in making you a "better individual." God is making you into a person who is more connected to others: joined to Jesus Christ and to all his other afflicted people whose center of gravity is also shifting outside themselves.

February 23

The unfolding of your words gives light; it imparts understanding to the simple. —Psalm 119:130

There's a big difference between knowing something by rote and actually understanding how it works. You think more insightfully and creatively when you understand something. Likewise, there's a big difference between doing something by rote and being oriented. You make skillful decisions when you're oriented. For example, a GPS offers rote guidance to get from point A to point B. So when you lose the signal in a strange neighborhood, you have no idea where you are (you are *dis*oriented!). But when you are driving in your own neighborhood and a road is closed, you have a half dozen different ways to get from where you are to wherever you need to go. You're oriented. You understand.

It's the same with how Scripture works in our lives. *Merely having Psalm 23 memorized won't persuade you that someone strong and caring is watching out for you. If you're to find any help in dark, vulnerable times, you need to understand what Psalm 23 means.* And saying the Lord's Prayer by rote will never convince you that God actually is your Father, or that he will provide what you need to live in his will today. But when you become oriented, then you mean the words you say. You understand how Jesus's teaching captures what you most need today—strength for today, mercy for your sins, protection from what afflicts you.

February 24

For we are his workmanship, created in Christ Jesus for good works,
which God prepared beforehand, that we should walk in them.
—Ephesians 2:10

The notion of calling provides a perspective on all of life and all of Scripture. The concept springs from the One who calls: God speaks. And because he is vocal, he calls forth all that exists. Because he is vocal, he proclaims who he is. Because he is vocal, when he comes in person, he is the Word becoming flesh.

And because he is vocal, you have a vocation, a calling. *Vocation is not a synonym for a professional career. Vocation is not restricted to those in "vocational ministry": pastors, missionaries, monks, and nuns. God's calling is personal with each of his children.*

How do we gain an awareness of our calling? It gets hammered out gradually in the process of living your Christian life honestly. I will ask you to reflect on five questions, each of which brings certain key matters into view.

What are your gifts? What is your life experience? What are your opportunities? How have you grown? What do you thrive doing? You will understand your calling as you understand the intermingling of these five things about you and your world. This calling is your true "vocation": what you are called to do in your life situation. What are those specific good works which God has prepared beforehand for you to walk in (Ephesians 2:10)? Your understanding of your specific vocation grows as you bring together these five strands of self-knowledge.

February 25

O Lᴏʀᴅ, you have searched me and known me!
You know when I sit down and when I rise up;
you discern my thoughts from afar.
You search out my path and my lying down
and are acquainted with all my ways. —Psalm 139:1-3

Because no two people and no two situations are exactly alike, God personalizes the way he acts and speaks. When we describe and confess our God, it might sound static. But he is kinetically connected to each of his people. It might sound like he was the Creator long ago. But he is also continually creating and recreating a people for himself. It might sound like he will become the Judge at the end of time. But he is also continually judging so that his plan for the safety and glory of his people prevails. It might sound like he was once the Savior when he died and was raised long ago, and that he will again save when he returns in the future. But he is also continually saving his sons and daughters by transforming them into the image of the Son. *He gets personal—with everyone, with those who long for him and with those who wish they could wish him away.*

God answers. He involves himself in the details of our lives, and life makes sense. In a fresh way we understand how our lives and the lives of others—believer and unbeliever alike—unfold in the ways Scripture portrays.

When he takes hold, everything moves at the right speed, not a mad scramble. We become our right size. The pressures on us become their right size. Our God becomes his right size. We are small; pressures are big; God is bigger.

February 26

And behold, there were two blind men sitting by the roadside, and when they heard that Jesus was passing by, they cried out, "Lord, have mercy on us, Son of David!" The crowd rebuked them, telling them to be silent, but they cried out all the more, "Lord, have mercy on us, Son of David!" And stopping, Jesus called them and said, "What do you want me to do for you?" —Matthew 20:30-32

When something is so wrong that you will never get over it, your reaction will either make you wise or will poison you. Great suffering puts a fork in the road. You will of necessity choose. It is no accident that—"Lord, have mercy"—is the essential prayer of the man or woman who faces facts honestly. It is no accident that "Blessed are the poor in spirit" is the first and foundational beatitude (Matthew 5:3). *A deep inner sense of need for help from outside yourself is the essential step of sanity.* It is this faith—"I am poor and needy. Help me."—that Jesus commends so often. Faith is not a leap into darkness and unreason, despite the cold hard facts. Faith is the honest reckoning with your need for help, and then the reasonable step in the direction of the person who can help you, given all the facts.

Our culture usually portrays suffering or anger or despair or anxiety as things with "how to" solutions. But the things that cause the deepest angers, fears, and despairs are betrayals at a depth that calls for a different way of thinking about solutions. You must learn to live honestly in the face of evils that don't necessarily go away. You must learn to honestly face down your own evil in the light of bigger mercies: "I am selfish and sinful, but God put his hands on me, that is all."

February 27

And you were dead in the trespasses and sins in which you once walked,
following the course of this world, following the prince of the power of the
air. . . . But God, being rich in mercy, because of the great love with which
he loved us, even when we were dead in our trespasses, made us alive
together with Christ—by grace you have been saved.
—Ephesians 2:1-2, 4-5

E veryone knows that "sin" means bad behavior—"the works of the
flesh are obvious" (Galatians 5:19 NRSV). But what else is it? Our
actions, attitudes, words, thoughts, and emotions do not arise in a vacuum. The Bible embeds and locates the obvious behaviors in an intricate, co-operating web of dark forces. Wise Christians have classically
identified three interlocking forces: the *flesh*, the *world*, and the *devil*.

The *flesh* describes the personal dimension of sinfulness. This
personalized iniquity not only "works" and takes action, it also "lusts"
inwardly. Sin's operations include an inner psychological dimension
that is relentlessly self-centering, self-exalting, self-willed . . . and
self-deceived. Ego usurps God and assertively self-destructs. We are
tempted by our own desires, which birth sins, which result in death
(James 1:14–15).

The *world* describes the situational dimension. Our social and
cultural surroundings marry the heart's proclivities to a buzz of
deceitful voices, values, vanities, promises and threats, pains and
pleasures. In other words, sin is highly sensitive to peer pressure. We
not only sin against others; we also are drawn into sin by the influence of others individually and collectively.

The *devil* adds a false-father, false-lord dimension. An active
enemy craves, schemes, lies, tempts, deceives, enslaves, accuses . . .
and murders. The enemy minds you, finds you, wines and dines you,
blinds you, binds you, and finally grinds you.

O merciful Father, lead us not into temptation. Deliver us from evil.

February 28

"Cursed is the man who trusts in man
and makes flesh his strength,
whose heart turns away from the LORD. . . .

"Blessed is the man who trusts in the LORD,
whose trust is the LORD.
He is like a tree planted by water,
that sends out its roots by the stream. —Jeremiah 17:5, 7–8

When you are angry, when you are anxious, when you want to escape, where do you choose to turn? Jeremiah describes a person who is turning away from God: "cursed is the man who trust in man and makes flesh his strength, whose heart turns away from the LORD" (17:5). We might call this anti-repentance, since it is the opposite of true repentance, which is characterized by turning toward God. Jeremiah is describing someone who is turning away from the fountain of living water and is becoming like a dried-up bush that lives in the desert. That accurately describes those who are caught in anger, anxiety, and escapism.

Usually when you feel stuck in anger, anxiety, or escapist behavior, you don't think you can choose to desire, feel, think, and act differently. But for those in Christ, they have the power of Christ. They have Christ's strength, truth, and righteousness. They have the Word of Christ and the power of prayer. Because of Christ, they can choose Christ. Because of the Spirit, they can keep in step with the Spirit.

Turning to Christ is to win spiritual warfare.

February 29

Again he entered the synagogue, and a man was there with a withered hand. And they watched Jesus, to see whether he would heal him on the Sabbath, so that they might accuse him. And he said to the man with the withered hand, "Come here." And he said to them, "Is it lawful on the Sabbath to do good or to do harm, to save life or to kill?" But they were silent. And he looked around at them with anger, grieved at their hardness of heart, and said to the man, "Stretch out your hand." He stretched it out, and his hand was restored. —Mark 3:1–5

I t is possible to say, "That's wrong!" and yet express our displeasure in ways that prove truly constructive. Actually loving. Even beautiful. Jesus saw wrong, called it wrong, and called out wrongdoers. Here is how he describes his purpose:

> God did not send his Son into the world to condemn the world, but in order that the world might be saved through him. (John 3:17)

Let's give this good anger a name: the constructive displeasure of mercy. Each of those three words matters. Good anger operates as one aspect of mercy. It brings good into bad situations. It stands up for the helpless and victimized. It calls out wrongdoers, but holds out promises of forgiveness, inviting wrongdoers to new life.

Your anger and mine can be remade into God's image. Strong mercy is the DNA of the entire Bible. Clear-minded mercy is the DNA of redemption. *Jesus gathers up our angers, not to neuter our sensitivity to evil, but to redeem how we respond. Strong, clear-minded mercy is the way we are meant to transmute feeling disturbed, uncomfortable, and bothered by what is.*

And by definition, mercy is consistently constructive. Mercy intervenes to address and solve whatever problem is in view. Jesus embodies this constructive displeasure of mercy. It is a rich, complex way of responding to life.

March 1

But I am poor and needy; hasten to me, O God! You are my help and my deliverer; O Lᴏʀᴅ, do not delay! —Psalm 70:5

Why do you pray? I suspect that your answer is the same as mine. The reason I pray is I need to pray. It is the door of life, and if I don't pray, I perish.

A good definition of prayer is that it is straight talk with the real God about what's really going on and what really matters. In prayer there is a kind of searing honesty about the things that really matter. When you become aware of what you really need and who God really is, you pray for one reason—you need to. You need a certain kind of help and you need things that God himself must give, or you perish. And when he gives them, you rejoice with gladness of heart.

What do we need, what exactly? We cannot fix what is wrong in us and around us without help from outside, and prayer recognizes this reality. We need everyday wisdom and understanding—understanding about how life actually works and what it is that we are to do with our lives. We need strength and power—power to live within the sufferings and afflictions of human life and to live well with courage, humility, hope, faith, and love. And we need protection God alone can provide.

When you become aware of what you really need and who God really is, you pray for one reason—you need to.

March 2

Likewise the Spirit helps us in our weakness. For we do not know what to pray for as we ought, but the Spirit himself intercedes for us with groanings too deep for words. —Romans 8:26

Why do we pray? We need hope. We need to know that the King will come and wipe away every tear from our eyes, that there will be no more death or mourning or crying or pain anymore. We need indestructible friendship. We need the presence of God himself in our lives. *We pray real prayers because we know that what we most need is to know him.*

So how do we pray? This flows straight out of the why. You must get down to your elemental need and get down to God's elemental promises. When you bring those together, then you speak straightforwardly to the one who can help you. Our needs correlate to these attributes of who God is—his character, what he does, what he thinks, what he promises.

We pray about things the Bible portrays: Protect me—I'm vulnerable, and you're strong (Psalm 72:4). Make me alive—I'm dying, and you are life (Psalm 119:50). Give me wisdom—write your words on my heart (Psalm 119:34). Don't let go of me (Psalm 38:21). Watch over me (Psalm 16:1). Give me strength (Psalm 119:28). Have mercy on me (Psalm 51:1).

As we pray prayers of need, they lead to prayers of praise for his goodness and mercy (1 Chronicles 16:34; Psalm 23:6). As we pray, the Holy Spirit intercedes to turn our confusion into something beautiful and fruitful.

Oh Lord, teach us to pray in such a way that our relationship with you is alive.

March 3

Then Jesus told his disciples, "If anyone would come after me, let him deny himself and take up his cross and follow me." —Matthew 16:24

J esus's amazing grace comes to sinners with everything needed to create children of glory. But the soul out of self-love resists the central activity of the Christian life: change. What gets in the way of living reliant on Christ's comfort and love? Of loving God with all that you are? Of looking out for the interests of others? *Something in you doesn't want to be seen for what it is. Yet the power and instruction of the Word and Spirit intend to remake you. God willingly and persistently will teach you to love, fear, trust, and serve him.*

The Bible calls this change by many names. Jesus says, "Become a disciple." A disciple self-consciously engages in becoming different. Jesus says, "Follow me." Follower, deny yourself, taking up your cross daily. Jesus says, "First take the log out of your own eye." Lightened of sin, you will treat other people very differently.

War with self comes paired with the peace of God that passes all understanding. The price is high: yourself. The reward staggers: God himself.

March 4

A Prayer for Us to Become Peacemakers

Our God and Father, we thank you that you have given to us Christ Jesus, fully God, fully a man. Thank you for his honest suffering, sweat, and blood, his entering our plight, being genuinely tempted, facing death itself, not recoiling in the face of horrors. A man of faith, a pioneer and perfector of our faith. And we beseech you that you will enable us to awaken, to see, to hear the Prince of Peace. Lord, we know that you have said that peacemakers are blessed, and you yourself are the peacemaker. We are war-makers so easily, or we are peace lovers who duck necessary conflict. *And we beseech you that you would make us men and women who are agents of peace in our world at war, who repent quickly when we are feisty or when we are fearful, who learn to go forward with our heads held high and to love people, who enter into difficult situations, recognizing that this is a world that needs redemption and that means stepping into hard places.* Help us not be lovers of comfort, protectors of reputation, wanting life to be on our terms, trying to create some little private paradise, a kingdom of peace and our own control. Let us live freely within the real world, the one that cries out for peacemakers. Lord, thank you that this is exactly what you are doing in our lives, one and all. Give us your own wisdom. Fill us with the Holy Spirit, who is the agent of a peaceable wisdom. Amen.

March 5

And because you are sons, God has sent the Spirit of his Son into our hearts, crying, "Abba! Father!" So you are no longer a slave, but a son, and if a son, then an heir through God. —Galatians 4:6-7

Who are you really? What defines you? You're not defined by your role in your family configuration, whether you are unmarried or married, whether you have children or not. You're not defined by your job or your money. You're not defined by your friendships. You're not defined by your local church or your denomination. You're not defined by your ethnic background.

If you were, you'd be cursed if you had to retire, a wreck if your best friend betrayed you, in despair if there was a split in your congregation, or despondent if your ethnic background was despised and mocked.

You're defined by your relationship with the living God. Getting that straight is the one thing that lets you actually engage rightly with all of these other roles, embracing the joys and positives and the good things and the blessings. And it lets you face whatever evils and darkness is there. Whatever your family history, whatever your current job, whatever your current friendship situation, role, whatever the future brings in gains or losses.

You must get who you are straight: You belong to Jesus Christ. You have been bought with his blood. You belong to your Father. You've been given the identity of a child who says, "Abba, Father." Your God is gracious to you. He is always gracious. He is always up to something good in your life. That is what defines you.

March 6

For we do not have a high priest who is unable to sympathize with our
weaknesses, but one who in every respect has been tempted as we are,
yet without sin. Let us then with confidence draw near to the throne of
grace, that we may receive mercy and find grace to help in time
of need. —Hebrews 4:15–16

A Prayer to Our Redeemer

Our Father, it is very good to know you. *And we thank
you that Jesus helps us. We thank you that Jesus forgives
us. We thank you for mercy and grace to help in moments
of need, real need.* Your summary of the struggles of the
human condition brings us to seek you. And we thank
you that Christ Jesus, the Lord of life, the Prince of Peace,
the Lord of love, wears many crowns. And these all speak
in various ways. All the things you have done, all that you
are speaks in various ways to the very concerns, needs,
struggles of people who need redeeming. And that is who
we gratefully are: people who need redeeming. We want to
grow into your image.

We pray that the significance of the mercies of God in
Christ—his dying love on the cross for us, in our place,
his gift of the Holy Spirit, his modeling a life he intends to
fashion in us, his choosing us before the foundation of the
world, his hearing us with the groans too deep for words,
interceding for us on our behalf—would change our hearts.
Would you make these great and big truths traffic down
into the places in life where we get bad attitudes, where we
get caught up in fear or anxiety, get bitter, or grumble? We
ask this for your name's sake, Amen.

March 7

Well might the sun in darkness hide
And shut his glories in,
When Christ, the mighty Maker, died
For man the creature's sin.

Thus might I hide my blushing face
While his dear cross appears;
Dissolve my heart in thankfulness,
And melt mine eyes in tears.

But drops of grief can ne'er repay
The debt of love I owe;
Here, Lord, I give myself away,
'Tis all that I can do.
— Isaac Watts, "Alas! and Did My Savior Bleed"

We live in a world of skeptical, laid-back, carefully measured commitments. We live in a world of half-hearted loyalties—to all but self-interest, private addiction, self-pity, and a sense of righteous grievance. But Christ wants whole hearts, believing, poured out, engaged, given away. How does he gain such? He tells us about himself and says, LISTEN.

Isaac Watts listened. He heard Jesus's message. His response? "Here, Lord, I give myself away." What so moved him? One supreme truth: Christ, the mighty Maker, died for man the creature's sin. One truth pierced him heart, soul, mind, and might. *One decisive truth made him respond with self-abandoning love: Christ, the mighty Maker, died for man the creature's sin.*

Are you listening? What do you need to stop and hear? The same message that Isaac Watts heard: Christ died for all, that they who live should no longer live for themselves, but for him who died and rose again on their behalf (2 Corinthians 5:15).

March 8

If any of you lacks wisdom, let him ask God, who gives generously to all
without reproach, and it will be given him. —James 1:5

A Prayer for Wisdom

Our Father, will you grant us nothing less than divine
wisdom? We thank you that you have promised
in your mercy to illumine us. Enlighten the eyes of our
hearts that we might know you as you are. Clarify our
self-understanding. Let us understand our world more and
more the way that you understand it. Above all else, will
you shield us from all evil and strengthen us in all good?
*Through our lives, be honored. And would our lives, by your
mercy, become fruitful, wise, and good.* Give us your wisdom,
that we might become peaceable, gentle, open to reason,
full of mercy and good fruits, impartial and sincere. Give
us your wisdom that we would become men and women
who delight that a God who is so spectacularly beautiful
has done such wondrous things. May your wisdom lead us
to consider others more important than ourselves instead
of seeing them as a problem to fix or a hassle we don't like.
Help us see the connection to how we can start to move in
your direction and learn to love and not be gripped by fear,
or hate, or confusion. Make it so. And we ask it in Jesus's
name, Amen.

March 9

Stand therefore, having fastened on the belt of truth, and having put on the breastplate of righteousness, and, as shoes for your feet, having put on the readiness given by the gospel of peace. In all circumstances take up the shield of faith, with which you can extinguish all the flaming darts of the evil one; and take the helmet of salvation, and the sword of the Spirit, which is the word of God, praying at all times in the Spirit, with all prayer and supplication. —Ephesians 6:14-18

In Ephesians 6, Paul describes the Christian life in simple terms. If we strip the metaphor out, he is telling us about the seven basic elements of what it means to be strong in the Lord and in his might. *What will make you able to stand against the world, the flesh, and the devil? Truth, righteousness, the gospel of peace, faith, salvation, the Word of God, and prayer.* These are the everyday, normal stuff of the Christian life. They are what you and I need every day to stand against the world, the flesh, and the devil. It is what we have been given in Christ to live in the strength of Christ. It is what we have to offer others in the middle of their everyday struggles with anger, fear, and escapism. There is hope for them and for you because Christ is our strength, and he has provided specific ways for us to live in his strength.

We can resist the devil by humbling ourselves, and he will have to flee (James 4:6–10). We can only do this out of total dependence on the Good Shepherd.

March 10

Be kind to one another, tenderhearted, forgiving one another, as God in
Christ forgave you. Therefore be imitators of God, as beloved children.
And walk in love, as Christ loved us and gave himself up for us, a
fragrant offering and sacrifice to God. —Ephesians 4:32–5:2

God's way of dealing with what is wrong in this world is wonderful and surprising, combining firmness with gentleness, honesty with forgiveness. But how do you put it into practice? How do you learn to let go of your wrong anger and express your just anger constructively?

Paul gives you practical help in Ephesians 4:29–5:2. He starts by telling us how *not* to express our anger. First, he says we are not to keep to ourselves and brood ("bitterness"). Second, he says we are not to go to the other person and dump our anger ("rage and anger"). Finally, we shouldn't go to others who aren't involved and gossip ("slander").

You have to go to God for help. As you go to him, you will learn how to think through your angry reactions, how to go to other people in such a way that you're actually asking for help, and how to go to the other person in a way that's constructive. *Your anger will be transformed when you understand deep in your heart how God, in Christ, treats you.* God's patience, mercy, forgiveness, and loving confrontation will only become real in your life as your relationship with him grows.

March 11

But the fruit of the Spirit is love, joy, peace, patience, kindness, goodness, faithfulness, gentleness, self-control; against such things there is no law. And those who belong to Christ Jesus have crucified the flesh with its passions and desires. —Galatians 5:22–24

How does God respond when something important in the world is wrong? He responds redemptively. Is God angry when people act like their own god, playing false to him, and bringing grief to themselves and others? Yes. But how did he express that anger? By sending his very own Son to this broken world to be broken on the cross. He sacrificed his Son so his people can be forgiven, transformed, and restored to a right relationship with him and others.

Your anger can also result in redemption. When you come to God and find forgiveness for Jesus's sake, you will be filled with God's Spirit. Because you are filled with his Spirit, it will be possible for you also to respond redemptively when you are angry. You can learn to say, "That's wrong," without ranting, exaggerating, cursing, yelling, or name calling.

Being filled with the Spirit means everything about you will start to resemble God. Instead of responding with sinful anger to unimportant things, you will start to see your life from God's perspective. You will begin to care about things that truly matter, instead of overreacting to relatively unimportant things.

When Jesus was on earth, he was not a stoic. No one cared more than he did about things that were wrong in this world. But his upset was driven by faith and love, not by pettiness, hostility, and aggression. Becoming like God means that you will care about the things Jesus cares about—the things that truly matter in God's world.

March 12

Beloved, let us love one another, for love is from God, and whoever loves
has been born of God and knows God. Anyone who does not love does
not know God, because God is love. —1 John 4:7–8

How do you seek intimacy with God? Meditate on the way he
treats you. *Love for others will come as you experience the love
of your Father in heaven.* God's love for us is the most wonderful
thing in this world—it's at the core of what makes life bright and
hopeful. Read these Bible verses and make them your own:

- You are never out of sight or out of mind to God (Psalm
  139:7–10).

- He creates intimacy with you by the way he treats you
  (Isaiah 42:3).

- He notices and cares about everything that happens to
  you (Luke 12:6–7).

- He speaks openly about himself (John 15:15).

- He listens to you (Psalm 6:8–9).

- He is a refuge in the midst of your sufferings (Psalm 46).

- He hangs in there over the long haul (Isaiah 49:14–16).

- He laid down his life for you (John 3:16; Romans 5:6–8).

- He forgives all your sins (Psalm 103:1–5).

- His mercies are new every morning (Lamentations
  3:21–24).

God wants you to respond to his love by trusting him with
your whole life. He has bridged the distance between you and him
through the life, death, and resurrection of his Son. Now he is
making you like him and walking with you every step of the way.
He's helping you step-by-step to love others the way he loves you.

March 13

For I am sure that neither death nor life, nor angels nor rulers, nor things present nor things to come, nor powers, nor height nor depth, nor anything else in all creation, will be able to separate us from the love of God in Christ Jesus our Lord. —Romans 8:38-39

As you read through Romans 8, you notice that Paul doesn't say that we won't have hardships. Instead he acknowledges that there will be "trouble . . . hardship . . . persecution . . . famine . . . nakedness, [and] danger" (v. 35). *But he does promise that none of these things "will be able to separate us from the love of God that is in Christ Jesus our Lord" (v. 39). Cling to this promise.* Cling to Jesus. Invite him into your struggles, your sorrows, and your questions. Fill your mind with his words.

When you read the Gospel of Luke, you read a very unusual biography of Jesus. Luke doesn't talk much about famous, smart, successful people. He focuses on little people, people who are powerless, bereaved, ignored, and neglected. Right now you may be there. You may be going through something far bigger than your ability to control or fix. As you read Luke, watch Jesus in action. Notice how he treats people with wisdom, love, and tenderness. Notice how he's content to do and say only one thing, or a few things. Take to heart that this is also the way he treats you.

March 14

"The secret things belong to the Lᴏʀᴅ our God, but the things that are revealed belong to us and to our children forever, that we may do all the words of this law." —Deuteronomy 29:29

Edith Schaeffer once used a tapestry metaphor to talk about the difficult things in life. She pointed out that the front of the tapestry was a beautiful pattern, but the back was a mass of knots and tangled threads. In life's broken, dark experiences you must find that the promises and presence of your God and Savior are real. One day, you will see the front side of the tapestry, instead of just the tangled back. One part of the beauty of the tapestry will be the way you learn to know God and love others by going through difficult experiences. Is that the whole answer to why God let it happen? No. There are things about his will and his purposes that are beyond us. The Bible says, "The secret things belong to the Lᴏʀᴅ our God, but the things revealed belong to us and to our children forever, that we may follow all the words of this law" (Deuteronomy 29:29).

What has been revealed is given so you can live. What hasn't been revealed to you is meant to be a secret thing. *Instead of trusting in your knowledge, you have to trust in God's love and goodness.* This is a lesson you will have to learn and relearn all through your life—not only now as you struggle with this heartache, but through all the ups and downs that life brings. Your relationship with God will be what brings you peace, not getting all of your questions answered.

March 15

But he said to me, "My grace is sufficient for you, for my power is made
perfect in weakness." Therefore I will boast all the more gladly of my
weaknesses, so that the power of Christ may rest upon me.
—2 Corinthians 12:9

As you turn to God in suffering, he will help you by changing the way you think about your life. Instead of despising your weakness, you will see that weakness reveals God's power. Pour out your heart to God just like Paul did in 2 Corinthians 12. He had a weakness that he called a "thorn in my flesh." He begged God to take his weakness away. He said, "Three times I pleaded with the Lord to take it away from me" (vv. 7–8 NIV).

Paul received from God this response: "My grace is sufficient for you, for power is made perfect in weakness" (v. 9, author paraphrase). God's power is perfectly revealed in our weakness. God will use your weakness to show you that what drives your life is not you, but the power and mercy of Another.

Paul responded to God by saying, "I will boast all the more gladly about my weaknesses, so that Christ's power may rest on me" (v. 9). The very things that the world despises become the occasions for the power of Christ to be displayed in Paul's life. Then Paul said, "For Christ's sake, I delight in weaknesses, in insults, in hardships, in persecutions, in difficulties" (v. 10 NIV). Such troubles are no fun to experience. But he's content in them for Christ's sake.

People value being strong and independent. But the dynamic of weakness and dependency makes Christ matter in your life. When Christ matters in your life, he shines through your life. People see the evidence of something wonderful—the hand of Another at work in you.

March 16

Do not be overcome by evil, but overcome evil with good.
—Romans 12:21

How you treat your enemies is a litmus test of your heart. Romans 12:14–21 is about how you deal with your enemies—whether you're a vengeance-taker or whether you're someone who is transformed to be able to do courageous good in the context of evil. It is out of the abundance of our hearts that we show ourselves. There's a major strand in the Bible about how we deal with the enemy-like behavior of our brethren who are acting contrary to their new nature. How will you react? Evil for evil, good for good? There are two dominant themes at play here. One theme is refuge. That's the theme of the Psalms. The second theme is repentance.

It's the repentance dynamic by which we are transformed—turning from the instinctive way we express displeasure, unhappiness, and anger—to the constructive displeasure that is glorifying to God. That response to evil expresses the person and character of Christ and demonstrates that there is a hope that is bigger than our circumstances. Revelation 21:4 reminds us that one day there will be a righting of all wrongs, no more sorrow, no more sighing, no more dying, no more tears. Every cause of stumbling, every cause of evil and heartache will be gone. And what will be left is joy and no more sin. The hope of heaven and all that means for those in Christ reframes how we view and respond to being sinned against.

March 17

"I the LORD search the heart
and test the mind, to give every man according to his ways,
according to the fruit of his deeds."
—Jeremiah 17:10

No one but God can see, explain, or change the human heart. We do not see anyone's heart. We cannot explain why anyone would have the behavior patterns they do. And we have no power to change another person's motives. But we can describe the human heart with the words of Bible. It gives us categories like fear of man, pride, lust of the flesh. The passage in Jeremiah 17 that says the human heart is unsearchable in terms of who can see it, explain it, and change it. It also gives you examples of hearts that are idolatrous or trust in the arm of flesh. So the description of what misrules us and hijacks us is often accessible and helpful to get on the table as we talk with people, and as we seek to understand ourselves.

Can you change what you want? Can your desires change? Of course your desires can change. It is the very heart of the Christian message. By the grace of God, such a person can actually learn to care about other people and reach toward someone else. It's a long, hard fight to break out of fear of man and actually learn to love. But that is a change that is exactly what redemption is about. Is it easy? No. Is it hard? Yes. Is that what redemption is about? Yes. Because you're not in control and someone else is, and you can learn to trust him. And that transformation is actually at the center of God's purposes for you.

March 18

To put off your old self, which belongs to your former manner of life and
is corrupt through deceitful desires, and to be renewed in the spirit of
your minds, and to put on the new self, created after the likeness of God
in true righteousness and holiness. —Ephesians 4:22–24

Desire language is the summary term for the sin nature in the New Testament epistles. The Old Testament captures the externalization of our desires with idols. In the New Testament, it's not as much a physical idolatry as much as a heart idolatry. The whole notion of desire, lust, and craving is a summary term, appearing in each of the apostles' letters. It answers the "why" question, the motivation question.

There's something you want, and it is your master. It is a desire that has become an evil lord over your life. Usually with Christians, the thing someone wants is a good thing. What's wrong with wanting a good thing? *The evil in our desires is often not what we want—the object—it's that we want it too much.* The desires themselves, what theologians historically have called *"natural affections"* can become inordinate—our thoughts and lives revolve around them. Our inordinate desires lead to anxiety, anger, fears, paranoia, escapism, aggression, domineering, obsession, and so on.

The world we live in views desires as needs that must be met, or drives that get conditioned for good or ill, neutral drives or instincts hardwired that are in conflict with each other or some other configuration. The single biggest defect with the modern personality theories is none of them understand our desires for what they actually are. But as we listen to God in his Word, we can understand our desires and learn to put off our inordinate desires and put on Christ.

March 19

Remember that you were at that time separated from Christ, alienated
from the commonwealth of Israel and strangers to the covenants of
promise, having no hope and without God in the world. But now in
Christ Jesus you who once were far off have been brought near by the
blood of Christ. —Ephesians 2:12–13

We usually try to measure our self-esteem by measuring ourselves against what we value the most and by comparing ourselves to others—both positively and negatively. It's one of the ways that fear of man and pride play a profound role in how we organize reality. In comparing myself to another person, I'm evaluating myself by what I call, "ladders to nowhere." If you're on the sixth rung and I'm on the fourth, you're better than me. But if I'm on the sixth rung and you are only on the fourth, I'm better than you. It's sad. But the gospel of our Lord and the entire revelation of Scripture rewrite these scripts and knock down the ladders to nowhere. God is the Creator, and he is sovereign. He creates differences. We could wish we were more athletic, prettier, had more money, had more brains, etc. But God chooses to place us in a context where we will be different from each other.

Before the living God, however, all of us are poor. We are all strangers, not insiders. We are all weak. We are all disabled. We are all dying. We're all slaves. We're all children. We are those who take refuge, unabashedly. We need a deliverer. *One of the ways the Bible reverses these false value systems is by actually taking degraded meanings and making them signs of relationship with God.* It's a complete inversion of the way that the false cultural values tend to operate.

March 20

"Blessed are the meek, for they shall inherit the earth." —Matthew 5:5

What is the defining characteristic of the Christian life? We usually (and rightly) say faith and love. But you can equally say that at the very center of the Christian life is meekness. Think of the first Beatitude: "Blessed are the poor in spirit" (Matthew 5:3). *Blessed are those who know their need. Blessed are those who are fundamentally needful of and oriented to the living God in the midst of life's sinfulness and sufferings and so forth.*

Think of the way in which in so many of the Psalms, even though the word *meekness* is not used, display this fundamental attitude of utter need: "Hear me, hear my cry, help me, be merciful to me" (Psalms 4:1; 57:1; 61:1–3). That's meekness. Meekness is this fundamental sense of being under somebody else. Meekness is not weakness. When you are meek you are simply acknowledging that your entire life force is absolutely under the control of another. This is the meekness of wisdom, the sense of not only being mastered, but of being dependent, of needing the grace of the one to whom you look. This sense of being attentive to the voice of another, attentive to the reign, the voice, and the will of the One who speaks to us.

The opposite of this mindset is to be self-exalting: you don't listen, you're a traitor, you want what you want, you're like Satan. Meekness is to die to yourself. It's life from the dead.

March 21

Even though I walk through the valley of the shadow of death,
I will fear no evil,
for you are with me;
your rod and your staff,
they comfort me. —Psalm 23:4

He has said, "I will never leave you nor forsake you."
So we can confidently say,
"The LORD is my helper;
I will not fear;
what can man do to me?" —Hebrews 13:5–6

It is interesting how the most commonly repeated command in the entire Bible is: "Don't fear." It's everywhere. It's also interesting that the way the Scripture deals with "Don't fear" is different from how it deals with "Don't commit adultery" or "Don't be a drunk" or "Don't steal." In those other sins, you're called to task, you're called to repentance, you're to repent and turn.

With "Don't fear," the Bible consistently, simply, gives you the good stuff. It says, "Don't be afraid, I'm with you." "Come out of the darkness, just come." "Don't be afraid, I will never leave you or forsake you. You're not alone." And you think about how in every fear in some way or other, you are alone. And there's something bigger than you that is out to get you, whether it's social humiliation or death by cancer.

But if you're not alone, the ground of the fear is cut away. We get tastes of that reality now. One day we will see it face-to-face. And on the last day, when we're face-to-face with Jesus, all fear will be gone forever.

March 22

Your words were found, and I ate them,
and your words became to me a joy
and the delight of my heart,
for I am called by your name,
O LORD, God of hosts. —Jeremiah 15:16

In considering your growth as a Christian, who and what most influenced you? Almost invariably, people tell stories.

When souls are being cured, people bear witness to their external troubles, their internal struggles, and their God of active providence and relevant speech. *Almost invariably, they specify how two means of grace served as vectors of their encouragement, instruction, and transformation: (1) the reorienting truth of a particular passage of Scripture; (2) the trustworthy love of a person who embodied Christ.*

I ask people to further describe these two factors by working through two sets of questions. The first set of questions considers how God works through his words.

What passage of Scripture has proved most significant in your life? What passage is most meaningful to you? Why? What does it touch? Why does this particular revelation from and about God have such an impact? How do these words make a difference?

The second set of questions considers two different perspectives on how God works through his people.

Who do you most trust? What about this most trustworthy person earns your trust? What changed in you because of that person's influence? What are you able to talk about because you trust?

Both of these factors matter supremely in the change process, because God's truth is spoken and embodied by loving people.

March 23

In this is love, not that we have loved God but that he loved us and sent his Son to be the propitiation for our sins. Beloved, if God so loved us, we also ought to love one another. —1 John 4:10-11

When hopes are crushed and dismembered, you must learn the one hope that can never be destroyed: "In this is love, not that we loved God, but that he loved us, and sent his Son to be the propitiation for our sins" (1 John 4:10). *Those words are not intended for "religious" people in "religious" contexts. They are words for the actual troubles we all must face, for the actual failings we all have, for all the things that prompt the Son's self-sacrificing love.*

When this holds you, as this takes root inside you, you learn how to live well up against all that is wrong: "Beloved, if God loved us in this way, we also ought to love one another" (1 John 4:11). You can be thankful. You can consider others. You can do small things gladly. Why else do we live? For what else are we born? You learn that you can make some difference. You can be merely helpful—not salvific. You will never think that you are better than any other human being. You will never think your efforts can right all wrongs. Beloved, you learn not to hate or fear or despair. You learn not to numb yourself. You learn to care.

March 24

I do not cease to give thanks for you, remembering you in my prayers, that the God of our Lord Jesus Christ, the Father of glory, may give you the Spirit of wisdom and of revelation in the knowledge of him, having the eyes of your hearts enlightened, that you may know what is the hope to which he has called you, what are the riches of his glorious inheritance in the saints. —Ephesians 1:17–18

O ur God gets personal with his children.

When we Christians say that we know and serve a "personal God," we are usually making a theological statement, confessing our faith. The God revealed in the Bible is a person—in fact, "one God in three persons." He is not an abstraction or an impersonal force. He is and does love, communion, intimacy, initiative, and cooperation within himself as well as with us. He acts. He speaks. He is this knowable yet unfathomable person. He thinks. He tells us what he thinks, so that we will know. And yet his thoughts are unsearchable, so that we cannot know. He is wise. He actively rules. His providential hand is gracious and just. He gives life. He builds up and nourishes. He tears down and kills. He renews. He does things a person does. And in the fullness of time, we are privileged to know him in personal, intimate, familial terms. *He is . . . our Father. He is . . . our Savior and our Lord. He is . . . our Holy Spirit. You and I are persons because he is this Person.*

And our personal God is not simply the one we describe and confess. He gets personal. He-who-is speaks to us and acts purposefully on our behalf. He is wholeheartedly hands-on with us.

March 25

With my voice I cry out to the Lord;
with my voice I plead for mercy to the Lord.
I pour out my complaint before him;
I tell my trouble before him. —Psalm 142:1-2

The standard practice for both public and private prayer is to speak so as to be heard by the Person with whom you are talking. Prayer is verbal because it is relational. Prayer *per se* is not a psychological experience. It is not contemplative immersion in an inner silence beyond words. It is an honest verbal conversation about things that matter, talking with someone you know, need and love.

I've known many people (myself included) whose relationship with God was significantly transformed as they learned to speak up with their Father. It is easy for prayer to become a kind of muttering to oneself, becoming a bucket list of requests, with little connection to who the Lord is and what he is up to. It is easy to slide into thinking of prayer as the evoking of certain religious feelings, or a set of seemingly spiritual thoughts, or a vague sense of comfort, awe, and dependency on a higher power. It is easy for prayer to meander into vague pieties, and to become virtually indistinguishable from thoughts. Sometimes it becomes indistinguishable from anxieties and obsessions! Sometimes prayer is confused with the act of stopping to ponder quietly and collect yourself. Sometimes prayer becomes a superstitious rabbit's foot, a ritual to keep bad things away and to ensure good things.

Do be quiet, and for the right reasons—so you can notice and listen, so you can find your voice. This living God is highly verbal and listens attentively to you.

March 26

Such is the confidence that we have through Christ toward God. Not that
we are sufficient in ourselves to claim anything as coming from us, but
our sufficiency is from God, who has made us sufficient to be ministers
of a new covenant, not of the letter but of the Spirit.
—2 Corinthians 3:4-6

Forgiven people don't simply rest in peace because their rest-less sins, corrosive guilt, and dark shame are now covered. You now have Christ's goodness and mercy to embody and to speak to others. You are God's beloved child—and that does not make you complacent and self-satisfied. You are beloved . . . so that you are able to love, to give your life away for others.

So you don't actually become a "self-confident individual." Your trust and confidence is decidedly not in yourself, but in the one who has loved you by saving you from misguided attempts at self-confidence. Your life will continue to be stressful. You are still mortal. You still live in a world of disappointments and dan-gers. You still fail. You still need the fragrant offering of the King and Savior who died at thirty-three. You serve this King and Savior, and his service is not always convenient. He puts you out of your comfort zone. He strips away the illusions that you can control people and events. He doesn't let you create a safe zone where you don't need to care about broken lives. *As a per-son whose confidence rests outside of yourself and in God, your life purpose is to love people who need the Savior who loves you.* You are only giving away a bit of what is being lavished on you.

March 27

Come now, you who say, "Today or tomorrow we will go into such and such a town and spend a year there and trade and make a profit"— yet you do not know what tomorrow will bring. What is your life? For you are a mist that appears for a little time and then vanishes. Instead you ought to say, "If the Lord wills, we will live and do this or that."
—James 4:13-15

You don't know how either your big decisions or your daily decisions will turn out. Trust your God. His providential control is the background for your entire life. Don't try to figure out what you can't know. Don't appeal to signs, hunches, impressions, coincidences. No need for magical thinking or reading the tea leaves. No need for paralysis waiting for guidance. No need for obsessive intercessions trying to pry an answer out of providence. *We will come to know God's providential will of control in retrospect. In the present, seek wisdom and make grown-up decisions about school, marriage, work, and the rest. There is no contradiction between making adult choices and having childlike trust.*

How he tells us to live and how he chooses to work meet in the mind and heart of God. In our sanctification, his revealed will and his providential working come hand in hand. Everything our Savior commands describes our sanctification: a life of purposeful wisdom, self-giving love, self-control, gratitude, and joy. And our Savior God is in control, continually working toward exactly these ends. He gives wisdom, love, self-control, and all other fine fruits—but along trajectories we could never predict or script.

March 28

Blessed be the God and Father of our Lord Jesus Christ, the Father of
mercies and God of all comfort, who comforts us in all our affliction, so
that we may be able to comfort those who are in any affliction, with the
comfort with which we ourselves are comforted by God.

—2 Corinthians 1:3–4

Affliction is where God develops you as a person so that your
trust and your love come into fruition. It's no accident that
Paul begins his second letter to the Corinthians by bearing witness to this dynamic. *His afflictions—and yours—are the door
through which God's love enters. His afflictions disciple him—and
yours disciple you—into compassion for others.* The afflictions of
others are the door through which Paul—and you—express genuine love and bear eloquent witness to the love of God. This
dynamic is so essential to understanding how life actually works
that Paul revisits this interplay of affliction and grace throughout
2 Corinthians.

I suspect that when most of us read 2 Corinthians 1:3–4 we
think first of the message of Jesus Christ. We are right to think
first about what God has promised and how he has acted on his
own words. He delivered us from sin and death. Jesus embodied
the Father's mercies. And God's message and action are not only
about what happened 2,000 years ago. He continually delivers
real-time mercies through the presence, strength, voice, and
hand of the life-giving Spirit. And he will deliver nothing less
than resurrection. If you live in him, you will never die; if you
die in him, yet you will live. The inexpressible gift of Christ—
past, present, and future mercies—is the heart of God's comfort.

March 29

But you are a chosen race, a royal priesthood, a holy nation, a people for his own possession, that you may proclaim the excellencies of him who called you out of darkness into his marvelous light. —1 Peter 2:9

Your true identity is who God says you are. *You will never discover who you are by looking inside yourself or listening to what others say. The Lord gets first word because he made you. He gets the daily word because you live before his face. He gets the last word because he will do the comprehensive life review.*

Your true identity inseparably connects you to God. Everything you ever learn about who God is—his identity—correlates specifically to something about who you are. For example, "Your Father knows your need" means you are always a dependent child. "Jesus Christ is your Lord" means you are always a servant.

Who God is also correlates with how you express your core identity as your various roles in life develop. For example, "The Lord's compassion for you is like a father with his children." You will always be a dependent child at your core, but as you grow up into his image, you become increasingly able to care for others in a fatherly way.

A true and enduring identity is a complex gift of Christ's grace. He gives a new identity in an act of mercy. Then his Spirit makes it a living reality over a lifetime. When you see him face-to-face, you will know him as he truly is, and you will fully know who you are.

Your new and true identity connects you to God's other children in a common calling. It is not individualistic. You are one member in the living body of Christ.

March 30

I have been crucified with Christ. It is no longer I who live, but Christ who lives in me. And the life I now live in the flesh I live by faith in the Son of God, who loved me and gave himself for me. —Galatians 2:20

When you live for the God who gave his only Son's life for you, you find genuine meaning for your life. This purpose is far bigger than your suffering, your failures, the death of your dreams, and the disillusionment of your hopes. *Living by faith in God for his purposes will protect you from despairing thoughts. God wants to use your personality, your skills, your life situation, and even your struggle with despair to bring hope to others.*

He has already prepared fruitful things for you to do. The apostle Paul says, in the Bible, "For we are God's workmanship, created in Christ Jesus to do good works, which God prepared in advance for us to do" (Ephesians 2:10). As you seek to work good in whatever circumstances you face, wherever God places you, you will find meaning, purpose, and joy. And when the race is over, it will be your Father in heaven who ends your days by calling you home. Until that time, may Jesus himself bless you, keep you, make his heavenly Father's face shine upon you, and give you peace.

March 31

Since therefore the children share in flesh and blood, he himself likewise
partook of the same things, that through death he might destroy the one
who has the power of death, that is, the devil, and deliver all those who
through fear of death were subject to lifelong slavery.
—Hebrews 2:14-15

When Adam and Eve believed Satan's lie—"you will not surely die"—and ate the fruit, death entered our world. Adam and Eve did die and ever since we too have been, as Hebrews says, subject to a lifelong slavery because of our fear of death (2:15).

How amazing then is the good news that Jesus is alive! Hebrews 2 explains how Jesus freed us from our slavery to death: Jesus became flesh and blood, so that he could fully enter into our life and fully enter into our death. When the Innocent One gave himself for the sins of the world, the power of death was broken. Jesus's life, death, and resurrection destroyed the one who has the power of death—the devil—and set free those who look to Jesus in faith.

When we face death, we have the same choice before us as we have in every area of life: Who will be our shepherd? Those who trust in Jesus have a Good Shepherd through the valley of the shadow of death into the house of the Lord forever (Psalm 23).

April 1

Hear my prayer, O LORD;
let my cry come to you!
Do not hide your face from me
in the day of my distress!
Incline your ear to me;
answer me speedily in the day when I call.
—Psalm 102:1–2

The Psalms are meant to be alive for us. As you read them, fill them with your life experience. This is exactly what God's people over the centuries and millennia have done. The Psalms, by and large, strip away the details of the writer's experience, and you are given patterns of experience that you can put your life into. You can use them as a container in which your exact life experience can be placed.

Psalm 102, for example, is labeled, "A prayer of one afflicted, when he is faint and pours out his complaint before the LORD." You can put lots of different things from your life into these categories. It allows you to put your life into this prayer: "Hear my prayer . . . let my cry come to you! Do not hide your face from me in the day of my distress! . . . answer me speedily in the day when I call!" (vv. 1–2). Lots of different things that happen in your life can go into the cry for help and the feeling of distress and affliction and being overwhelmed, unable to face all that's happening.

There are both psalms of sorrow and psalms of joy and gratitude. Live in both types of psalms. In the flow of the Psalms you get this picture of how life actually moves—through sorrow to joy.

When you get down to basics, you have reason for joy and you have reason for heartache, and the Psalms show you how to be honest with God in both.

April 2

Count it all joy, my brothers, when you meet trials of various kinds, for
you know that the testing of your faith produces steadfastness. And let
steadfastness have its full effect, that you may be perfect and complete,
lacking in nothing. —James 1:2–4

The testing of your faith produces something absolutely lovely: steadfastness, endurance, courage, and a mature faith. Whatever you are facing, God is doing something. Hard things are only a part of what God uses. Good things are also a trial. Everything is a test and a trial, to help you figure out what's wrong or needs maturing.

Every one of us is a beta version of what we will be. There are corrections needed, and God uses all sorts of situations as testing grounds to fix what's going on inside of us. Trials can show up as poverty or wealth, failure or success, illness or good health.

Another example of a test is what happens when you open your mouth. What will come out? James has a lot to say about that, especially if what comes out is angry or starts fires instead of helping people. Likewise, how do you respond to the suffering of others? Do you care? How will you help? Every good and bad situation you're in, whether it's happening to you or happening to other people, is a test.

As you see the ways you need to grow and mature, keep in mind that the Father gives more grace. Ask God for help. Why ask him? Because you lack something that you need; you need more of what he only can give. He will not reproach you for needing his help. He's not going to scold you. We're supposed to need him. We're made to need him, to lean upon his grace.

April 3

"Therefore do not be anxious, saying, 'What shall we eat?' or 'What shall we drink?' or 'What shall we wear?' For the Gentiles seek after all these things, and your heavenly Father knows that you need them all. But seek first the kingdom of God and his righteousness, and all these things will be added to you." —Matthew 6:31-33

Our fears must be attended to. We must do something with them. Our tendency is to try to ignore them, to try to barrel through life. Remember the Parable of the Sower in Luke 8? One of the features of the soil that is unfruitful is worry. The last thing in the world we want is to be unfruitful, given the fact that we have the Spirit of the living God. When worries and stresses come, we don't want to simply wait for panic attacks—these explosions of fear—we want to attend to them.

We want to stop. We want to speak to the Lord. We want to listen. Notice your anxieties creeping in today, tomorrow, this coming week. This is the perfect situation, to be familiar with our frailties and finiteness and weakness—what an ideal place to be to be able to speak about the Lord in new ways. Weaknesses and fears are an opportunity to move into Scripture and see the right Person, Jesus Christ himself.

Focus on today because the One who loves you, he will be the One who cares about tomorrow. You don't have to worry about tomorrow because he will worry about tomorrow on your behalf. And if the One of compassion and the One of strength is the One worrying about tomorrow, then you in your finitude can simply be focused on today. That's the beauty that we have in knowing Christ.

April 4

In him you also, when you heard the word of truth, the gospel of your
salvation, and believed in him, were sealed with the promised
Holy Spirit. —Ephesians 1:13

W ho is God? Everything we learn about him makes a
difference.

- *God makes us know him.* "Oh, continue your steadfast love
  to those who know you" (Psalm 36:10).

- *God acts according to his purposes.* "Whatever the Lord
  pleases, he does" (Psalm 135:6).

- *God gives grace.* "Surely goodness and mercy shall follow
  me all the days of my life" (Psalm 23:6).

- *God demonstrates power.* "Once God has spoken; twice I
  have heard this: that power belongs to God" (Psalm 62:11).

- *Christ invades to make peace between God and all nations.*
  "Praise the Lord, all nations! Extol him, all peoples!"
  (Psalm 117:1).

- *God's wrath will fall on enemies.* "Kiss the Son, lest he be
  angry, and you perish in the way, for his wrath is quickly
  kindled" (Psalm 2:12).

- *God inherits us and we inherit him.* "You are my Lord; I
  have no good apart from you. . . . The Lord is my chosen
  portion and my cup" (Psalm 16:2, 5).

We and God will inherit each other, will possess each other,
will share together in his glory. We live in this hope. In the fullness
of time all shall be well and all manner of things shall be well. The
Holy Spirit who rivets Christ into your heart now is the down payment of every good inheritance then and forever (Ephesians 1:13).

April 5

For the word of God is living and active, sharper than any two-edged
sword, piercing to the division of soul and of spirit, of joints and of
marrow, and discerning the thoughts and intentions of the heart.
—Hebrews 4:12

The Word of God is living and active: it strikes home, con-
victing you of sin and convincing you of the grace of God in
Christ Jesus. This Word effectively elicits your love; powerfully
renews your mind; wisely guides, guards, and shepherds your
walk.

Why is the Word so powerful? It is powerful because it is
"Thy Word, O Lord." The Word is not a noble human philosophy. It is not a magic incantation. *The Word is what God says:
about himself, about you, about the world you live in, about his
will. The Word reveals the Person who speaks it, a Person who tells
you what you need in order to repent and learn to trust, love and
obey him.* The Word received changes you; good soil bears good
fruit. The Word rejected or ignored also changes you; the heart
becomes increasingly hard, blind, and deaf.

Applying the Word wisely to real human life is work—hard,
prayerful, observant, thoughtful work. The first few verses of
Proverbs 2 say you need to listen hard; you need to cry out for
help; you need to search and dig. Listen to the Lord who speaks.
Love him and what he says.

April 6

We all once lived in the passions of our flesh, carrying out the desires
of the body and the mind. . . . But God, being rich in mercy, because of
the great love with which he loved us, even when we were dead in our
trespasses, made us alive together with Christ—by grace you have
been saved. —Ephesians 2:3a, 4-5

Sometimes we are right to be angry because we are experiencing true wrong. Then the problem is not getting angry, but how we express our anger. It's not right when your spouse is indifferent or inconsiderate. It's not right if your boss treats you unfairly or your child refuses to obey. It's not right when you are abused or attacked.

Anger has been given to us by God as the way to say, "That's not right and that matters." In our broken world, you will have many good reasons to be angry. But because we are part of the broken world, we express our anger at true wrongs in the wrong way. We blow up. We get irritated. We gossip. We complain. We hold a grudge. We shut people out. We get even. We become embittered, cynical, hostile. Something really wrong happened . . . and we become really wrong in reaction.

Anger is merciless. Anger sees, punishes, and gets rid of all offenders. *But God has chosen to be merciful to wrongdoers, including someone like you, who struggles with taking God's place in the world (Ephesians 2:1–5).* God's mercy brings life to you. If you struggle with bitterness, if you grumble, if you yell and argue, then you need God's mercy. You will receive mercy and help when you confess to God your struggle with trying to control everything and with judging those around you.

April 7

Be angry and do not sin; do not let the sun go down on your anger and give no opportunity to the devil. —Ephesians 4:26-27

Anger is an inevitable response to living in a troubled world where things can and do go wrong all the time. God does care about what makes you angry, but he also cares about how you express anger. If you don't learn how to deal with your anger, you will become bitter and estranged from God and people.

Anger is our God-given capacity to respond to a wrong that we think is important. God also gets angry at things that are wrong in this world. Your capacity to be angry is an expression of being made in his image.

God knows well that stuffing your anger deep inside is destructive. And learning tricks for keeping calm never discovers the purpose for which God designed anger. Anger needs to be acknowledged and expressed in a positive way, as a form of doing what is good and right.

God's way is for you to express your anger in a way that actually redeems difficult situations and relationships. How does this happen? It starts with understanding what anger is, where it comes from, and how a right relationship with God will actually change the way you view and express your anger.

April 8

For you did not receive the spirit of slavery to fall back into fear, but you
have received the Spirit of adoption as sons, by whom we cry,
"Abba! Father!" —Romans 8:15

People change when the Holy Spirit sheds the love of God abroad in their hearts through the gospel. Whoever receives the Spirit of adoption as God's child learns to cry out, "Abba, Father." People change when they catch hold of their responsibility for what they believe about God. Life experience is no excuse for believing lies; the world and devil don't excuse the flesh. *People change when biblical truth becomes more vivid and louder than previous life experience. People change when they have ears to hear and eyes to see what God tells us about himself.*

Even if your father or mother didn't love you, you *can* know the love of the Father. God the Father *is* faithful, merciful, consistent. God *is* aboundingly merciful (Psalm 103; 2 Corinthians 1:3). God *is* committed to meet his children directly, to teach, to bless, and to transform (John 15:2; Hebrews 12:1–14).

Here is a simple summary of the way to grow in the knowledge of God your Father: identify and take responsibility for the specific lies, false beliefs, desires, expectations, and fears that rule you and poison your relationship with God. Find specific truths in the Bible that counter your internal falsehoods and expectations. Turn to God for mercy and help, that the Spirit of truth would renew you, pouring out his love freely. Identify the specific sins committed against you. The love of God gives courage to look evil in the eye. Identifying wrong helps you know what to forgive. Find wise believers to pray for you, hold you accountable, encourage, and counsel you.

April 9

Jesus said to her, "I am the resurrection and the life. Whoever believes in me, though he die, yet shall he live, and everyone who lives and believes in me shall never die. Do you believe this?" —John 11:25-26

The biggest evidence for the fear of death ruling people lives is that they won't think about it. We live in a culture that can't face death. People organize their lives around illusions of substantiality, the idea that my life has meaning because I've got family, my life has meaning because of things I've achieved or because of what I've acquired. Those may be all good things, but they aren't good enough to stand up to death.

What is your life about? What makes life meaningful? As we face the fact of death, we must also face the fact that there is a man who lived who said, "I am the resurrection and the life." Jesus is the door out of the vortex of the darkness of death.

Where do you set your hopes? What do you actually live for? This question tells you where your heart is anchored. *Your hope is either in the one person who has defeated death, who is the resurrection and the life, or your hope is in something which may be a perfectly good thing but is not good enough and will perish with you.* There is a hope that stands up to death.

Be enriched (and enrich others) on these promises of God:

- "I am the resurrection and the life" (John 11:25).
- "I will never forsake you" (Hebrews 13:5).
- "Your life is hidden with Christ in God (Colossians 3:3).
- You have "an inheritance that is imperishable, undefiled, and unfading, kept in heaven for you" (1 Peter 1:4).

April 10

Now Jesus was praying in a certain place, and when he finished, one of his disciples said to him, "Lord, teach us to pray." —Luke 11:1

It's hard to learn how to pray. We can sometimes make an intelligent, honest request from capable friends whom we trust for something we need. But somehow when making a request is termed "praying" and the capable party is termed "God," things tend to get tangled. You've seen it, heard it, done it: the contorted syntax, formulaic phrasing, meaningless repetition, artificially pious tone of voice. If you talked to your friends that way, they'd think you'd lost your mind!

But if your understanding of prayer changes . . . if your practice of prayer then changes . . . if the prayer requests you make change, then you will change, and so will your relationship with God and his people.

When you pray, remember the three emphases of biblical prayer: circumstantial prayers, wisdom prayers, and kingdom prayers. Sometimes we ask God to *change our circumstances*: heal the sick, give us daily bread. Sometimes we ask God to *change us*: deepen my faith, teach us to love each other, forgive our sins. Sometimes we ask God to *change everything* by revealing himself more fully: your kingdom come, your will be done on earth as it is in heaven.

When any one of these three gets detached from the other two, prayer tends to go sour. If you just pray for better circumstances, then God becomes the errand boy—no sanctifying purposes, no higher glory. If you only pray for personal change, then it tends to reveal a self-absorbed spirituality detached from engagement with other people and the tasks of life. If you only pray for the sweeping invasion of the kingdom, then prayers tend toward irrelevance and overgeneralization.

Learn to pray with the three-stranded braid of our real need.

April 11

Blessed be the LORD!
For he has heard the voice of my pleas for mercy.
The LORD is my strength and my shield;
in him my heart trusts, and I am helped;
my heart exults,
and with my song I give thanks to him. —Psalm 28:6-7

It is unsettling to *need* help. Even when it ends up joyous and peaceful, dependency often doesn't feel very good in the process. You must cast your cares on God, who cares for you, because you're helpless in yourself (1 Peter 5:7). Your cares are bigger than you. You are under pressures. You are vulnerable, and you know it. You are burdened about matters you cannot control or fix. Life is hard. You feel crushed, careworn, threatened. You come as a refugee, not boasting of your assets, but bringing your cares. And your Father cares for you. He is strong and good. Safe at last! In the end, you rest peacefully.

Psalm 28 captures the whole cycle in a short space. David basically cries out, "Help! If you won't listen to me, I will die." This is not a comfortable feeling. He is threatened, battered, and exposed. He is powerless, with nowhere else to turn. The Lord does listen. The outcome is exultant and grateful. The voice of need becomes the voice of joy: "You are so good!" The cry for help becomes a shout of gratitude: "Thank you!" *It's not pleasant to need help. But it's a sheer joy to find help.*

April 12

[I pray] that the God of our Lord Jesus Christ, the Father of glory, may give you the Spirit of wisdom and of revelation in the knowledge of him, having the eyes of your hearts enlightened, that you may know what is the hope to which he has called you, what are the riches of his glorious inheritance in the saints, and what is the immeasurable greatness of his power toward us who believe. —Ephesians 1:17–19a

When people think about God by instinct, not by revelation, they ask many of the wrong questions. Will he meet my felt needs? Will he be copilot in my life? Can I get him to make my day, my spouse, my kids, my health, and my finances work out? Is he like a rabbit's foot? If I do my bit for God, will he do his bit for me? Is it tough to figure out what he's up to or what he wants? Is it possible he might disappoint me?

What would God have you know? Himself. His glory. Nothing less than the Lord who is the centerpiece of the universe and history. Jesus Christ. Reconciliation between yourself and God. The breakout of his light into every nation: the mystery now revealed. Our participation in his mission to invade darkness. Reconciliation between peoples as outcasts are welcomed into the community of promise. How to live in the way of peace and wisdom in all relationships. All this and more. You come to know wonder upon wonder.

The letter to the Ephesians tears the doors off mysteries. The love of Christ beyond knowing, now known. The unfathomable riches of Christ, now fathomed. Things exceedingly far beyond all you can ask or imagine, now revealed in front of your eyes.

April 13

Open my eyes, that I may behold
wondrous things out of your law. —Psalm 119:18

How do you bring your life to Scripture? I write in my Bible all the time—I underline, highlight, and mark up Scripture. I think about it, try to understand it, jot down things I might hear someone else say, and jot down my own thoughts. A simple excerpt of Scripture, even a one-liner, that you revisit in your head and your heart before you go to sleep, as you're driving the car, or at other times throughout the day, is going to actually make a difference in your life. When you're stressed, when you walk into a difficult situation, it's there, and it reminds you that there is a God who speaks to us, who promises to be with us.

Scripture comes to life when there's an intersection between what's going on in my life and who God is and what he says. A simple example is Philippians 4:5–6. It comes to life when I can say, "Lord, here are the things I am anxious about today," or "Here are my pressure points today, where I know I'm going to be stretched." I need God's help. I need a personal connection about what it means to trust him. I'm wanting to bring who I am to who he is.

I have been so struck by Psalm 119 and how in its 176 verses about our encounter with the God of Scripture, the God who speaks, *the three most common requests are: "Teach me," "Help me to understand," and "Make me alive to this." I can read the words on the page, but God must make it alive to me and alive to who he is.*

April 14

If we confess our sins, he is faithful and just to forgive us our sins and to cleanse us from all unrighteousness. —1 John 1:9

The beauty of the gospel is that our confession is always linked with God's promise of good. What are God's promises to you? Here are a few specifics to take to heart. Stop and think over each promise. What would it mean for you to truly believe and trust this? How does this promise change the meaning of your failures and sins? Think about these promises. Say them aloud. Turn to God on the basis of these promises.

I will never leave you or forsake you (Deuteronomy 31:6–8). Imagine—you will never be abandoned. He will not walk away.

The Lord make his face shine on you and be gracious to you (Numbers 6:25). Imagine—the Lord promises to turn a beaming face toward you. He will treat you with true kindness. Grace means undeserved kindness, and God is willingly gracious.

The Lord turn his face toward you and give you peace (Numbers 6:26). Imagine—he promises to never turn away from you. He gives peace. He does not get disgusted and give up. He does not leave you in trouble, turmoil, and confusion.

All the promises of God are YES in Jesus Christ (2 Corinthians 1:20). Jesus fulfills all these promises and more. Because Jesus loved you to the uttermost, you have true hope. He personally took your shame and guilt onto himself. Because of Jesus's death for you and because of his resurrection to life, you can bring your darkest sins into his bright light. Ask God for mercy because in Jesus he has shown that what he promises comes true.

April 15

And the peace of God, which surpasses all understanding, will guard
your hearts and your minds in Christ Jesus. . . . What you have learned
and received and heard and seen in me—practice these things, and the
God of peace will be with you. —Philippians 4:7, 9

The Lord is guarding you with his peace (Philippians 4:7). Here
is another consolation that will "delight your soul" in the
midst of anxiety. Paul says, "The peace of God, which transcends
all understanding, will guard your hearts and your minds in
Christ Jesus." The peace of God guarding and watching over us
is a theme that runs through the entire Bible. In Psalm 121, for
example, David says seven different times that God is watching
over you. Who is watching you? The Lord, the Creator of the
whole universe, and the one who has ultimate power over every
circumstance. And when is he watching? By day and by night.
Nothing that happens during the day or the night can harm you,
because the Lord, your Good Shepherd, is on guard.

When the Good Shepherd is present, his peace is present.
Paul says, "The God of Peace will be with you" (Philippians 4:9).
When you read about David in the Bible, the constant refrain is
that the Lord was *with* him. His life was blessed because the Lord
was *with* him. He failed, he sinned big, he often blew it, and yet
the Lord was *with* him. He grew very frail, and yet the Lord
was *with* him. His life was a picture of living faith—a faith that
faced trouble squarely and still knew the peace of God because
he knew that God was *with* him.

When you are anxious, remember that your God is guarding
you with his peace.

April 16

Stand therefore, having fastened on the belt of truth. —Ephesians 6:14a

The topic of truth is an interesting place for Paul to start the conversation on spiritual warfare, because the truth that is in Jesus, which Paul has been speaking of all through Ephesians, is completely outside of human imagination or experience. No one could have made this up. It's too good to be true—Christ died for sinners! Christ is raised to life by the power of God. We have life in him. We are raised with him. God dwells with his people. At the very core of Ephesians is the revelation of Jesus Christ, and it is this revelation that holds everything together.

We gird ourselves with Christ. Just like a belt holds us together, so the truth of who Christ is and his saving work hold us together. This Christ who was crushed and humbled unto death, even death on a cross, has triumphed over sin, death, and the grave. The belt of truth must come first. If Christ is not raised, then faith is futile, we are still in our sins, and the darkness wins. But if Christ is true, then all the old rules and rulers are overthrown. Death and moral darkness lose. All that is wrong will become untrue. Christ is true. And by speaking truth in love, we grow up into him who is truth (Ephesians 4:15).

April 17

Stand therefore . . . having put on the breastplate of righteousness.
—Ephesians 6:14

For at one time you were darkness, but now you are light in the Lord.
Walk as children of light (for the fruit of light is found in all that is good
and right and true) and try to discern what is pleasing to the Lord.
—Ephesians 5:8–10

Often we imagine that the breastplate of righteousness is only defensive and protective. The righteousness of Christ does protect our core. Because Christ's righteousness is now ours, we are protected from the death that we deserve for our sins. But Paul also wants us to envision Christ's righteousness in action. He is describing the goodness, love, faith, and humility that Jesus lived while here on earth. The same righteousness that is now ours must express itself in how we treat others. It protects us because it's the opposite of hate and pride and unbelief—which tears us and others apart.

Throughout Ephesians Paul calls us to the simple beauty of righteousness. "Walk as children of light, since the fruit of light is in all goodness, righteousness, and truth, proving in your life what is pleasing to the Lord" (Ephesians 5:8–10). *Righteousness is the way to take on all that is hurtful and false. Christ's battle strategy is to do what is right and good, and to say what is true and helpful.*

April 18

He restores my soul.
He leads me in paths of righteousness
for his name's sake. —Psalm 23:3

What is your hope? I'm talking about your hope that it's all going to turn out okay in the end. The Bible is clear: he who began a good work in you will bring it to completion (Philippians 1:6). Jesus came. God sent his only Son. How does that give you an indestructible hope? It's the little phrase: "for your name's sake." God is at work because of who he is. You're the beneficiary. God is acting to complete the work because of who he is.

Just think of a couple of passages with this phrase. Psalm 23:3: "He restores my soul. He leads me in paths of righteousness." Why? For his name's sake. Think of Psalm 25:7. Here, David has been talking about his sins: "Remember not the sins of my youth or my transgressions; according to your steadfast love remember me, for the sake of your goodness, O LORD!" We see four verses later in Psalm 25:11: "For your name's sake, O LORD, pardon my guilt, for it is great."

I think this is perhaps the most pointed description of our utter dependence on God's mercy. That is absolute dependence outside of yourself. Why does he have hope? "For your name's sake."

You could paraphrase it this way: "Oh Lord, when you think of me, think of yourself." When you remember me, remember who you are. When you think about my sinfulness and my failings, remember your mercies. You are good, compassionate, faithful, loving kindness, forgiving. It's all based on the fact that God is true to who he is. That is the absolute foundation of any confidence that we would have.

April 19

Therefore let anyone who thinks that he stands take heed lest he fall. No temptation has overtaken you that is not common to man. God is faithful, and he will not let you be tempted beyond your ability, but with the temptation he will also provide the way of escape, that you may be able to endure it. —1 Corinthians 10:12-13

One of the basics of a biblical worldview is knowing that you have all the same weaknesses and struggles as the rest of people in your life. You, like me, deal with pride. You, like me, deal with some perversion in the way you treat money. You, like me, deal with fear of man. We all put a different spin on it but pride, fear of man, love of pleasure, mammon worship, this is human nature 101, isn't it? Our differences are matters of degrees, not differences of kind. In kind, you and I deal with all the same kinds of sufferings. There are people who do you wrong, there is creeping mortality that besets you, there are financial pressures and temptations, and there are voices in the culture that try to lead you astray. There are huge commonalities between us all.

There is a fundamental gentleness in the way we deal with people that comes because of fellow-feeling, a sympathy of heart in what we face. We're all in the same boat. We're all in need of mercies. There is wonder in the argument of passages like Hebrews 4 and 5 that Jesus Christ himself, who was without sin, entered into human experience, cried out to God and needed God to be his Savior and refuge just as much as we do, and trusted his Father even in the face of death. Thus, he can help us, and thus, we can help each other.

April 20

And whatever you do, in word or deed, do everything in the name of the
Lord Jesus, giving thanks to God the Father through him.
—Colossians 3:17

As you experience the process of biblical change, you start to
see life and its difficulties as existing within a wider, higher,
deeper set of purposes. You may have never really realized that
the events of your life actually serve the purpose of glorifying
God. *As you grow as a disciple, you start to reinterpret or reorient
all the events of your life—whether it's a traffic jam or a diagnosis of
cancer—and understand them as opportunities to better know and
love the Lord.* You can also be positioned to minister to someone else in a difficult, unexpected situation because that's exactly
how the living God in Christ met you, very tenderly and very
clearly. So maybe your ministry will be ignited by the way you
handle some little dinky episode out on the highway.

Our Father, please have mercy on us. We live so carelessly,
and we have these little moments of illumination, it's as
though our head bobs above the ocean. And then we sink
for a long time. We beseech you to awaken us and make us
float, make us breathe, make us see. Let us take seriously
the delightful call of Christ, calling us out of darkness
into light. Let us embrace your call in ways that are life
rearranging, the call that we would become men and
women who contribute to the quantum of light in the dark
world, and don't just bumble along as one more person
stumbling through darkness. Have mercy on your people.
Make us beautiful. Carry us forward. Amen.

April 21

"Be merciful, even as your Father is merciful." —Luke 6:36

Goodness and steadfast love walked among us, took on flesh, was tempted as we are yet without sin, and was touched with the feeling of our infirmities. He deals gently with the ignorant and wayward.

Such love is a communicable attribute of God—therefore he commands us to learn patience and kindness. In taking us on—we who are too often impatient, too often unkind—and in making us into the image of Jesus Christ, the Holy Spirit will make us patient and kind. He will teach us to be "in it for good" with other people, amid the ups, the downs, the exigencies. This is the lifelong goal of Christian ministry.

The Lord's heart is revealed in this beautiful description: "The LORD, the LORD, a God merciful and gracious, slow to anger [in the Greek, "patient"], and abounding in steadfast love and faithfulness, keeping steadfast love for thousands, forgiving iniquity and transgression and sin" (Exodus 34:6–7). He is in it for good with all who take this revelation to heart as God's great gift of himself, as our greatest need, as the goal of our moral transformation.

It is striking that when revealing his glory and goodness, the Lord chose to show forth communicable attributes. He could have mentioned his omniscience, omnipotence, omnipresence, self-existence, eternity—things infinitely beyond the creature. But he chose to reveal his mercy, what is within our comprehension, within our experience, within our grasp—by grace. We, too, learn to become merciful and gracious, slow to anger, abounding in steadfast love and faithfulness, forgiving.

April 22

O LORD, you have searched me and known me!
You know when I sit down and when I rise up;
you discern my thoughts from afar.
You search out my path and my lying down
and are acquainted with all my ways. —Psalm 139:1-3

The Psalms communicate a warmth and immediacy of our relationship back to God: honesty, gratitude, bewilderment, anguish, hope, trust, and the rest. But what do all these things mean? Consider with me the following inexpressibly wonderful truths.

God watches you and watches over you. The Searcher of hearts sees everything, inside and out. The Christian life is the absolutely open life and can be lived in the wide open. God also oversees, guards, protects, provides, and looks out for the well-being of his children. You are never out of sight of the one whose steadfast love has been set on you.

God's hand is involved in every circumstance. God is present in the midst of every trouble. There are no accidents in the lives of God's children. He is up to something good in the lives of his own. God's providence means that a guiding hand rests on every event.

God's voice speaks to you in all circumstances. The Holy Spirit is the final author of the Bible, and the Bible speaks to all of life. A Christian is and must be a person of the Book, because Christ himself lived by the Book. Those sheep who hear Jesus's voice hear the Bible.

God pours out his love in your heart through the Holy Spirit. He makes you understand the message of grace in Jesus Christ. The Spirit's power makes the Spirit's message a joy in the hearts of listeners.

To become party and witness to God's redemptive love is an intimacy worth shouting about.

April 23

Refrain from anger, and forsake wrath!
Fret not yourself; it tends only to evil. —Psalm 37:8

To be made new means dying to what is old . . . to be made new means awakening to new life. We might say it this way: you and I must become Christians with respect to our anger. We must learn to stop complaining, criticizing, arguing, and being bitter and hostile. To do that, we need the mercies of Christ—and Christ freely gives himself to the needy. Because of our tendency to flip out and revert to old ways, we need to enter lifelong rehab. The Christian life begins with an awakening and continues with a reorientation process. It presses forward until you see Jesus face-to-face. You and I are in process.

I know many people who have relearned to do anger, who have had their anger significantly transformed. Each of them bears witness to the active hand of God. It takes grace. And each of them bears witness to the diligence of humility. It takes grit. You must honestly and patiently wrestle with yourself. You must consciously choose to become a different kind of person. You must work it out over a lifetime. *None of us will be perfect in this life. But each of us can grow. Any headway you make in the reorientation of your anger is worth more than any amount of money: "nothing you desire can compare" (Proverbs 3:13–15).*

The goal is to keep changing in the right direction.

April 24

"But I say to you who hear, Love your enemies, do good to those who hate you, bless those who curse you, pray for those who abuse you. . . . If you love those who love you, what benefit is that to you? For even sinners love those who love them." —Luke 6:27-28, 32

It is easy to glaze over when you hear, "Love your enemies, do good to those who hate you." It is easy to write off Jesus, as if he must not really mean it, as if in saying this he is being a rather gentle-souled, naïve idealist. Does Jesus's call imply that he hopes that people can "just be nicer to each other"? Is Jesus unaware that this sounds like, "Let people walk all over you"? Nothing of the sort. The love and goodness he is talking about has more grit than sweetness, more hard-as-nails realism than niceness. You can't separate what he did for us—blood, and sweat, and tears—from what he calls us to do. He means what he says.

To do good to someone who does wrong, who has hurt you or others—this is a marvel. It's so much easier to give back in kind. Charity does what the recipient doesn't deserve. Someone deserves payback because they did you or others wrong. But you do charity.

Anger grips tightly a wrong, points it out, prosecutes it, punishes it. Mercy acts generously toward a wrongdoer, rather than claiming your pound of flesh. Anger thinks this way: "I've been wronged, so I will deal out fair and just punishment to the malefactor." But generosity, like patience and forgiveness is "unfair." You treat with purposeful kindness someone who treated you or others badly.

April 25

Trust in him at all times, O people;
pour out your heart before him;
God is a refuge for us. —Psalm 62:8

Search me, O God, and know my heart!
Try me and know my thoughts! —Psalm 139:23

God wants to know what's on your heart. He wants you to need him, to go to him, and to plead with him about your real problems. He wants you to tell him all about your troubles—the health problems, the financial worries, the straying child, the struggling church, and the grief and loss you have experienced. He wants you to confess to him the sins that drive your sinful anxiety—the idols that have hijacked your life. He wants you to ask for his forgiveness for your lack of trust and faith, and for times you've desired his good gifts more than him.

Begin with total honesty and say, "Lord, I don't understand; help me to understand you." *Admit to him that, although your words say you believe he is in control, your anxious thoughts reveal the truth: You still desire to be in control.* Ask God to teach you how to close the gap between what you say you believe and how you think and function on a day-by-day basis. God will use your honest confession to build a relationship with him that will give you true and lasting peace. Your growing and deepening relationship with God is what will transform your anxious thoughts into humble faith and trust.

April 26

"The secret things belong to the LORD our God, but the things that are revealed belong to us and to our children forever, that we may do all the words of this law." —Deuteronomy 29:29

Scripture is tailored for human relevance. As we read in Deuteronomy 29:29, the things revealed are for us—and are relevant for every generation. Scripture shows no interest in abstract theological dogmas disconnected from life. Scripture shows a great deal of interest in what people are like, and how God directly connects. While teaching us who God is, Scripture simultaneously teaches us to know what he sees in us, and what concerns him about us, and what his purposes are in working with us. This reality has many implications. Here's one implication worth taking to heart and pondering long and hard: *Anything God reveals about himself, whether in words or actions, simultaneously reveals something about us.*

Here are some simple examples:

- God makes and sustains everything that exists. This means you and I depend on him for life, whether we recognize it or not.

- God clearly sees and fairly evaluates everything we do. This means that whatever you want, fear, think, do, feel, or say matters. People are accountable. And it means we have a problem. By nature, nurture, choice, and habit, we stray into self-destructive delusions.

- God is merciful. This means that we need mercies and gifts of many kinds—rescue, forgiveness, reconciliation, protection, strength, help, hope, wisdom, a new heart, a new life. Every promise and gift of God is embodied in Christ.

To be a human being is to live, move, and have our being under his care, under his eye, and under dire need for his grace.

April 27

The steadfast love of the LORD never ceases;
his mercies never come to an end;
they are new every morning;
great is your faithfulness. —Lamentations 3:22-23

Learning how to live well is the most complex skill imaginable. It is the work of a lifetime. But isn't it odd that a musician who recognizes and acquires the intricate skills and sensibilities that go into playing the violin, will build her personal life by rote as a pastiche of formulas, truisms, mechanisms, and mantras? And isn't it odd that a man who knows how much learning, experience, close observation, trial and error, and heart go into crafting fine furniture, will destroy his life through automatic and unquestioned impulses of unbelief, anger, immorality, fear, greed, and ambition? And isn't it odd that a Christian would assume that a theological pat answer and a behavioral quick fix will suffice for living the Christian life, when it's obvious that our struggle with failures, missteps, pain, and vulnerability will not cease until we have faced down our last enemy and see the face of God?

We are meant to stop and think hard. Wisdom is a way of seeing and understanding the world, ourselves, other people, and the Lord God.

We are meant to develop increasing skill. Wisdom is a way of engaging the world, ourselves, others, and the Lord.

We are meant to seek out mentors, role models, wise friends. He who walks with the wise becomes wise.

We are meant to learn how to acknowledge and recover from failures. What hides in the dark grows darker; what comes to the light becomes bright as day.

We are meant to face pain. Mercies are new every morning because mercies are needed.

April 28

Fear not, for I am with you;
be not dismayed, for I am your God;
I will strengthen you, I will help you,
I will uphold you with my righteous right hand. —Isaiah 41:10

W hy do you feel anxious? There are two reasons, and they interlock. The first reason is objective, and it is true. You live in a world that is uncontrollable. You face things that are threatening. You are indeed vulnerable. The second reason you feel anxious interlocks with the first. Your heart tells you that in this world of dangers, threats, and uncontrollable things, you are all alone. That second reason is a lie.

God tells us all throughout Scripture to not be afraid. He says it in a note of reassurance and promise related to his presence with us: "Don't be afraid; I'm with you. I'm here. I am committed for the duration. I began a good work. I won't give up on you. I am yours. You are not alone."

God speaks directly to the core experience of anxiety with the fundamental reality of his presence. That false prophet in your heart is speaking half-truth. We are indeed in a very vulnerable world. But probe the claim that you're all alone to face it and you discover that to be a lie. There's someone who is here. You're not alone.

April 29

The LORD your God is in your midst,
a mighty one who will save;
he will rejoice over you with gladness;
he will quiet you by his love;
he will exult over you with loud singing. —Zephaniah 3:17

All relationships come with purpose. *God himself is intentional in his relationships. His relationship with you did not happen by accident—it happened on purpose. He has sought you out to be his own.* It is an on-purpose relationship with you. At the beginning of Philippians, Paul reminds us that he who began a good work in you will bring it to completion on the day of Christ Jesus (Philippians 1:6). This shows an intentional beginning, middle, and finale to his work in you. This is a powerful reminder that you are not alone, no matter what is happening.

What do you most need? You need strength from outside yourself, his ear to listen to your need—someone who will listen when you cry to him. You need protection and wisdom and help. To this end, you are loved by the God of creation, the God of redemption, the God who made all things, and the God who redeems all things—the Father who is compassionate toward his children, the Word of God that became incarnate for us, full of grace and truth.

God knows each one by name. He takes each one of us to heart. He knows us by heart, and his thoughts toward every single person are more than the grains of the sand on the seashore. As you grow in this understanding, you begin to know you are not alone.

April 30

Be not far from me,
for trouble is near,
and there is none to help. —Psalm 22:11

You may know that as a child of God, you are not alone. But you often feel alone. So much of human life is experienced in a lonely, isolated, overwhelming way. You may feel isolation related to sin or various forms of suffering. Other people can and do come into your struggles, but they can only come halfway at best.

God has designed his universe so that only he can go all the way into your experience. Only God can come all the way in and be on the inside of your experience. That's the simple, objective part of the fact that you aren't alone.

How do you find your way from alone to not alone? Psalm 22 climbs into the heart of Jesus's experience of being alone as he was dying. As we read this Psalm, we are watching someone else deal with that essential problem of aloneness. We are watching Christ deal with it. He has been there. He is one of us.

It's so encouraging to see this psalm is an honest process of wrestling between what Jesus knows of God's faithfulness and the suffering he is experiencing. The hinge of the psalm comes in verse 21b when he knows God is helping him. The psalm then moves to worship as the cry for help has been met with God's care—God has answered him. *Jesus shows us how to move from alone to not alone—clinging to the promises of a loving and faithful God and waiting to see how he will meet you.*

May 1

Remember your mercy, O Lord, and your steadfast love,
for they have been from of old.
Remember not the sins of my youth or my transgressions;
according to your steadfast love remember me
for the sake of your goodness, O Lord! —Psalm 25:6-7

Having the right expectation of the change process—of the struggle of sanctification—is so important. To the end of our days there will be a struggle. It won't be completely resolved until we see Jesus face-to-face, when tears are wiped away, and we are made like him.

How do you think about failure? You need to have a vision of ongoing growth that is colored by ongoing failure. You can expect to see both increments of growth in your life, as well as moments of battling sin. Within this wrestling, you can be both tremendously encouraged about your growth, while still always being aware of the fight with darkness.

The nature of the growth process is that you gradually see an increase in the rapidity of your repentance, an increase in your self-awareness, and an increase in your appreciation of God's grace and your dependence on his power and promises. You learn to echo the psalmist when you cry out to God, "You are a God of steadfast love. When you think of me, think of you. When you remember my sin, remember your mercy."

You can have joy, even in the midst of continuing imperfection, not just by fighting sin well, but by growing in doing good. Every single person who makes any progress with persistent sin starts to care for other people. They discover that they have something to give away. With the mercy you have received in your affliction, you are able to comfort those in any affliction (2 Corinthians 1:4), as you grow toward the goal of a pure heart and a good conscience and a sincere faith (1 Timothy 1:5).

May 2

For the word of God is living and active, sharper than any two-edged
sword, piercing to the division of soul and of spirit, of joints and of
marrow, and discerning the thoughts and intentions of the heart.
—Hebrews 4:12

Why do people do what they do? The Lord God has a great deal to say on the issue. He vigorously rebuts counterfeit explanations by demonstrating that human motivation has to do with *him*. Scripture claims to search out the "thoughts and intentions of the heart" according to the specific criteria by which the Searcher of hearts evaluates what he sees in us (Hebrews 4:12).

Good questions provide aid in discerning the patterns of a person's motivation. They aim to help people identify and unveil the ungodly masters in their hearts. Good questions reveal "functional gods," what or who actually controls particular actions, thoughts, emotions, and attitudes. Consider when you become anxious, preoccupied, and filled with fretful concern. As the sin of worry tightens its unpleasant hold on your soul, perhaps you jump for some escapist quick fix: raid the icebox, watch TV, go shopping, drink a beer, play a game. Or perhaps you mobilize to seize control: make a string of phone calls, work all night, build a faction of supporters, clean your house, get mad. Why is all this going on?

You profess that God is your rock and refuge, a very present help in whatever troubles you face. You profess to worship him, trust him, love him, obey him. *But in that moment—hour, day, or season—of anxiety, escape, or drivenness, you live as if you needed to control all things. But grace reorients us, purifies us, and turns us back to our Lord.*

May 3

If your law had not been my delight,
I would have perished in my affliction. —Psalm 119:92

Psalm 119 has it all. It makes readers attach love and need to truth, and it makes prayers attach truth to need. This psalm is addressed to the God who speaks and acts. Listen to these statements and consider how they impact your life:

- You answered me (v. 26).
- The earth is full of your steadfast love (v. 64).
- You are good and do good (v. 68).
- Your rules are righteous and in faithfulness you have afflicted me (v. 75).
- I am yours (v. 94).
- You are my hiding place and my shield (v. 114).

This psalm tells you how the Lord sees sufferings and what they mean, and he tells you how he sees you. It takes a hard look at the fact that life has hardship, pain, difficulty, and suffering.

As the psalmist talks to God, you see a template for living, thinking, feeling, reacting, and responding to suffering. He gets specific with God about what he is going through and where he is tempted, and he asks God for what he needs. There's a continual plea for God to do things. He's asking for God to teach him, to open his eyes, to revive him. He knows he needs someone outside of himself to help him in what he is facing. *He reaffirms his commitment to God, and you see the resulting joy: "I am your servant" (v. 125). This is the direction he will head, even if he gets blown out of the water by sin, suffering, and affliction.*

Lord, would you enlarge our hearts, that we might live, walk, move, think, feel, and relate in the light of what has been said to us by you and by a person who loved you?

May 4

He does not deal with us according to our sins,
nor repay us according to our iniquities. —Psalm 103:10

Mercy traverses the exact same ground as raw anger. Mercy says that what is wrong matters. Evil matters and is offensive.

Mercy does something about what is wrong. It's not passive, nor is it happy about what's going on. The dominant key, however, is love, not hostility or destruction. Mercy sees what is wrong and sets about a long, slow repair.

Mercy is an expression of love in the face of something that is wrong. Here are four different aspects of what the constructive displeasure of mercy looks like:

1. *Patience.* It is slow to anger. Patience is willing to work with wrong over time. When you are truly patient, you often see the wrong more clearly, because you do not immediately react with your own wrong. It is an act of courage; a clear-minded choice to engage for the long haul with something that needs repair.

2. *Forgiveness.* It is a kind of holy unfairness that names the wrong for what it is but doesn't give back what is deserved. Forgiveness sees the wrong and then lets it go.

3. *Generosity.* Doing good to someone who has done wrong. Loving your enemies. Not returning evil for evil.

4. *Constructive conflict.* It attacks the problem, confronts evil, rescues victims, and calls wrongdoers to accountability. It is an act of love to bring about what is good and beautiful.

How do you learn to do this? You learn because Jesus has already treated you this way, with patience, forgiveness, generosity, and a willingness to engage with what is wrong in your life.

May 5

So teach us to number our days
that we may get a heart of wisdom. —Psalm 90:12

Psalm 90 is an invitation for you and I to think about our mortality and all that it means. The closing six verses are all tied to a plea to God for his loving kindness and his favor to lead to something permanent: "Establish the work of our hands" (v. 17). Make what we do permanent, not just flying away like the mist.

What lasts? What holds up? The call to daily die to our sinfulness is really the same as asking yourself this question. One of the ways you learn to both die well and to live well is that you do battle with sin. This battle does not end until you see him face-to-face and are made like him.

At the end there are things that last. What are they? *When I faced a sudden need for open heart surgery and was confronted with the fact that I could die on the table, I found that everything else fell away but these two things: love for God and love for people.* All the clutter, all the distraction went away, and what was left was a God to know, love, adore, seek, and trust, and then to love people well—my wife, my children, friends, etc.

For we who are in Christ, what we do is not in vain (1 Corinthians 15:58). All works done unto the Lord stand the test of time. As you learn this perspective, you can then start to touch other people's lives in ways that help them understand what really lasts.

May 6

Now may the God of peace . . . equip you with everything good that you
may do his will, working in us that which is pleasing in his sight, through
Jesus Christ, to whom be glory forever and ever. Amen.
—Hebrews 13:20-21

Consider the graces that God steadily works to produce in us. They are certainly different from what we naturally gravitate to. In that sense, his purposes are extreme, radical, on fire, and exceedingly beyond all you can ask or even imagine!

But then again, the Holy Spirit seems on fire to produce a life afire with rather unfiery things. His view of what is significant cuts "awesome" down to size (while being the farthest thing from dull). He is forming in you things that are good for the long haul. Good for times when your feelings are marked with pain or loneliness. Good for days or months or years of perplexity and struggle. Good for the small deaths of old age and then for dying. Good for helping others going through the same troubles. He is forming what is good for living life well, wisely, and on purpose.

We long for dramatic action, but right now, we need good graces to carry us through all that happens until the Day when the dramatic finally happens once and for all.

Consider this list of "ordinary" graces that are set on fire with the odd fire of God's purposes. Ponder each one for a moment: mercy, patience, gratitude, commitment, constructive candor, bearing one another's burdens, reliance on another, peacemaking, endurance, humility, love.

Not one of these sets off conspicuous fireworks. But these are worth more than anything else you could ever desire. They deliver even more than you think. Jesus lived these good graces. He is making you into this image.

May 7

To you, O LORD, I call;
my rock, be not deaf to me,
lest, if you be silent to me,
I become like those who go down to the pit. —Psalm 28:1

In prayer we connect human need with the promises of God. All true prayer comes forth when our need and God's promises meet. We need everyday wisdom and understanding. We need power to live within the sufferings and afflictions of human life. We need courage, humility, hope, faith, and love. We need forgiveness every single day. We need the presence of God himself in our lives. We need provision, both tangible and spiritual. We need hope. We need to know that the King will come. We need indestructible friendship.

These needs correlate to the attributes of God—his character and his nature. Deuteronomy 31:8 says, "It is the LORD who . . . will be with you; he will not leave you or forsake you. Do not fear or be dismayed." Your need for courage, for God's presence, and for hope are answered by who God is.

Understand that faith has two moods. One side of faith is need. The other side of faith is gratitude. You have reason for both joy and heartache in life. So be honest about both in your prayers.

Be specific and talk straight to God. I often use the Psalms to pattern my prayers. The Psalms are general and open so that your life experience can be placed in them. Over the centuries our spiritual forebears have done this with the Psalms. *You want to have a straightforward conversation at the intersection of where you really are and who God really is. When this conversation happens, redemption explodes onto the plane of our earthly existence.*

May 8

Because he inclined his ear to me,
therefore I will call on him as long as I live. —Psalm 116:2

Our God teaches us to have meaningful conversations with him. Prayers in Scripture are candid, constructive, relevant and grace-filled. They teach us to remember who he is. As we listen, we learn to talk honestly about what is good or bad about us. We learn to speak of hard things as well as happy things in our circumstances. We learn to cry out where we need help and sing about how we are grateful. Our prayers can express care and concern for others—"I pray that your love will abound more and more with knowledge and all discernment" (Philippians 1:9).

God then teaches us to have meaningful conversations with each other. The way we talk with him directly relates to how we talk with each other. Ephesians 4:15 says that we grow up in Christ by lovingly speaking truth with each other. How do we encourage each other daily in the face of sin's deadly deceitfulness? How do we comfort each other in whatever afflictions and difficulties each one of us faces today? How do we talk about what matters in a way that makes a difference?

Listen in to how Scripture shows us what it's like to talk with God. Then talk about the same kinds of things with other people.

Our Father teaches us to traffic in reality—addressing the best and the hardest things in life. You can't live in reality without seeing both and remembering your Lord in the midst of it. Facing the hard things, you can be honest about your need. Receiving the good things, you can express joy and thanks. As you learn to pray about what matters, you are also learning to talk with other people about what matters.

May 9

Blessed be the LORD,
for he has wondrously shown his steadfast love to me
when I was in a besieged city. . . .

Be strong, and let your heart take courage,
all you who wait for the LORD! —Psalm 31:21, 24

We tend to have a perspective that suffering is a moment and not a condition. We think of it as seasonal, where life is miserable for a few weeks and then we're fine. But the overarching reality is that the human condition includes chronic and degenerative suffering. It's a gift from God that some of our suffering is seasonal and momentary, but in the bigger picture, we live in a broken world with mortal bodies that are chronically wasting.

This notion should be fundamental to our understanding of suffering. Jesus did not just come to alleviate the little aches and pains of life; he came to deal with our chronically destructive condition and give us hope. Those dealing with chronic suffering can live with a fundamental realism about what life is and who they are and who Jesus is—broken humans can shine with the simplicity of faith.

When tough things happen, what do you live for? Hardship can be used by God to create a living and true faith, or it can shatter people. There's a lot of fluff in Christendom, but only the living core can stand up to death and evil. *The way you can be strong and let your heart take courage is to hope in the Lord. This is where the peace of God begins to outweigh the suffering.* Jesus Christ, the Holy Spirit, the promise of peace, and the presence of our Father aren't just religious theories and niceties. If we seek him, we find him, and he brings comfort and he brings joy.

May 10

"But I say to you who hear, Love your enemies, do good to those who
hate you, bless those who curse you, pray for those who abuse you."
—Luke 6:27-28

*G*odly anger does not need to "win." It does not have to succeed
*in bringing malefactors to justice. Its purposes are more modest
on the surface, but more extravagant under the surface: the glory of
God and the eternal well-being of God's people.* Godly anger has
good effects for all concerned. So when you are confronted with
unrepented evil, when your best efforts seem to have had no
good or lasting effect, you don't have to become angrier. You can
instead become more objective and matter-of-fact.

On the inside, mercy works to soften your heart. Jesus
would have you pray for their well-being, which includes their
repentance unto life. On the outside, you are called to persistent,
straightforward acts of unmerited kindness: "If your enemy is
hungry, feed him; if he is thirsty, give him something to drink"
(Romans 12:20). Also, on the outside, you may be called to join
with others in those corporate activities that impose objective
consequences on wrong behavior: church discipline, severance
from a job, an eviction notice, calling the police, criminal pro-
ceedings, enacting better laws, voting in new leaders, etc. Such
good activities are also "judgments against perceived evil," but
they operate in a more dispassionate mode. They are objective,
sober necessities. They set limits on our more personal labors
to help people. As such, they are a great comfort and good. It
is often a great relief for a person facing persistent evil to know
that others are also taking responsibility for making it right. It
reduces the temptation toward vigilante action.

May 11

The humble faith that makes for peace is just as objective as the proud craving that makes for conflicts. Many people view faith as their feelings of trust, confidence, peacefulness, contentment, or happiness. Many people view prayer as an experience of certain religiously-colored emotions: fervency, stillness, joy, familiar comfort. Such feelings are sometimes associated with faith and prayer, but the Psalms illustrate how the faith that talks to God can express itself in many different feeling states, some pleasant, some rather unpleasant. And we should never forget that many forms of falsehood may feel peaceful or fervent or confident. *The state of your emotions is no accurate register of whether you are actually relying on God.*

Faith lives as though what God says is true. God does give more grace to the humble. Humble yourself. God does oppose proud warmakers. Come out with your hands up and surrender. He truly forgives those who open their eyes to their sins. Stop, open your eyes, confess. He sealed his promise in the blood of Jesus. Count on it. He actually gives the Holy Spirit to his children who ask. Ask. "If any of you lacks wisdom, let him ask God, who gives generously to all without reproach, and it will be given him." (James 1:5). Ask unafraid, knowing your need. "You do not have, because you do not ask. You ask and do not receive, because you ask . . . to spend it on your passions" (James 4:2–3). Ask, repenting of your lusts. God himself will empower fruit-bearing. He gives wisdom to walk in the image of Jesus Christ.

May 12

I therefore, a prisoner for the Lord, urge you to walk in a manner worthy
of the calling to which you have been called, with all humility and
gentleness, with patience, bearing with one another in love, eager to
maintain the unity of the Spirit in the bond of peace. —Ephesians 4:1-3

The Lord calls you to please him by humility, forbearance, candor, generosity, and tenderheartedness to all others. This common calling operates irrespective of the social roles you fill. It establishes a core attitude of mutuality that threads through every single relationship. *We are one with each other and we are equals, leveled before God, whether apostle or new convert, tycoon or welfare recipient, CEO or janitor, competent adult or helpless infant. We live as peers before him who is no respecter of persons.* Differences of competence, power, wealth, intelligence, achievement, opportunity, sex, age, and ethnic background vanish.

All of Ephesians 1:1–5:20 and 6:10–24 applies always, to every Christian, in every relationship. You have been given God's grace and are commanded by your Lord Jesus to give grace to others. Whether you are married or single, male or female, child or parent, employee or boss, you live, move, and have your being within a mutuality: one church, saints together, members of one body, fellow citizens, neighbors, God's household and dwelling, brothers and sisters to one another. You are a *we*. So you are called to be patient and constructive in every relationship and every interaction. You dare not do otherwise. No superiority, no double standard, no favoritism.

May 13

For you did not receive the spirit of slavery to fall back into fear, but you have received the Spirit of adoption as sons, by whom we cry, "Abba! Father!" —Romans 8:15

If your father was demanding, critical, neglectful or selfish, are you crippled from knowing God as a loving Father? Must you first experience a corrective human relationship in order to make "God is my Father" a nourishing reality? This statement proves false under examination. It distorts the nature of the human heart and why it is that people believe lies about God. It flatly denies the power and truth of God's Word and the Holy Spirit. This is not to say that people with poor human parents don't often project those images onto the true God.

But think about this. In the normal course of life, none of the words God uses to describe himself have wonderful experiential correlates. Sinful human fathers are not unique in misrepresenting God. Does your experience of figureheads, politicians, tyrants, and grafters cripple you from knowing God as King and Judge? It needn't. Consider also the shepherds of God's flock whom you've known. Some people can point with joy to a "godly pastor who made such an impact on my life." But other people grew up under false teachers, greedy willful, arrogant, and careless men. Does this mean that you can gain no comfort from the fact that the Lord is a shepherd until you have the corrective experience of knowing a godly pastor? Ezekiel 34 (and then John 10) argues the opposite. *God assumes we can hear comfort straight from him even if people have betrayed our trust. The Holy Spirit weighs more than fallen experience.*

May 14

For the Lord disciplines the one he loves, and chastises every son whom he receives. —Hebrews 12:6

God's love is active. He decided to love you when he could have justly condemned you. He's involved. He's merciful, not simply tolerant. He who abhors sin pursues sinners by name. God is so committed to forgiving and changing you that he sent Jesus to die for you. He welcomes the poor in spirit with a shout and a feast. God is vastly patient and relentlessly persevering as he intrudes into your life.

God's love actively does you good. God's love is full of blood, sweat, tears, and cries. He suffered for you. He fights for you, defending the afflicted. He fights you. He pursues you in powerful tenderness so that he can change you. He's jealous, not detached. His sort of empathy and sympathy speaks out words of truth to set you free of sin and misery. He will discipline you as proof that he loves you. He himself comes to live in you, pouring out his Holy Spirit in your heart, so you will know him. He puts out power and energy. God's love has hate in it: hate for evil, whether done to you or by you. *God's love demands that you respond: believe, trust, obey, give thanks with a joyful heart, work out your salvation with fear, delight in the Lord.*

May 15

"Man does not live by bread alone, but man lives by every word that comes from the mouth of the LORD." —Deuteronomy 8:3

A s you study God's Word, how do you widen your personal application of Scripture? Keep your eye out for straightforward passages. Typically, they generalize or summarize in some manner, inviting personal appropriation. Such words give you promises, principles, templates for experience.

Core promises and self-revelations of God. Exodus 34:6–7, Numbers 6:24–26, and Deuteronomy 31:6 state God's foundational promises that repeatedly appear and are variously applied throughout the rest of Scripture. Pay attention to what God says about who he is, what he is like, his purposes, his promises. Make such promises and self-revelations part of your repertoire of well-pondered truth. Get a feel for how all these words come to a point in Jesus Christ.

The joys and sorrows of many psalms. Consider how the Psalms generalize to all of us. They intentionally flatten out specific details, so anyone can identify. We are given a template flexible enough to embrace any one of us.

The call of commands. In matters of obedience, the Bible often proclaims a general truth without mentioning any of the multitude of possible applications. In such cases, the Bible speaks in large categories, addressing countless different experiences, circumstances, and actions. Sorting out what it specifically means is far from automatic, but the application process follows a rather direct line.

Stories interpreted. A story communicates on many levels, showing nuances of relationship and experience that are incommunicable otherwise. Frequently a single comment or incident speaks repeatedly and deeply to a person. *You are changed by knowing that it matters when you take the time to listen, to think, to take to heart.* You are changed by knowing that bigger purposes are at work.

May 16

This is my comfort in my affliction,
that your promise gives me life. —Psalm 119:50

What words can I say to you when your life is hard and you are hurting? I certainly don't think there is some magic word that will make everything better, but when it comes time to say something, I might say this: Jesus is a most sympathetic friend, fellow sufferer, and Savior. He has walked a hard road. He has felt his own anguish and crushing pain (Isaiah 53). He understands. He is compassionate toward you. By the comfort of his presence and sympathy, he intends to draw you out and draw you to himself.

I encourage you to go to him and speak to him. There is something about our ability to find words to express what we're experiencing that makes a genuine difference. *A wise Christian of many centuries ago said, "To open one's heart to one's friend—it doubles our joys and cuts our griefs in half."* I have found this to be true. There's something about speaking to someone who truly cares about you that soothes your wounds.

May you cry out to our God. He calls you his friend. He deeply cares for you. He is your Savior. Trust him. He has walked down this road before you. He promises to walk with you in this.

And I might say one more thing. Suffering must be walked through one step at a time. Be honest. Don't take any shortcuts. Let each day's trouble be sufficient for that day. Seek your Father. If you seek him, you will find him.

May 17

"And if anyone gives even a cup of cold water to one of these little ones
who is my disciple, truly I tell you, that person will certainly not lose
their reward." —Matthew 10:42 NIV

What could shake you out of plodding along through life, going through the motions in your Christianity? Let me share something I've found that has affected my own lethargy and apathy. I often look at myself in light of the seven deadly sins. The one that always gets me is sloth. Sloth doesn't just mean you're just sitting around watching TV all day. Sloth also means indifference. Feeling apathetic. It's a pretty accurate characteristic of the modern era, a mild cynicism that questions whether or not anything really matters.

The thing is, everything actually does matter. It matters a whole lot. The tiniest things we do, the most careless words we say, the smallest act of kindness toward another person— all these things actually count. From God's perspective, there's nothing we do that's outside his concern or gaze.

Think of how Jesus chose to single out giving a glass of cold water to somebody who is thirsty and talked about how you won't lose your reward in heaven when you do something that small. He thought that spotting someone else and serving them in some small way really, really mattered. Someone else's need matters to the point that you put yourself out.

Every choice, every thought, every word, every deed, and every attitude—really, truly matters. As you awaken to that, you awaken to the fact that you really need help. You're able to say, *"God, I really need you. I need your strength. I need your forgiveness. Give me the grace to care about things that really matter."*

May 18

Now may the God of peace himself sanctify you completely, and may
your whole spirit and soul and body be kept blameless at the coming of
our Lord Jesus Christ. —1 Thessalonians 5:23

The anger your sin deserves fell on Jesus. God's anger at sin was expressed—but for your well-being. Once and for all in the past, God set you free from ever experiencing his wrath against your sins. In steadfast love, he freely offered his innocent Son to bear the wrath deserved by the guilty. God's anger punishes and destroys, giving our sin its due—but it was taken by Jesus, the Beloved Lamb, the Savior of sinners. Because he loves us, he offers himself to bear the fire of anger; the way of our deliverance is his glory and our joy. God's loving anger, expressed in a way that brings us blessing, is the basis of life from the dead: it assures us of true forgiveness. Justification by faith and adoption as the children of God rest upon that form of love called substitutionary atonement. *What we deserve, another bore because he chose to love us. In this supreme act of self-giving love, we experience God's anger acting FOR us. In response, we confidently repent and believe.*

In love, God's anger works to disarm the power of your sin. His anger at sin is again expressed for your well-being. In steadfast love, he remakes us, not by tolerating our sin, but by hating our sin in a way that we learn to love! The process is not always pleasant because suffering, reproof, guilt, and owning up don't feel good. But deliverance, mercy, encouragement, and a clearing conscience do feel good. God remakes us progressively into love, joy, peace, and wisdom—his own image.

May 19

For where jealousy and selfish ambition exist, there will be disorder and every vile practice. But the wisdom from above is first pure, then peaceable, gentle, open to reason, full of mercy and good fruits, impartial and sincere. And a harvest of righteousness is sown in peace by those who make peace. —James 3:16–18

Anger problems are only one strand in the larger problem of interpersonal conflict. To understand and solve anger problems, we must deal with conflict in all its forms. People fight with each other and with God; sinful anger is but one of the weapons. As sinners, we naturally contend for our presumed self-interest.

Peacemaking is about God in Christ and about human beings renewed in his image. The Lord is the supreme Peacemaker. *Christ made peace once for all between us and God; he continues to make peace, teaching us to do the same with each other; and he will make peace, finally and forever.*

We could look in many places, but James 3–4 is the classic, extended passage that speaks the mind of Christ to this issue. In James 3:13–4:12, the Holy Spirit summarizes the problem and solution: (1) The demanding, self-exalting heart will bear the fruit of chaos and conflict; (2) God is jealous for our loyalty, destroying his enemies, but gracious and generous to the repentant; (3) The wise, humble, receptive heart will bear fruit of a life of peacemaking. These themes appear in many variations. No more accurate, profound, and thorough analysis of the dynamics of conflict has ever been written. No more powerful promise of aid has ever been given. James 3–4 places us in the light of the unrelenting gaze of God, and promises grace upon grace.

May 20

What causes quarrels and what causes fights among you? Is it not this,
that your passions are at war within you? —James 4:1

W/*hy* do you fight? The biblical analysis is straightforward and cuts to the core. You fight for one reason: because you don't get what you want. You fight because your desire, what pleases or displeases you, what you long for and crave, is frustrated.

The expectations that lead to conflict reveal something fundamental about where combatants stand with respect not just to each other but to God himself. Our cravings rule our lives; they directly compete with God himself for lordship. No problem is more profound and more pervasive. James 4:1 says that such God-playing desires "battle" within us. This does not mean that desires battle against us or with each other. These are our desires, expressing who we are.

What's wrong with what I want? Scripture, the Holy Spirit's X-ray of the heart, makes clear that when such desires rule, they produce sin, not love, and so they show themselves corrupt. God sees into the heart of conflict; he sees the private kingdom we each create.

What exactly do you want that makes you warlike, when Christ's rule would make you peaceable? Answer honestly, and you will have identified why you participate in sinful conflict.

James 4:6 makes a staggering promise: God gives grace to the humble. Grace is more and greater than sin. When god-players admit the truth, they find amazing grace in Jesus: forgiveness, mercy, sanity, a fresh start, cleansing, power, and freedom. Every facet of the grace of God is tailored to cleanse and renew angry, critical, fearful, proud people.

May 21

Do not be anxious about anything, but in everything by prayer and
supplication with thanksgiving let your requests be made known to God.
And the peace of God, which surpasses all understanding, will guard
your hearts and your minds in Christ Jesus. —Philippians 4:6-7

We have good reasons to be afraid, but better reasons to not be afraid. Here are six practical tips for dealing with anxiety. First, *identify your form of anxiety*—learn your triggers and response to worry and stress. Are you nervous, driven, compulsive, irritable, or escapist? Second, *consider your reasons for trust*. The Lord is on your side (Romans 8:31). He will remain faithful (1 Corinthians 1:9). He will provide (Philippians 4:19). These are examples of promises that can help you rest. Third, *name your real troubles and anxieties*. What do you worry about? What keeps you up at night? Fourth, *identify what hijacks your heart*—what captures you so that you forget these promises and actually live in functional unbelief. What is it you want? What do you desire to control? Fifth, *have an honest conversation with God*. Name your exact troubles, be upfront about where you go wrong, and earnestly ask him for help. Last, *do what needs doing today*. Each day has enough trouble of its own (Matthew 6:34). We're called to trust, and then we're called to do the calling of today.

The kind of sanity that is the end result of living your life in this way is both simple and complex. It's not a magic answer, but it is a way forward that allows you to get a grip on your anxieties.

May 22

Be not wise in your own eyes;
fear the LORD, and turn away from evil.
It will be healing to your flesh
and refreshment to your bones. —Proverbs 3:7–8

There is something distorted in our self-knowledge. It's like keys out of tune on a beautiful piano. We may have eagle eyes for the faults of others but be blind to where we are out of tune or qualities we are entirely missing. When our evaluative capacity misfires, we are wise in our own eyes and repress the knowledge of God. It can invert the conscience. One of the most significant ways Christ engages his people is in this life-long retuning and repairing of the piano, to restore our evaluative capacity to sanity, to see the world the way it actually is. Distortions can come from wrong tendencies in our churches, deep-seated tendencies in ourselves, or high pressure from the culture. God is in the business of renewing the conscience.

When you struggle with low self-esteem, the biggest question is, whose eyes matter? Who judges me or gets last say in my life? To whose opinion do I orient? Your opinion of yourself and what others think of you is a half-truth. There's Someone else whose opinion matters more—God's. His opinion matters because when his comes first, the other opinions are put into secondary perspective and don't serve as a primary cause in your life. When this priority order is put in place, you can then appropriately profit from others' opinions or your own self-evaluation. *An appropriate self-understanding is derivative of the one whose opinion really matters.*

May 23

By this we shall know that we are of the truth and reassure our heart
before him; for whenever our heart condemns us, God is greater than
our heart, and he knows everything. —1 John 3:19–20

What assuages your guilt and delivers you from what is wrong? We launch many self-salvation projects in an attempt to self-atone for our sin and guilt. We try to find more affirming friends. We try to go live a worthwhile life so we have something to be proud of. We affirm ourselves and tell ourselves we are okay. One of the core messages in our culture about how our failures are made better is that we are justified by faith in our own intrinsic goodness.

The message of Christian faith both parallels and is utterly different from this message. You are made right by faith in the Savior of the world who has loved you and accepted you, washed you, included you, will bear with you your whole life, and will bring to completion the good work he started in you. He will have compassion on you as a father has compassion on his children.

Those who are truly free from sin and guilt understand the fear of the Lord—the orienting of life to Someone else's opinion and standards. This is the beginning of wisdom and sanity. This is where all true peace and self-understanding begins. *You don't find self-esteem by following the wrong standard, but the Lord gives you intrinsic self-worth when you depend on his standard.*

May 24

Pardon for sin and a peace that endureth
Thine own dear presence to cheer and to guide
Strength for today and bright hope for tomorrow
Blessings all mine with 10, 000 beside
Great is Thy faithfulness
Great is Thy faithfulness
Morning by morning new mercies I see
All I have needed Thy hand hath provided
Great is Thy faithfulness, Lord, unto me
—Thomas Chisholm, "Great Is Thy Faithfulness"

Your God—who has promised to be gracious, and who demonstrated it at extreme personal cost—can be trusted when you are afraid. God is for you. I know this because he says so, and he does what he says. Your story is still being written, and you can trust him and not be afraid.

Jesus is both patient and urgent with you. Patient means he's committed to you for the long haul. This is good news because you will struggle with sin your whole life. Urgent means there is always something to do today: someone to love, some way to think, some way to seek him, something to repent of, or to ask others for help with. What makes these two elements work together is that his patience is always purposeful. His urgency is always full of mercies.

At the center of change, you are taken out of yourself: out of willful sin, unbelief, and guilt, all of which tend to create an inward vortex. *Change is extraspective. At the core of change is faith awakening to God, moving in his direction, seeking him, growing in love toward God and others. This leads you to acts of love and courage. These acts make us more like Jesus.* Every obedience makes us more like him and part of the triumph of light over darkness.

Our Father, we thank you that you are not ashamed to call us brothers and sisters, and that we all can walk before you in the light of life. It is the story of what Jesus has done, is doing, and will do. Each of our stories is unique and beautiful. We are so grateful that you change us into people of radiant beauty.

May 25

The aim of our charge is love that issues from a pure heart and a good conscience and a sincere faith. —1 Timothy 1:5

Christ's transformational work in our lives simultaneously operates in two dimensions, the vertical and horizontal. God is always reorienting both our worship and our walk, our motives and our lifestyle. Paul summarizes the purpose of his ministry this way: "The goal of our instruction is love from a pure heart and a good conscience and a sincere faith" (1 Timothy 1:5). Love summarizes the renovation of horizontal relationships. A pure heart, good conscience, and sincere faith capture the reconfiguration of vertical relationship. An impure or double-minded heart serves multiple masters. A bad or distorted conscience misinterprets, misguides, and misevaluates, failing to process life God's way. A hypocritical faith professes, sings, and prays one way, but trusts something else when push comes to shove. Restoration of heart, conscience, and faith produces acts of obedience.

Who or what is your functional God/god? What do you love, trust, fear, hope, seek, obey, and take refuge in? The Bible—the penetrating and light-giving Word of the Searcher of hearts—is concerned to pierce below behaviors and emotions in order to expose motives, to lay people bare before him with whom we have to do. Reorienting motives through the grace of the gospel can follow when there is conviction of particular forms of disorientation. *Intelligent repentance will make the love of Jesus your joy and hope. The grace and power of Jesus Christ change both root and fruit.*

May 26

"You shall love the Lord your God with all your heart and with all your soul and with all your mind." —Matthew 22:37

The following sampler of questions will get you thinking fruitfully about how human life is exhaustively God-relational. Human beings inescapably love God—or love something else. We take refuge in God—or in something else. We set our hopes in God—or in something else. We fear God—or something else. Scripture will come to life in new ways as you develop an alertness to how the man-before-God verbs play out in real life.

What do you love? Hate? There is no deeper question to ask of any person at any time. There is no deeper explanation for why you do what you do.

What do you seek, aim for, pursue? What are your goals and expectations? Where do you bank your hopes? Human motivation is not passive, as if hardwired needs, instincts, or drives were controlled from outside us by being "unmet," "frustrated," or "conditioned."

What do you fear? What do you tend to worry about? Where do you find refuge, safety, comfort, escape, pleasure, security? This is the Psalms' question, digging out your false trusts, your escapisms that substitute for the Lord.

What or whom do you trust? Trust is one of the major verbs relating you to God—or to false gods and lies. Crucial psalms breathe trust in our Father and Shepherd. Where instead do you place life-directing, life-anchoring trust?

By seeing the God-relatedness of all motivation, you see that what is wrong with us calls for a God-related solution: the grace, peace, power, and presence of Jesus Christ. Living faith in Jesus Christ is the only sane motivation, the radical alternative to a thousand forms of deviance.

May 27

"Beware of practicing your righteousness before other people in order to be seen by them, for then you will have no reward from your Father who is in heaven." —Matthew 6:1

What might it mean to be addicted to *religiosity*—religion gone bad? Ask yourself the following questions: What do you make of God? How do you relate to him and treat him? How do you then treat people? What do you do with your troubles and heartaches? How do you deal with your failures and sin?

Perhaps you pray to be seen by other people (Matthew 6:5–13) or you put a lot of stock in religious behavior, but are self-deceived, self-righteous, and despise strugglers (Luke 18:9–14). Religiosity is fundamentally built around show and how you're perceived. There's no sap of a living relationship in your practices.

We must work against religiosity, whether it's addiction to religious practices, to power, or the love of status and reputation. In these situations, you turn God into a puppet and a whole host of human desires and fears all run amok in your heart. There is no real love, honesty, or real humility in religiosity. The core graces of the Christian life are invariably washed away.

How do you address it? You begin to live out the reality of your true needs meeting the true mercies of the living God. *When you face pain, hurt, hardship, and vulnerability, look for the opportunity to meet, need, know, love, trust, and seek the living God.* Instead of distracting yourself when you meet trouble, you seek to know the Lord who is with you (Psalm 23:4). You come to know him as a stronghold, a shelter, and a shade (Isaiah 25:4). You come to see how his mercies are tailor-made to exactly help you with what you are dealing with.

May 28

The law of the LORD is perfect,
reviving the soul;
the testimony of the LORD is sure,
making wise the simple;
the precepts of the LORD are right,
rejoicing the heart;
the commandment of the LORD is pure,
enlightening the eyes. —Psalm 19:7–8

The Word is alive with the love of God in Christ Jesus. He invades our darkness. His words are so clear. He vividly portrays the human struggle. The wise will of God is realistic and directly relevant. Truth comes in person, attached to names and places, to weather and food, to troubles and joys. God shows himself operating in the midst of the worst and the best and all the muddling in the middle. Scripture came as a timely text, adapted to the varied conditions and experiences of real people, because God is a timely Redeemer.

How do you then bring truth to life? How do you apply the Word of God? *Always ask two questions of yourself and others: What is your current struggle? What about God in Christ connects to this?* You might be facing sufferings and troubles of various kinds (James 1:2). You might be sinning—doing and thinking various troublesome things (James 3:16). Usually it's a tangle of both. God talks exactly about these things. How does the Savior enter these struggles? What does he say? How does he help? What will he change?

Keep the big picture in view, then act on some detail. Know the themes both in Scripture and in person. Then apply one relevant thing from our Redeemer to one significant scene in your story. Apply this first and foremost to your own life. You can then give away what you are being given. What you give out of your own life will be life-giving to others.

May 29

The law of the LORD is perfect,
reviving the soul;
the testimony of the LORD is sure,
making wise the simple;
the precepts of the LORD are right,
rejoicing the heart;
the commandment of the LORD is pure,
enlightening the eyes. —Psalm 19:7–8

Both in your own life and in the lives of those you help, it helps to keep in mind this simple goal: *connect one bit of Scripture to one bit of life*. What is your current struggle? How does God in Christ connect to you in this? When you are learning kindness from your Savior, you will be able to teach unkind people. When you are learning to endure suffering well, you will be able to reach sufferers. It is the same with any other radiancy of the Spirit: clarity, courage, humility, patience, joy, wisdom, gratitude, mercy, teachability, generosity, and honesty.

Knowing general truths about yourself—your tendencies, typical patterns, themes that replay in your personal history—doesn't change you. You must be able to identify where your current struggle lies, what it means, what exactly is at stake, and where to go. Today, what is your particular battlefield? You must be able to trace the difference between truth and lies, clarity and confusion, hope and illusion, right and wrongs, insight and self-deception, true need and wild desires, love and self-serving, living faith and functional godlessness.

Where do you need God's redemption and help? When you are disoriented in your current struggle, you don't even know your choices. When your way is deep darkness, you don't know what makes you stumble. The right bit of Scripture—six words, two verses, one story—reorients you. You need help, and the Lord is a very present help in trouble.

May 30

Therefore, since we have been justified by faith, we have peace with God through our Lord Jesus Christ. —Romans 5:1

Are we changed by knowing that we are justified by faith? Yes and amen. To consciously remember and take to heart that you are justified and accepted by God because of what Jesus Christ has done for you makes a big difference in your Christian life. In some counseling and discipleship situations, it is exactly the message that needs to be featured. This truth is theologically foundational to being a Christian, to being forgiven, to being made right with God, to having the courage to be candid about our sins. It is elementary in the sense of being basic, fundamental, essential, constitutive. Consciousness of this truth does not only work to change people at the inception of Christian faith. The New Testament letters are written to Christians. As an aspect of apostolic pastoral care unto sanctification, they often remind God's people of what Christ did for us. It is no surprise that I have known many true Christians who only gradually came to understand the significance of what Christ did on the cross. Growing in such knowledge was a part of their sanctification, their growing assurance and confidence, their understanding of sinfulness, their gratitude. Growth in those things was often slow and hard-won.

Justification by faith often powerfully affects people who are oriented toward their own performance. It comforts those disturbed by the sting of their failures. It disturbs those who are comfortable and self-satisfied in their successes. *So whether you think you are too bad or think you are good enough, it makes a difference to know that justification before God comes by faith in Christ and what he has done.*

May 31

But truly God has listened;
he has attended to the voice of my prayer.

Blessed be God,
because he has not rejected my prayer
or removed his steadfast love from me! —Psalm 66:19-20

In your honest conversation with God, use the Psalms. God has given us the Psalms so we have many different ways of talking with God about the things that really matter to us. Some psalms speak to God about our sins: e.g., Psalms 32 and 51. Other psalms speak about suffering injustice at the hands of others: e.g., Psalms 10 and 31. And many psalms speak of both: e.g., Psalms 25 and 119. All the Psalms speak of God and reveal what he is like, what we need from him, and how we express love for him. The Psalms are poetic, but they are not poetry; they are living examples given to teach us how to talk honestly with God about things that matter. Your relationship with a living person is what sets the Bible's approach to anger apart from self-help books, medications, and mind control.

Your willingness to be mastered by Jesus and to make following him your first priority will allow you to imitate him in expressing things like anger in a redemptive way. Then your conflicts won't end with slammed doors, hurt silences, and sharing others' sins. Instead, there will be a constructive back-and-forth that is colored by mercy and a desire for each of you to grow in God's image. *Your real, living relationship with the God who loves you to the uttermost will allow you to grow in having real human relationships, where the conflicts you have will become an opportunity for growth, understanding, and expressing the fruits of the Spirit.*

June 1

"Would that we had died in the land of Egypt! Or would that we had died in this wilderness! . . . Would it not be better for us to go back to Egypt?" —Numbers 14:2–3

In the book of Numbers, we read about a typical human response to the hard things—the "heat"—of life. Things are not going well for the people of Israel, so they grumble and forget God is good. They forget he is in control and that he will give what he promised. To go blind to God is an instinctive human response.

Like the Israelites in the wilderness, my grumbling and complaining always includes a false view of myself—I believe I am right and have the right interpretation of what's going on. I am justified in complaining against God. That's often accompanied by a false view of the past, just as Israel reinterprets Egypt as the promised land.

There's also a false view of the future. Here God has promised his people a land flowing with milk and honey, fruit trees, fields, and houses. The supreme blessing was that it would be the dwelling place of God with his people. Israel forgot that. The journey from Egypt was intended to be a two-week trip, but by miscalculating God, themselves, their past, and their future, they brought on forty years of wandering in the wilderness instead.

How are you responding to your heat? Are there any areas where you have allowed false beliefs to develop into false views of God, yourself, and your situation? You can always turn to the Lord for healing and rest (Isaiah 30:15).

June 2

And it is God who establishes us with you in Christ, and has anointed us,
and who has also put his seal on us and given us his Spirit in our hearts
as a guarantee. —2 Corinthians 1:21-22

What a wonderful truth—it is God who establishes us with you in Christ! We are in Christ because of his work. He has put his seal on us, and he has given his Spirit in our hearts as a guarantee, a down payment of glory. *The Holy Spirit is the one who writes the promises of life on the human heart. The Holy Spirit is our counselor—God himself on the scene at work transforming our lives.*

The Holy Spirit transforms us right in the middle of our most significant sufferings, whether they are pervasive, atmospheric kinds of things or sharp, knife-edge things. Those are the things that actually make us little "Christs" in this world. They conform us to his image. They make us people who are, even in the hardest things, full of redemptive purpose.

Biblical comfort, as referred to earlier in this chapter of 2 Corinthians, is something far wider than our English word. It's *parakaleo*, the word for the Holy Spirit used in John 14–16. He is the one who comes beside a person to provide immediate, needful help. This comfort is describing a real experience of relevant mercies and truth. So it includes actual aid and it includes words that illumine the world, reveal our sinfulness (the wisdom of our flesh), show us the mercies of God, and invite us to him. We serve a God who is up to something redemptive for those who are his beloved children. He is always working to transform us into his image.

June 3

> "Blessed is the man who trusts in the Lord,
> whose trust is the Lord.
> He is like a tree planted by water,
> that sends out its roots by the stream,
> and does not fear when heat comes,
> for its leaves remain green,
> and is not anxious in the year of drought,
> for it does not cease to bear fruit." —Jeremiah 17:7–9

Real change in our lives is worked out in moments where we are different than what we would be by nature and nurture. God tells us in his Word that in each moment of our lives we can either be what we are like naturally—full of thorns (like a thornbush in a desert) or transformed into those full of fruit (like a tree planted by water). What makes the difference? Who we are trusting: "blessed is the one who trusts in the Lord."

One of the ways you can understand change is that it occurs at the intersection between what rules your heart and what is impacting you in your world (the "heat"). Thorns exist at the intersection of heart and heat. Good fruit also exists at the intersection of heart and heat. All issues of the heart are relational. Fear of man, for instance, is to turn away from God and to orient my life toward another person. To turn away from fear of man is to turn back to God and relate to God. This is a relational change. This is about where you are putting your trust. What is the heat? What are the thorns? What are the mercies of God? How do they apply? How do I draw near to him? How then do I live in a different way? *This is the heart of the gospel, the good news of the Messiah who invades lives to offer mercy and to transform who we are and what we live for and how we live.*

June 4

Put off your old self, which belongs to your former manner of life and is corrupt through deceitful desires, and . . . be renewed in the spirit of your minds, and . . . put on the new self, created after the likeness of God in true righteousness and holiness. —Ephesians 4:22–24

Sanctification is the word that describes God making of us into the image of Jesus who is holy, loving, humble, true, joyous, self-sacrificing. It is a process of transformation and it is progressive, which means it's not done until we see him face-to-face. It's not a one-and-done transaction. Sins like fear of man, pride, desire to control my world, desire to feel good, have comfort or pleasure are all things just wired into the DNA of our fallenness. Change is not going to be just a machete stroke that suddenly cuts off all the wrong in us. But there will be progress—the Spirit will make us more like Jesus.

A famous metaphor for the nature of the Christian life and the nature of the work of Christ is a World War II metaphor. Post-Christ, is like the Allies landing at Normandy. The defeat of Germany has begun. But there will be tens of thousands of young men killed and lots of death and blood and heartache until Germany is fully defeated. The spiritual victory has been won, but there will be battle after battle, after battle, after battle, until the victory is fully realized at the end. That picture of the Christian life is very helpful. *There is the up-and-down experience, but the ups and downs over the long haul are going somewhere. Christ has pledged by his blood to complete the work that he has begun. He will do it!*

June 5

And I am sure of this, that he who began a good work in you will bring it to completion at the day of Jesus Christ. —Philippians 1:6

A Prayer for the Lord to Meet Us

*O*ur *Father, we thank you that in your tender mercies, we have been caught up into a most wonderful kingdom, into the purposes of a Savior and King who will complete what he has begun.* And that there will be a day when every one of us is no longer a person prone to fears and confusion and irritation and little selfish acts. And there will be a day that we'll be unafraid to live an utterly open life. There will be a day that we will live in the light as children of light. And would you make it so. Lord, we are coming from many different places, different churches, and different life experiences. Some of us feel like we haven't really suffered in very significant ways. Some of us have been shattered by things that have happened. We pray, Lord, that you would meet us, one and all. And we would, one and all, grow into wisdom. And I do pray for my brothers and sisters that this would be a good week—a week of careful thought, close reading, helpful meditation, and self-awareness. And most of all, a living faith that takes other people to heart. We ask this in Jesus's name, Amen.

June 6

But he gives more grace. Therefore it says, "God opposes the proud but gives grace to the humble." Submit yourselves therefore to God. Resist the devil, and he will flee from you. Draw near to God, and he will draw near to you. —James 4:6–8a

You can read stacks of books on conflict resolution, mediation, and interpersonal conflict, and they will never say that at the heart of conflict is a heart that is far from the living God. Because they never get to the core of the problem, they never get to the core of the solution, which is simply repentance. It is coming back in need to the one who promises to give more grace.

James 4 is so rich in portraying what is the root of righteousness, faith, love for God, and need for God. It looks like humbling yourself, submitting yourself to God, resisting the devil, drawing near to God, cleansing your hands, purifying your hearts, mourning, weeping, and humbling yourself before the Lord. This is honest reckoning with the God who is gracious.

James does not content himself with just a list of abstract resolutions for conflict like, "Well, I should have faith," or "I should commune with God," or "I should trust him," or "Next time, instead of getting irritated at my kids, I'll just trust God more." Instead of that, James comes right into the moment and asks, "What do you do now?" Right now you can humble yourself before the living God. Right now you can turn from your own way and go God's way. Right now you can bring your cares to the living God. *God wants you to bring your real-life struggles with the problem of evil, sin, and sufferings to the God who is merciful and powerful. You will find grace!*

June 7

Bless the LORD, O my soul,
and forget not all his benefits,
who forgives all your iniquity,
who heals all your diseases,
who redeems your life from the pit,
who crowns you with steadfast love and mercy. —Psalm 103:2-4

*E*xtrospection means looking outside of ourselves. This is at the heart of everything that the living God is doing in your life and mine. Faith awakens and seeks a God of mercy and power. We can break this into three slices. Part one is the wake-up. There's something fundamental about the transformation of our lives that involves an awakening. Blind people start to see, deaf people hear, the sleepers awake, and the dead are alive.

The second aspect of a genuine change process is a growing persuasion that life is a moral drama. This is really crucial. What I mean by a moral drama is that every day we have to answer basic questions about our direction: Will I be a fool or will I be wise? Will I be hateful or loving? Will I be proud or humble? Will I worship myself or God? These are the daily choices that will shape your life. As you recognize the importance of these choices, you will begin to see that all of the little and big moments of life make up a moral drama where you either turn toward God or away from him.

Third, an essential part of the change process is a growing persuasion that God is truly gracious, that his grace is your sole hope. This is essential. If you realize that life is a moral drama, you know you need utter and complete help, right? Sin puts us in this very tiny little cramped world. And mercy puts us in a very large and spacious world. *God's grace gives us the power to turn toward him—the one who crowns you with steadfast love and mercy.*

June 8

Consequently, he is able to save to the uttermost those who draw near
to God through him, since he always lives to make intercession for them.
—Hebrews 7:25

There is a present ministry of Jesus Christ to you, interceding for you. There are descriptions of Jesus Christ as the living mediator that just thread through Scripture. Hebrews reminds us that Jesus is able to save us when we draw near because "he always lives to make intercession." Paul reminds us that Jesus is at the right hand of God interceding for us (Romans 8:34). You might think that Jesus's mediation happened only several thousand years ago. But the Lamb is still standing. He is continuing to work out a living salvation for all who call on him by faith. The High Priest is *now* mediating. It's an ongoing ministry to us as his children. He's with us to the end.

It's my prayer that these truths would sparkle in your life and would form the way you think about other people, the way you process your own life, your deepest struggles, and the fine china of where you are weak, vulnerable, struggling with sin, feeling overwhelmed, and having a sense of life being out of control. God's grace is tailored to these things. *The very strengthening and shielding and help and forgiveness that you need, you are able to find in your Savior, who is a present tense mediator.*

June 9

> For we do not have a high priest who is unable to sympathize with our weaknesses, but one who in every respect has been tempted as we are, yet without sin. Let us then with confidence draw near to the throne of grace, that we may receive mercy and find grace to help in time of need.
> —Hebrews 4:15-16

G od will use your difficulties and suffering as the door into a deeper knowledge of his love. As you read the Psalms, you see that those who know God well know themselves to be afflicted, weak, oppressed, broken, humble, and needy. Psalm 31:5—"Into your hands I commit my spirit"—was on Jesus's lips as he hung on the cross, powerless and in great pain. He became this for us.

Jesus lived in weakness. He knows what it's like to depend on the mercies of God for every breath. *Jesus's experience of weakness is the door to one of the most marvelous promises of God in our passage above: "Let us then approach God's throne of grace with confidence, so that we may receive mercy and find grace to help us in our time of need" (Hebrews 4:16 NIV).*

You are struggling. Life is hard. You need. Your Lord sympathizes with your need. He promises you grace and mercy—immediate help in the context of your need.

June 10

The LORD is my shepherd; I shall not want.
He makes me lie down in green pastures.
He leads me beside still waters.
He restores my soul.
He leads me in paths of righteousness
for his name's sake.

Even though I walk through the valley of the shadow of death,
I will fear no evil,
for you are with me;
your rod and your staff,
they comfort me. —Psalm 23:1–4

How does the way you live change as you take to heart truths about your weakness and God's power? Depend on Jesus one day at a time. Jesus says, "Therefore do not worry about tomorrow, for tomorrow will worry about itself. Each day has enough trouble of its own" (Matthew 6:34 NIV). Jesus wants you to depend on him one day at a time. Learn to not worry about tomorrow. Whatever your future, you are called to live by faith today.

To do this you must meditate on who Jesus is. More than any other passage, Psalm 23 brought Jesus to life for me in my struggles with weakness. The psalm is full of promises—he provides, he restores my soul, he is with me, his goodness and mercy pursue me all of my days. Make this psalm your own. Jesus, your Good Shepherd, will fill you with confidence. God doesn't meet us the way we want, but he does restore us. *No matter what you are facing, you have a Shepherd who is with you, restoring you, and bringing good things—himself—into your life.* Learn to trust him and you truly have something worth living and dying for.

June 11

You have kept count of my tossings;
put my tears in your bottle.
Are they not in your book? . . .

This I know, that God is for me.
In God, whose word I praise,
in the LORD, whose word I praise,
in God I trust; I shall not be afraid. —Psalm 56:8, 9b–11a

Sometimes Christians make you feel that if you just get the right answers to your trials, you can apply them and your problems will instantly be solved! But that's not God's way. God is a vinedresser who carefully and slowly prunes his vines through the years. God works in us on a scale of years, over a lifetime.

So look for slow, steady change. What can you expect? When your pain is raw and overwhelming, you can expect that your pain will lessen as you start to bring it to God by using Psalms 55, 56, and 57.

Healing and peace will grow not in an instant, but over time. Perhaps there will be parts of your difficulties that will not leave you until Christ returns. Only at the return of Christ, when he makes all things new, will every tear be wiped away (Revelation 21:4). You may be marked by suffering, but you've learned to take small steps of obedience, wise love, and hope. Most amazingly, you will be able to help other suffers. God has a purpose for you that flows out of your life experience, a high and holy calling. *As you learn about how Jesus Christ meets, enters, and transforms your particular affliction in life, you can begin to help others who are facing all kinds of affliction.* Your compassion, wisdom, and hope for redemption will bring the light of God to a world dying in darkness and suffering.

June 12

"Blessed is the man who trusts in the Lord,
whose trust is the Lord.
He is like a tree planted by water,
that sends out its roots by the stream,
and does not fear when heat comes,
for its leaves remain green,
and is not anxious in the year of drought,
for it does not cease to bear fruit." —Jeremiah 17:7–8

It is right in the middle of hard realities that your faith and trust in God grows. In Jeremiah 17:7–8, Jeremiah is talking about living in a desert where life is hard and brutal. The desert in the Bible is the place of death. There's no water, no food. It's hot. There are dangerous predators and poisonous snakes. It is the place where your faith is tested. Do you feel that grief and confusion have brought you into a spiritual desert? As you deepen your trust in God, your desert will become the place where you find God's living water of hope, mercy, and blessing.

God's living water is his presence. He says, "I am with you." He is the only person who can profoundly reassure your heart. Though you may be feeling alone, he is with you. His presence means that even in the darkest of circumstances you can be unafraid. Let me say it again: He is with you. He is with you.

Because God is with you, you will be fruitful, even in the aftermath of heartache and perplexity. He promises that one day all sorrow, pain, and tears will be wiped away (Revelation 21:4).

June 13

What then shall we say to these things? If God is for us, who can be against us? —Romans 8:31

Beloved, never avenge yourselves, but leave it to the wrath of God, for it is written, "Vengeance is mine, I will repay, says the Lord."
—Romans 12:19

God expresses his love for his people by each of the three ways he expresses his anger at wrong. God's loving anger resolves the entire problem of evil in a way that brings him inexpressible glory and brings us inexpressible blessing: justly condemning evil, severing the power of remnant evil, and bringing relief from suffering. Numerous psalms connect the steadfast love and mercies of the Lord to this loving wrath by which he delivers his children both from their own sins and from those who harm them.

It's important to make proper distinctions. God's wrath has become the hope of his children though it is the despair of his enemies. But those enemies who are willing to believe the staggering message of how wrath is converted into grace through Jesus Christ will be changed into friends. The truth is that you can't understand God's love if you don't understand his anger. This is simply the message of the book of Psalms, that royal road into the heart of redeemed humankind, with its otherwise inexplicable interweaving of joy and sorrow, hope and anguish, confidence and fear, contentment and anger.

God's loving anger on our behalf nourishes and encourages our faith. *God's beloved children hope and trust that at the return of Christ, his anger will make things right. In anticipation, we groan and eagerly wait.*

June 14

"My sheep hear my voice, and I know them, and they follow me."
—John 10:27

God is with you, immediately and personally at work. He is at work both in you and in those whom you seek to help by speaking the truth in love. John 10:27 and John 15:1–5 are foundational sources of confidence for God's children: Christ's sheep hear his voice; the Vinedresser prunes those who are in Christ. God works within his people; therefore, we can reach out to others. Those in whom he begins to work, he will continue to work until the day when glory and joy are revealed, until the day when the intimacy of faith becomes the intimacy of sight.

The apex of all hope and happiness can be stated in four words: God is with us. This is one of Jesus's names: Emmanuel. *This is the supreme promise: I will be with you. This will sustain you while you live and when you die. When you are elated, your happiness will be infused with thankfulness. When you agonize, your suffering will be infused with hope because of "Christ in you, the hope of glory"* (Colossians 1:27).

The Bible is about the subject of intimacy with God. What does it look like? What are his purposes? He can and will meet you, and me, and those to whom we minister. God has not left us groping to understand his ways. He has not left us afloat in the ambiguous ecstasies and despairs of both experience and circumstance. He has revealed his ways. He has revealed himself. The living faith that listens to the living Word of the living God will experience the sort of living intimacy that gives foretastes of heaven.

June 15

"Fear not, little flock, for it is your Father's good pleasure to give you the kingdom." —Luke 12:32

Your heavenly Father cares tenderly for you, like a parent for a beloved child. The One who touches base with you and connects with you is your Shepherd. He plans to walk with you today. So he can keep an eye on you? That's part of it. He will protect you and nourish you. But the one who catches your ear is also your Counselor whose intimate voice speaks wisdom to your heart. That is the God we serve, the one we want to love, the one who wants us to walk with him every day.

> *Our Father, will you hear us, will you help us? Will you meet us? Give to us your Holy Spirit, your very self. Shepherd us, master us, protect us, and encourage us.* Where we are weak, strengthen us. Where we are anxious, calm us. Where we get frustrated, will you soothe what troubles us? Will you in every way meet us one and all? Each of us, Lord, that we'd be encouraged, that we would live our lives with more light and more tenderness for others and more genuine joy and gratitude and need toward you. Please help us and meet us. And we pray in the name of Jesus Christ our Savior, Amen.

June 16

And hope does not put us to shame, because God's love has been poured into our hearts through the Holy Spirit who has been given to us. —Romans 5:5

The grace of the Lord Jesus Christ and the love of God and the fellowship of the Holy Spirit be with you all. —2 Corinthians 13:14

Bear one another's burdens, and so fulfill the law of Christ. —Galatians 6:2

A Prayer for a Tender Heart

Lord, we thank you that you have called us to bring our true need to the one who loves us. Thank you that, like a father, you have compassion on us. We thank you that you care for us like a good father who cares, feels tenderly, supports and even carries his child. We pray that you give us hearts receptive to the love of God in Christ Jesus, that we would rejoice in you and love you, that we would be lifted up to you, that we would have a greater degree of confidence and steadiness and hope and love for you and a tender heart that bears others on our hearts. *I pray that we would increasingly see beyond our own small frame of reference and take into ourselves the needs of a great and wide kingdom—the needs of brothers and sisters who suffer and struggle, the needs of the poor, that we would have the same kind of heart that you have.*

Lord, not only speak to us through your Word, but make those words alive in us and us alive to you. And we ask this in the name of Jesus Christ who embodied all this and more, Amen.

June 17

In him we have obtained an inheritance, having been predestined according to the purpose of him who works all things according to the counsel of his will. —Ephesians 1:11

As God reveals himself, what do we come to know? The letter of Ephesians opens by relentlessly pressing on us that God is in control. Things happen by his will (Ephesians 1:1, 3, 5, 8, 11). The universe works according to God's plan to glorify himself in Christ and in all true believers who incorruptibly love Jesus.

Listen to Ephesians, and you will know that life is not a sloppy, confusing mess. Perhaps you've heard the metaphor that we look at life from the tangled, knotty side of the tapestry, and later we'll see the beautiful, coherent pattern on the top side. That's a useful metaphor, but Ephesians lets us see the top side of the tapestry now. God says, in effect, "It's all working out according to a definite plan. A hand is on the controls of history and of your life, with the power to perform what he chooses."

When Paul says you have the hope of glory because you were "predestined according to the purpose of him who works all things according to the counsel of his will" (1:11), he's not trying to stir up debate about esoteric doctrines and philosophical riddles. God is utterly in control. Any other view would be absurd—this God spins galaxies and hold atoms together, after all. *Because his purposes will not be thwarted, you can leap to the call, learning to be courageous, optimistic, persevering in love through troubles. His purposes sustain you through it all.*

June 18

Be at peace among yourselves. And we urge you, brothers, admonish
the idle, encourage the fainthearted, help the weak, be patient with them
all. See that no one repays anyone evil for evil, but always seek to do
good to one another and to everyone.
—1 Thessalonians 5:13b-15

You and I have been given a gift with a purpose. The gift is life in Christ. That purpose is that we become Exhibit A in demonstrating real love at work in the real world: the constructive displeasure of mercy. It means nothing less than treating people the way Jesus treats you. When we do wrong, he demonstrates his constructive displeasure and mercy to us. *He is patient with us, not quick on the draw. He forgives us and doesn't turn against us. He is generous to us, giving us grace upon grace. He talks straight to us, bringing what's wrong to light in order to set us free of what blinds and perverts us.*

You and I learn to do the same as is being done to us. You may well have gotten a taste of this dynamic from a good parent, a wise boss, an excellent coach, a thoughtful teacher, a mature friend, a genuine pastor. Have you noticed that when you are treated in this fine way, it tends to bring out the same in you? You get a glimpse from someone else of a higher purpose for your life. You get a bigger perspective on troubles and troublesome people.

June 19

He has told you, O man, what is good;
and what does the LORD require of you
but to do justice, and to love kindness,
and to walk humbly with your God? —Micah 6:8

M ercy. Because Jesus hates suffering and loves sufferers, sufferers find help and joy. Mercy. Because Jesus hates sin and loves sinners, sinners find forgiveness and joy.

This response to something that is wrong in our world is complex. It involves a constructive mix of justified anger combined with mercy and active efforts to make true peace where there is trouble. The constructive displeasure of mercy traverses exactly the same ground as simple anger. But it's on a different spectrum altogether. It does not act like the typical hostilities. Like simple anger, it says, "That matters. It's wrong and offensive. I want to do something about it." But unlike just getting mad, it says, "That's wrong—and I will be constructively merciful in pursuing whatever is just, whatever makes things right, whatever does good."

Mercy is an entirely different way of reacting to offenses, to things we think are wrong. Think about this: mercy is not a non-reactive indifference—because it cares. And it's the furthest thing from approval—because what's happening is wrong. Mercy includes a component of forceful anger, but anger's typical hostility, vindictiveness, and destructiveness does not dominate.

True mercy proceeds hand in hand with true justice. It brings mercy to victims by bringing justice. While working hand in hand with justice, it offers mercy to violators. Mercy contains a combination of attitudes and actions that proceed in a constructive, instead of destructive, way.

June 20

The Lord is not slow to fulfill his promise as some count slowness, but is patient toward you, not wishing that any should perish, but that all should reach repentance. —2 Peter 3:9

Patience is a curious response to something that is wrong. Why is it curious? Because when you are truly patient, you agree with the moral evaluation that anger makes: "That's wrong. What you're doing does not please me. It offends me. It hurts people." True patience is not about passivity, indifference, or tolerance of evils. You do not just put up with bad things. It's not an easygoing tolerance and neutrality. It does not accept anything and affirm everything. *Patience hates what's happening. Then it rolls up its sleeves to redress what is wrong.*

Patience sees wrong, but it is "slow to anger." This is a prime characteristic of the Lord God. He is gracious, compassionate, and slow to anger (Exodus 34:6). It is the first characteristic of love. "Love is patient" (1 Corinthians 13:4). God is love, and God is slow to anger. He intends to make us like himself. To be slow to anger means you are willing to work with wrong over time. "The Lord is not slow about his promise as some count slowness, but is patient" (2 Peter 3:9). God chooses to work over a scale of moments, days, years, decades, centuries, millennia. And he will accomplish what he has set out to do.

June 21

"Pay attention to yourselves! If your brother sins, rebuke him, and if he repents, forgive him, and if he sins against you seven times in the day, and turns to you seven times, saying, 'I repent,' you must forgive him."
—Luke 17:3-4

Forgiveness comes in two forms. First, and foundationally, you forgive another person before God, whether or not that person admits or even recognizes any wrong. This is *attitudinal forgiveness.* Listen to how Jesus speaks of this vertical-dimension forgiving of another person:

"Whenever you stand praying, if you have anything against anyone, forgive, so that your Father also who is in heaven may forgive you your trespasses." (Mark 11:25)

You stand alone before God your Father dealing with your own attitudes. This vertical aspect of forgiveness deals with our attitudes. Its purpose is to change you, not to deal with the other person. It prepares you, so you will go to the other person already willing to be merciful. You are no longer holding the grudge, building up bitterness, on the defensive, on the offensive.

The second aspect of forgiveness is *transacted forgiveness.* Again, listen to how Jesus describes it: If your brother sins, bring it up with him directly, and if he repents, forgive him, and if he sins against you seven times in the day, and turns to you seven times, saying, "I repent," you must forgive him (Luke 17:3-4, author's paraphrase).

Notice that here Jesus envisions a conversation with the other person. You bring it up constructively; the other person asks to be forgiven. The interpersonal interaction is able to be both candid and full of mercy (a rare combination!) because the attitudinal forgiveness has already happened.

This combination of attitudinal and transacted forgiveness helps make sense of many common and extremely tangled situations.

June 22

For all the promises of God find their Yes in him. That is why it is
through him that we utter our Amen to God for his glory.
—2 Corinthians 1:20

I t is easy to forget that God is an actual person. We so easily forget. That is why he so often reminds us: Remember! He takes
the initiative. He willingly comes to you. He is not an idea, an
energy, an experience you work up within yourself. We hear his
words to us in the Bible, revealing how Jesus embodies the Yes!
to all his promises and purposes. But he is not bound within the
pages of the book. His book reveals the one who speaks, who
is I AM. He is active. He walks with us. He tells us his names
so we can talk with him. He is your hands-on Father. He is the
Vinedressser at work pruning you to make you fruitful. He is
your Good Shepherd who gave his life for his sheep. He walks
with you and watches over you. He is the Holy Spirit who makes
his home in you so that you become a person of faith and love.
This most wonderous Person is the game changer.

God's Word speaks of who he actually is. *Cancer is my true
enemy, one of the many shadows of death, one of the many evils. But
Christ willingly walks with me through every valley shadowed by
death. He is willingly your Shepherd too.* Remember. It takes looking to him in the neediness and dependency of faith. Ask and
you will receive. Ask for mercy for all the ways you do not follow
him. Trust his death in your place, the price for all your wrongs.

June 23

Do not be anxious about anything, but in everything by prayer and supplication with thanksgiving let your requests be made known to God.
—Philippians 4:6

The Lord is listening. Paul tells us in this passage to make our request known to God. Think about that for a minute. If the Lord is near, if he is someone who knows what's on your heart, who knows what weighs heavily on you and preoccupies you, then he is a hearer of his beloved children.

Many psalms start out by pleading with God—Lord listen to me, bend your ear, you must hear me, I need you to listen and act on my behalf. These are not calm psalms; they are intense and pointed. In Psalm 28, David tells God that if God doesn't hear him, he will die. This is faith talking, and David talks this way because God is listening.

God's listening does not guarantee that what is making you anxious will go away—that your financial problems will be solved, that you will be cured of cancer, or that whatever else is worrying you will disappear. You may not be healed, people you love may die, and you may struggle with financial stress. But God comforts, strengthens, and gives hope in the mist of the most difficult circumstances. Jesus did not want to drink the cup of God's wrath. But God strengthened him, and he was fully willing. There's help from him for whatever worries you.

So when you are anxious, pour your heart out to God. He is listening.

June 24

I know how to be brought low, and I know how to abound. In any and every circumstance, I have learned the secret of facing plenty and hunger, abundance and need. I can do all things through him who strengthens me. —Philippians 4:12-13

God taught Paul a secret we all need to know: the secret of contentment. Contentment, unlike indifference, is the godly opposite of worrying and obsessing. When you worry, you're trying to hold onto what you might lose, or you're grabbing for what you don't have. Indifference means you are trying not to care about what you don't have or might lose. But that's not contentment. *Contentment offers a fundamental stability that comes from knowing that the all-powerful Lord of the universe is near. He is listening to your cries and guarding you day and night.*

Paul learned contentment by depending on his Lord. He said, "I can do everything through him who gives me strength" (Philippians 4:13). Paul knew that, no matter how the circumstances of his life changed, God would be his constant, faithful, loving protector.

You are his child, and he wants a relationship with you. God's peace comes to us as our relationship with him becomes deeper, more honest, and more intimate.

June 25

Having the eyes of your hearts enlightened, that you may know what is
the hope to which he has called you, what are the riches of his glorious
inheritance in the saints, and what is the immeasurable greatness of
his power toward us who believe, according to the working of his great
might that he worked in Christ when he raised him from the dead and
seated him at his right hand in the heavenly places. —Ephesians 1:18–20

God's present grace to sinners demonstrates that he is with us and in us. How do you know he is with you? The love of God has been poured into our hearts through the Holy Spirit who was given to us, by whom we cry out, "Abba, Father" (Romans 5:5; 8:15). The good news is not simply what happened long ago and far away. What Jesus now does reshapes what we do. God is present with us and works powerfully in us. Our Father gives wisdom for the asking. The Holy Spirit comes for the asking. Good gifts are for the asking. The Bible repeatedly invites us to need, ask, receive, and live on present grace. Would you die to yourself and live a new life? Present grace gives you the confidence to seek help, to question those old felt needs, desires, opinions, and lifestyles, to put to death what is not beautiful. Present grace nourishes faith working through love.

June 26

He also told them a parable: "Can a blind man lead a blind man? Will they not both fall into a pit?" —Luke 6:39

Do you ever talk with people about their problems or about your own? Perhaps your role is designated by some title that defines you as a counselor. Or you might be "just" a coworker, neighbor, friend, parent, spouse, sibling, child, or grandparent. How do you help a person you love to think straight, when he or she thinks crooked? How do you learn to see straight and think straight, when something inside you compulsively bends in the wrong direction?

You need a clear-eyed realism about the human tendency toward self-blinding. Only then will you bring a buoyant sense of the centrality of the grace of Jesus Christ in counseling ministry. And only then will you help people make the most essential change of all, learning to know God in real life.

But the soul's blind self-love resists this sort of change. What keeps us from loving and needing God with all that we are? Something in us doesn't want to face the Someone who insists on having the first and last say about our lives. Naturally, that something in us does not want to be seen for what it is. It is allergic to the truth about ourselves because we have an allergic reaction to "spiritual submission to God." We say No, No, No to life on God's terms, and we forfeit self-knowledge in the bargain.

Yet the words of the personal Word and the power of the personal Spirit go patiently about the business of remaking us. *God persistently teaches us to fear him, to trust him, to love him, and so, when we have ears to hear, we begin to serve him.*

June 27

Then Jesus told his disciples, "If anyone would come after me, let him
deny himself and take up his cross and follow me." —Matthew 16:24

Only if you face up to your sin and your resistance to God
can you see clearly and act gently, helping others to face
up to themselves as well. The Bible calls this essential change
dynamic by many names. Jesus says, "Become a disciple." In
other words, sign on for life learning. A learner is committed
to becoming different. Do your opinions, feelings, choices, and
habits currently have the status of divine right? Is how you are
a given, something you insist on? As soon as I'm willing to say,
"Not necessarily," I step off the death spiral and onto the learning curve.

*Jesus says, "Follow me." To follow somebody else runs com-
pletely opposite to the self-will that characterizes what I do instinctively.* Listening to him runs directly opposite to the opinions I
obsessively think. This change dynamic will make you radically
counterintuitive. To follow somebody else runs flat opposite to
the entitled self-assertiveness that western culture reinforces in us
every day. This change dynamic will make you radically countercultural, while every alternative to "Follow me" is just another way
of going with the flow.

June 28

Your testimonies are righteous forever;
give me understanding that I may live. —Psalm 119:144

You should ask the same things of the Bible that you ask of people. Why not? The Bible is about people, troubles, mercies, choices, struggles, and hope. So ask of Scripture, *What were those people facing back then? What did God choose to reveal to them?* Today's specific situations and choices are never exactly the same, but there are always common themes. And though our saving God never works in exactly the same way twice, he is the same yesterday, today, and forever.

The Word of God reveals God's person, promises, ways, and will on the stage and in the story of real human lives. At every turn, the Word of God shows people facing particular challenges and choices. Amid the troubles and opportunities of their lives, they are tempted to believe particular lies, to choose particular wrongs, and to live in ways that are ugly, perverse, and complicated. Scripture also shows us the Lord of life, the true and living God who enters the human condition redemptively, making wrongs right, speaking wisdom that we need.

Scripture shows some people believing what is true, choosing what is good, and living in ways that are simply beautiful—people after God's own heart. They need, seek, and turn to the Lord. Supremely, we witness the true Man after God's own heart, that bright Lord, Word made flesh, living with us, touched by our weakness, full of grace, truth and glory, loving God and neighbor. This is the goal of our discipleship.

June 29

For from his fullness we have all received, grace upon grace. —John 1:16

There is past, present, and future grace. Each aspect of grace is what you and I need in order to walk more steadily in the light and to run from darkness. Some days we need one aspect of grace more than another. But always we need grace.

There is a past tense aspect of grace in how God has chosen to work in you and to complete the work. It has to do with all the historical work of Jesus Christ. He left his Father's throne above, came down, and emptied himself of all but love. He died for us, supplying justification by faith, adoption, and regeneration by the power of the Spirit. If you are dealing with guilt and anxiety about yourself and feeling like you're a failure, you need past grace. Past grace is the door of mercy. Past grace speaks of a reconciled relationship.

Second is present grace. Present grace tells you that God is with you. He is on the scene, ready, willing, and a present help. He is working in you. Present grace is the dynamic that is emphasized in prayers about God's power and presence, when we call on God to reveal himself to us and through us, to shield and strengthen us for what we face.

And then there is future grace. God will come for you. Everything that's wrong now is going to be made right. Future grace is about the confidence that one day all tears will be wiped away, and the things that are difficult now will be filled with joy.

The medicine for what ails you is all of grace—God's great working of past, present, and future grace.

June 30

And I am sure of this, that he who began a good work in you will bring it
to completion at the day of Jesus Christ. —Philippians 1:6

A Prayer of Thanksgiving for Christ at Work in Us

Our God and Father, thank you that you have given
us Jesus, your Son, and that the Lamb of God—the
Lion of Judah, the King of kings, the long-awaited Messiah
has come for us. Thank you that Jesus is a very present
help, guide, friend, shield, and Savior. He keeps us.
And we thank you that we cry out to one who is a living
Shepherd, one who does not leave the universe and the
church to bumble along, does not leave us to our own
devices. We are so grateful that you persevere with us. We
are so grateful that there is evidence in our lives that there
is someone else who is at work, someone who will bring us
into daylight. Someone who has begun good work and will
finish it.

*We beseech you that you will continue to work in us even right
to the finish line, that you will bless us and keep us and watch
over us and make us alive to you, make your words bright
and shining with life and rich with meaning and deep with
hope, powerful to transform us.* We ask these things in your
name, Lord Jesus, and we ask it, thanking you that you are
faithful to do all that you have promised. Amen.

July 1

And, as shoes for your feet, having put on the readiness given by the
gospel of peace. —Ephesians 6:15

The gospel of peace—reconciling Jews and Gentiles to God and to each other—is a central theme in Ephesians 2–3. In the gospel of peace, relationships are reconciled, forgiveness triumphs over anger, and a community of mutual kindness is established. This comes through powerfully in Ephesians 4:25–5:2. The gospel embodies peacemaking power.

Where did Paul find this picture? It is a rich allusion to Isaiah 52:7:

> How beautiful upon the mountains are the feet of him
> who brings good news,
>> who publishes peace, who brings good news of happiness, who publishes salvation,
> who says to Zion, "Your God reigns."

Whose feet are beautiful with the good news of peace? Isaiah 52:6–10 makes clear that the shoes belong to the Lord who is coming in person. Every eye sees the Lord returning to Zion, bringing comfort and redemption. A few sentences later, Isaiah 53 will tell us how he will do it. The Lamb of God will bear the iniquity of us all.

Jesus Christ is the good news of peace to the ends of the earth. The man wearing those shoes is on the march. Stand up and join him.

July 2

In all circumstances take up the shield of faith, with which you can
extinguish all the flaming darts of the evil one. —Ephesians 6:16

We are on the march, but the enemy fights back—hard. He lies, he schemes, he accuses, he hurts, he divides. He would enslave you and kill you, if he could. Ephesians has reminded us that wherever lies and hostility control a relationship, the devil dominates (4:25–27). We are to stand against the devil's purposes and plans (6:11).

The shield is the only piece of weaponry that intends to communicate a protective role as we face counterattacks of lies and hostilities. In every life circumstance, our shield repels "the flaming darts of the evil one." *Where does this shield image come from? The Lord himself is a shield to those who take refuge in him when faced with enemies.* In numerous psalms, our enemies are characterized as liars and murderers. They hate the Lord and his people.

Psalm 18 is an example of faith seeking protection and strength in the Lord. In the first few verses David piles up every safe-place metaphor he can think of. This is what it looks like when a person takes up the shield of faith:

> I love you, O Lord, my strength.
> The Lord is my rock and my fortress and my deliverer,
> my God, my rock in whom I take refuge,
> my shield and the horn of my salvation, my stronghold.
> I call upon the Lord, who is worthy to be praised,
> and I am saved from my enemies. (vv. 1–3)

Notice, the Lord is the shield. Faith looks with confidence to the one who protects and strengthens. This is how Christ took up the shield. This is how we, who are in Christ, continue to abide in Christ and strengthen ourselves in him.

July 3

And take the helmet of salvation . . . —Ephesians 6:17a

Christ is our salvation from death and sin. Salvation! A Savior! He comes in person for people who have lost their way and are dying. He came for us, and we go forth for others. We are living the message, wearing this helmet of salvation. Paul has spoken about this Gift of gifts throughout his letter. What was that truth with which we first girded ourselves as we sought the Lord's strength?

Ephesians 1:13 tells us, "When you heard the word of truth, the gospel of your salvation, and believed in him, you were sealed with the promised Holy Spirit." And what was that breastplate, footgear, and shield? It is the reality that Jesus Christ saves us from death, depravity, and the devil.

We were dead, and the Spirit made us alive (Ephesians 2:5). He awakened faith by his power. The Lord freely gifts all good, and we gratefully receive. *The gift of the new covenant in the coming of Christ our Savior, and the gift of the life-giving Spirit, and the gift of words of salvation—this is Ephesians. This is the light that we bring against the darkness.*

July 4

And take . . . the sword of the Spirit, which is the word of God.
—Ephesians 6:17

The Bible often fills out a metaphor from multiple angles. As we listen, as we stop and think, we get the point. Paul is doing this in Ephesians 6 as he piles up pictures of Christ's strong weapons of lifesaving war. What we see in Ephesians 6 are different ways of saying the same thing—how to strengthen yourself in the Lord, how you walk in the light, how you respond to the word of truth. He wants us to get the point.

This final piece of weaponry is another allusion to Isaiah. Isaiah 49:2 provides the most obvious reference to a weapon of divine words. These are the words of the servant of the Lord, the Messiah, who says, "He made my mouth like a sharp sword." This sword expresses the wisdom of the Spirit, destroying evil and bringing in the peaceable kingdom.

We are now invited to take up this sword of the Spirit and proclaim the one who was made "a light for the nations, that my salvation may reach to the end of the earth" (49:6). *Strengthen yourself in this Lord, and go where the darkness reigns.*

July 5

Praying at all times in the Spirit, with all prayer and supplication. To that end, keep alert with all perseverance, making supplication for all the saints, and also for me, that words may be given to me in opening my mouth boldly to proclaim the mystery of the gospel, for which I am an ambassador in chains, that I may declare it boldly, as I ought to speak.
—Ephesians 6:18-20

Faith responds to God's truth by interceding for the real needs of others. Paul had prayed for us to know the Lord's strength, love, and presence (1:16–23; 3:14–21). He called each of us to find strength in the Lord (6:10) and to take refuge in the Lord (6:16). Now, personal need moves to concern for the needs of others. *Faith cascades into love. We pray for our fellow saints who have the same need for the Lord's truth, strength, love, presence, and protection.* Others need your prayers for strength in the Lord. And the people they love need the same care from them.

What Paul says next is astonishing. He has called us to pray for each other. Now he puts himself first in the queue of needy ones in verses 18–20. He needed our Lord's help as much as you do. He, too, needed the weaponry of strength to enable him to engage in Christ's mission—this belt, breastplate, shoes, shield, helmet, and sword of life that invades darkness with truth, faith, and love.

July 6

The heart of the wise makes his speech judicious
and adds persuasiveness to his lips.
Gracious words are like a honeycomb,
sweetness to the soul and health to the body. —Proverbs 16:23–24

We're called to speak encouraging words to others. Here are a few tips as to how you might do this. First, the word that's helpful to somebody else is usually short and sweet. I can rarely take in more than a line or two of Scripture in a way that makes a difference. There's a place for reading chunks of Scripture, but at a tense moment in life, that's probably a bit much to swallow.

Second, you need to help people slow down to make their intake of Scripture personal. Help them see themselves in Scripture in detail. For instance, in James 1:3, when you read "count it all joy . . . when you meet trials of various kinds," help them apply this to their trial. Think together about why it is so hard to find joy in this situation. Look at how tender God is about our faith in the following verses. He doesn't even call our reactions foolish. He says if we lack wisdom, to ask for it, and he'll help us (v. 5). Help people put their lives into passages like these.

Our tendency when someone is struggling is to use Scripture to paint the moral landscape by looking up passages directly related to their struggle, be it a temper, bitterness, or something else. And it's valid that you would do that, but *it's also so important that you always connect their struggle to the diversity of the promises of God and the grace of God.* Our imaging of God in these situations is like a three-watt night-light helping the person connect to the God who is the Sun of life.

July 7

But immediately Jesus spoke to them, saying, "Take heart; it is I. Do not be afraid." —Matthew 14:27

What is the most frequent commandment in the entire Bible? Fear not. Don't be afraid. Don't be anxious. This is a very different kind of command—it's more a voice of reassurance to you. It's speaking to a place we struggle.

We have very good reasons to be afraid, because everything that we value is fragile and vulnerable and out of our control. We've got to understand that this "command reassurance" is radically realistic about all that is fragile, so it's not just whistling in the dark hoping you won't be afraid. Fear and anxiety are responses to something that seems overwhelming and out of control.

In saying, "Don't be afraid," God is very concerned to give us reasons to trust. The whole book of Philippians is giving you reasons to not be anxious: "He who began a good work in you will bring it to completion at the day of Jesus Christ" (1:6). This anchors your life as a journey, dignified by the hope that one day the struggle is going to be over. "Christ Jesus . . . did not count equality with God a thing to be grasped, but emptied himself, by taking the form of a servant . . . by becoming obedient to the point of death" (2:5–8). Jesus came into our plight. He wore what we wore and faced what we face. He died in our place and is alive. "My God will supply every need of yours according to his riches in glory" (4:19).

You have very good reasons to be afraid, tense, anxious, and stressed, but you have better reasons not to be afraid.

July 8

Then the Lᴏʀᴅ said to Moses, "Behold, I am about to rain bread from
heaven for you, and the people shall go out and gather a day's portion
every day, that I may test them, whether they will walk in my law or not."
—Exodus 16:4

Imagine this: you've left Egypt. Your food is gone and you're in the desert. There are good reasons for anxiety, because you don't know where food is going to come from. You, your family, and your people could die.

In the middle of this trouble, God himself hears and he gives you manna. You open your tent the next morning, and there is manna all over the place— it's exhilarating. You know you're not supposed to take too much, but you're afraid about tomorrow, so you take more than you need, and it rots.

That night you go to bed a little less anxious. Someone said that the manna is going to be there tomorrow, and you wake up and sure enough, there it is. This time you gather just enough for the day. And then you repeat this process over and over again. Could you imagine by around day 1000 that you're finally getting to the point that you wake up confident because you know the manna is going to be available to you?

The New Testament version of manna is grace. God will give you all the grace that you need today. But he's not going to give you all the grace you need for tomorrow, because if you had manna for the next week, you would trust in your storehouses and forget about God.

There are good reasons why the Lord's strategy is to give you all you need for today but not for tomorrow. That's this principle of manna. The grace you need to face tomorrow will be yours just when you need it.

July 9

But you, O LORD, know me;
you see me, and test my heart toward you. —Jeremiah 12:3a

A Prayer to the God Who Knows Us

Almighty God, to whom all hearts are open and all desires known, and from whom no secrets are hidden. You know us. You know our thoughts; you know our fears. You know things about us we don't even know about ourselves. You know our sorrows and our joys. You know the places where we have been given wisdom; you know the places where we are still foolish. You know what breaks our hearts and what delights us.

This day we are open before you and we ask you that you will cleanse the thoughts of our hearts by the inspiration of your Holy Spirit. Breathe upon us, meet us, and give to us your very self. Our Father, wash, strengthen, and shelter us. Protect, lead, and guide us throughout this day, that we would trust you and would know you.

Teach us to love you and to magnify your holy name. Teach us to treat others with the kindness and clarity of purpose that expresses your love. Make us come alive to you and your Word. We commit ourselves to you through Jesus Christ, our Savior and our Lord, Amen.

July 10

Let your speech always be gracious, seasoned with salt, so that you may know how you ought to answer each person. —Colossians 4:6

Let no corrupting talk come out of your mouths, but only such as is good for building up, as fits the occasion, that it may give grace to those who hear. —Ephesians 4:29

Every one of us has been significantly helped by hearing someone else talk personally. Hearing from others about their struggles, goals, and experiences instructs us, builds us up, and encourages us.

How do we best talk about our experiences, thoughts, struggles, and lessons learned when ministering to others? How do we balance this with listening well? *We need to become wise in how to approach others so that we can help connect them to Jesus, who best understands people and their suffering and sin. We want every word out of our mouths to be constructive, according to the need of the moment.*

We were made to know others and to be known by them. When we are isolated and there's no one we can trust, we cannot thrive. Others need to hear God's words from us. We need to hear God's words from others. A vision for the Christian life is that we would imitate God, who loves us with a purposeful patience that is willing to keep pursuing good ends all the way to the finish. It's not that we have to figure out a quick fix to our or others' problems today. The change process has a lifetime as a framework, and this gives you hope as you seek to take the next step, say the next helpful word, in each moment. God is patient with his people, so we can be too.

July 11

No temptation has overtaken you that is not common to man. God is
faithful, and he will not let you be tempted beyond your ability, but with
the temptation he will also provide the way of escape, that you may be
able to endure it. Therefore, my beloved, flee from idolatry.
—1 Corinthians 10:13–14

I'm going to speak to you as one who is beloved, as one who is
tempted, and as one to whom there is a way of escape. When
you are struggling with a persistent sin, what does change start
to look like?

There is always some kind of wake-up call. You wake up to
three things. For starters, you wake up to who you really are. You
realize you have been in a dream and that you have been lying
to yourself. You begin to understand that your life is a moral
drama. You own up to your personal responsibility for your sin,
and you realize that the whole purpose of your life is to be in a
transformative process going from darkness and folly to light
and wisdom.

Secondly, you wake up to what's really going on in your
world. You have been misunderstanding the nature of the world
in which you live. It is full of temptation, trial, lying voices, and
false pleasures.

Lastly, you wake up to the fact that you need exactly who
God is. *You need exactly the things that God promises to give, to be,
and to do. You reach out for his mercy, you flee sin and temptation,
and you run for daylight. You cry out to God in your need and you
ask for help.* This leads to opening yourself up to other people
and letting them in on the struggle, because we were never made
to change alone.

July 12

*"And forgive us our debts,
as we also have forgiven our debtors." —Matthew 6:12*

*Be kind to one another, tenderhearted, forgiving one another, as God in
Christ forgave you. —Ephesians 4:32*

Change is a is an interpersonal process. We need each other.
You do not change on your own. Talk to people about your
troubles. Confess your sins to one another. Where you have hurt
others, ask for forgiveness. You must also forgive others when
you have been sinned against.

Jesus is unrelenting here. You must forgive, even if they are
dead, even if they are still your enemy, even if they never come
and ask. There must be a vertical attitudinal forgiveness, whether
there's ever transactional forgiveness within a real relationship.
Every alternative to forgiveness is evil—anger, bitterness, clamor,
slander, and malice.

You've got to grapple with what people have done, just as
you've got to grapple with what you have done. As you do this,
*where will you turn amidst your pain and trouble? You must take
refuge in the living God. God as your refuge stands against every
alternative refuge.* Hard times will come, but there is a fountain
of living waters—the Lord, who can be trusted. And you will
not fear when the heat comes. Your leaves will remain green, you
will not be anxious in the year of drought, and you will not cease
to bear fruit (Jeremiah 17: 7–8). Alternately, you will die if you
take refuge in yourself.

July 13

This is my comfort in my affliction,
that your promise gives me life. —Psalm 119:50

What is the usual effect suffering has on you or the people you know? You turn in on yourself. You become preoccupied with your pain, preoccupied with being betrayed, preoccupied by your physical pain or disability. It just hurts. It's just hard.

What is the intrinsic effect of sinning, of forgetting God, of straying and wandering? I turn in on myself. My mental universe consists of me. Sin curves into itself. I conduct a monologue in the theater of my mind.

Psalm 119 also conducts a monologue, but in a different direction. It's a dialogue in the theater of God's world. *The psalmist is getting outside of himself by declaring to God who God is and what God says. He then tells God what he's facing, both internally and externally. Then he asks God for help.* This is an out-loud relationship. You see honest cries of need coming from this person to God.

As you experience suffering, take your cue from this psalmist. You need fresh strength as you face this suffering. Ask God to revive you, to give you life (vv. 25, 107, 156). You are afflicted, prone to wander, and you need the Lord near to help you. Ask God to give you understanding (vv. 34, 73, 125, 144). Then recommit your way to God, in trust of him and his character (vv. 57–62). Cling to his promises in hope (vv. 49–50). He himself will be your "comfort in affliction." What better comforter could you have?

July 14

Beloved, do not be surprised at the fiery trial when it comes upon you
to test you, as though something strange were happening to you. But
rejoice insofar as you share Christ's sufferings, that you may also rejoice
and be glad when his glory is revealed. —1 Peter 4:12-13

God's hand is intimately mixed up in our troubles. Each day will bring you "its own trouble" (Matthew 6:34). Some difficulties are light and momentary—in your face today and forgotten tomorrow. Other hardships last for a season. Some troubles recur and abate cyclically. Other afflictions become chronic. Some woes steadily worsen, progressively bringing pain and disability into your life. And other sufferings arrive with inescapable finality—the death of a dream, the death of a loved one, your own death. But whatever you must face changes in light of the resurrection of Jesus Christ and the promise that you, too, will live. You can learn to say with all your heart, in company with a great cloud of witnesses: "We do not lose heart. Though our outer self is wasting away, our inner self is being renewed day by day. For this light momentary affliction is preparing for us an eternal weight of glory beyond all comparison" (2 Corinthians 4:16–17). We can learn to say it and mean it because it is true.

If you are someone who has taken the book of Psalms to heart, if you've pondered the second half of Romans 8, if you've worked your way through Job, if you've let 1 Peter sink in, then you've already got the gist of how God's grace works in hardships. But there are always new challenges. *The wisdom to suffer well is like manna—you must receive nourishment every day. You can't store it up, though you do become more familiar with how to go out and find what you need for today.*

July 15

Your words were found, and I ate them,
and your words became to me a joy
and the delight of my heart,
for I am called by your name,
O LORD, God of hosts. —Jeremiah 15:16

What chunk of Scripture has made the biggest difference in your life? What makes these words frequently and immediately relevant? Your answer will likely embody four foundational truths about how to read the Bible for wise application.

First, this passage became your own because you listened. He is saying this to you, and you need these words. You must act on this call to faith and love. When you forget, you drift, stray, and flounder. When you remember, and put it to work, bright truth rearranges your life.

Second, the passage and your life become fused. A specific word from God connects to some pointed struggle inside you and around you. Something God says invades your darkness with his light. He meets your need with his mercies. Application depends on honesty about where you need help.

Third, God meets you before you meet him. The passage arrested you. God arranged your struggle with sin and suffering so that you would need this exact help. Without God's initiative, you would never make the connection. The Spirit chose to rewrite your inner script, pouring God's love into your heart, inviting you to live in a new reality. He awakens your sense of need, gives you ears to hear, and freely gives necessary wisdom.

Fourth, the application of beloved passages is usually quite straightforward. God states something in general terms. You insert your relevant particulars. *A passage becomes personal when your details come to participate in what is said. The gap across centuries and between cultures seems almost to disappear. Your God is a very present help in trouble—this trouble.* Application occurs in specifics.

July 16

Speaking the truth in love, we are to grow up in every way into him who is the head, into Christ, from whom the whole body, joined and held together by every joint with which it is equipped, when each part is working properly, makes the body grow so that it builds itself up in love.
—Ephesians 4:15-16

The Lord's people are called to help each other grow up. We are called to know and be known by each other. We are called to counsel each other, to be change agents in each other's lives. We are called to speak the truth in love, and make a difference as brothers and sisters, shepherds and sheep.

To pick one example, Jesus is a wonderful counselor. He cuts to the heart. He's inconceivably generous and merciful. He's eminently approachable. He asks great questions. He's fiercely tough-minded. And he turns lives upside down. In comparison, we might be bumbling, misguided, ignorant, ineffectual, harsh, or timid. We might not even want to think of ourselves as counselors—though from Jesus's point of view, all of us are always counselors, whether foolish or wise. *Sure, we've got a long way to go. But it is into that image of Jesus that we are all being transformed. It is our joy that such a transformation turns churches into communities of wise love.*

We rightly see that public ministry from the pulpit is crucial, but we often fail to see that interpersonal ministry in conversations is equally so. In fact, the quality of conversations in the church is proof of whether public ministry is succeeding or failing to achieve Christ's goals.

July 17

"Truly, truly, I say to you, whoever hears my word and believes him who sent me has eternal life. He does not come into judgment, but has passed from death to life." —John 5:24

Because of Jesus, you don't have to fear that when you die you will experience God's judgment. Jesus has already experienced that for you. What is waiting for you after death is real life—eternal life. You don't have to earn this life. It is God's gift to those who put their trust in Jesus. This is how the apostle Paul explains it: "For the wages of sin is death, but the gift of God is eternal life in Christ Jesus our Lord" (Romans 6:23). *We all deserve death, but Jesus died in our place. When you trust in him, you no longer have to fear death, because now you share in Jesus's life.*

The eternal life Jesus gives is life the way it was meant to be—free from evil, sorrow, and sadness, and rich in everlasting joy, peace, and purity. The natural, well-earned wages of human life bring death and grief, but God's mercy and grace bring the delights that are at his right hand forever.

Sharing in Jesus's life is how you face all the shadows of death in this unhappy, fallen world and how you face the final darkness of death itself. Because he is alive, you know he will be with you when you die. Because he is alive, you know he will be waiting for you after you die. Because he lives, so do you.

July 18

How precious is your steadfast love, O God!
The children of mankind take refuge in the shadow of your wings.
They feast on the abundance of your house,
and you give them drink from the river of your delights.
For with you is the fountain of life;
in your light do we see light. —Psalm 36:7-9

You cannot face death with true, honest courage unless you are looking forward to meeting Jesus—the one who faced death for you and is now alive and with you. Are you looking forward to meeting the Lamb of God who took away your sin? Do you long to hear your Good Shepherd call you by name? Are you looking forward to going to your heavenly Father's home? It's a home of glory, filled with the radiance of the Holy Spirit. *In God's home all wrongs are made right, all darkness becomes bright, all losses are restored, and all tears are wiped away.*

When you pass through death, you will pass through to the moment when faith becomes sight, when you will actually see the one whom you love sight unseen. To die in the hope that God is with you is to pass through the loss of all things into the gain of all things, into the gain of Christ.

If you are facing the living God, the Lord of life and the giver of all mercies, you have every reason to look death straight in the eye. You're able to look past death toward something that is good, lasting, and wonderful. When you look past death with the eyes of faith, you will see a river of delight in the presence of the Lord himself; you will see yourself feasting at his table and drinking from the fountain of life (Psalm 36:7–9).

July 19

The Lord is my shepherd; I shall not want.
He makes me lie down in green pastures.
He leads me beside still waters.
He restores my soul.
He leads me in paths of righteousness
for his name's sake.
Even though I walk through the valley of the shadow of death,
I will fear no evil,
for you are with me;
your rod and your staff,
they comfort me.

You prepare a table before me
in the presence of my enemies;
you anoint my head with oil;
my cup overflows.
Surely goodness and mercy shall follow me
all the days of my life,
and I shall dwell in the house of the Lord
forever. —Psalm 23

Take a moment to rewrite this psalm to reflect your life. How has Jesus been your Good Shepherd? What places of beauty, peace, and safety has he led you to? Thank him for the ways he has guided you. What hard times has he walked with you through? Can you say with faith that "goodness and love will follow me all the days of my life" (v. 6)? When these things are hard for you to pray, ask Jesus to teach you about himself. Go to John 10 and read about Jesus, the Good Shepherd. Ask him to give you the joy of hearing him call you by name, of knowing that he is walking with you. These are prayers that God delights to answer. *He promises that when you seek him, you will find him (Jeremiah 20:13). When you find God, you find the greatest pleasure there is.*

July 20

The Lord is my shepherd; I shall not want.
He makes me lie down in green pastures.
He leads me beside still waters.
He restores my soul. —Psalm 23:1-3a

When I say Psalm 23 to myself, lingering over each phrase, every word lands relevantly. My life depends on the watchful mercies of the one who willingly restores my soul—and he is bringing me home. David's life experience inhabited every word of Psalm 23. *The Holy Spirit inhabits every word. And when I inhabit every word, I live. Every Christian has an intuitive feel for this. The Bible's counsel—God's message about how reality actually works—is uniquely personal, always relevant, and simply true.* We are not reading just one more theory about human nature. We are encountering the person who intends that we need him and know him, trust him, and love him. God's counsel reveals himself.

In the light of who he is, you discover who you truly are: a dependent creature, a stray and renegade, a beloved child, a much-afflicted human being. You learn that life is a stormy conflict between true and false, good and evil, right and wrong, faith and fear, love and hate, refuge and threat, life and death. You awaken to the everyday, cosmic drama in which you fully participate. You come to know the Giver of life even when you must walk through the valley of the shadow of death. The Bible's counsel awakens us, reorients us, and redirects us.

July 21

Open my eyes, that I may behold
wondrous things out of your law.
I am a sojourner on the earth;
hide not your commandments from me! —Psalm 119:18–19

We've all experienced times when Scripture seems irrelevant, and when our relationship with God waffles somewhere between distracted, indifferent, and complaining.

What can you do about that? Let me offer two suggestions. One asks God to do something for you, and the other asks you to notice some things about yourself.

Ask God: First, what can you ask the Lord to do when he and his words seem distant and dull? Psalm 119 teaches us to say: "Make me understand. Make me alive. Teach me. Open my eyes. Don't forsake me." The psalm-writer was no super-saint. He knew the same struggle you and I have. You can take this to heart. "God, awaken me to what is written." We can give voice to the very experience of disconnect that is given a voice in this psalm.

Notice Your Own Life: Second, when Scripture and God seem hazy to us, we are also hazy about ourselves. We become hazy about how we are doing and about what we are facing. If God seems far away, where are you? When we are far off, we are also asleep to where we need specific help today. What are you facing? Where are you struggling? *Whenever you become vividly aware of where you actually need outside help—today—then the kingdom of God comes near and Scripture sparkles.* Promises speak exactly the hope you need right now. Commands give exactly the guidance that will set you free. God's perspective is exactly the perspective that will reframe whatever you are facing.

July 22

Who is the man who fears the LORD?
Him will he instruct in the way that he should choose.
His soul shall abide in well-being,
and his offspring shall inherit the land.
The friendship of the LORD is for those who fear him,
and he makes known to them his covenant.
My eyes are ever toward the LORD,
for he will pluck my feet out of the net. —Psalm 25:12–15

Consider how the Psalms are written. Unlike the stories in the Bible, here the personal details are stripped away. Instead, a psalm speaks in experiential categories, inviting you to fill in details of what you are facing and how you are either struggling or being blessed. Psalm 25, for example, grapples with feeling the assaults of a godless world. It breathes an awareness of personal failures, and thus a need for the Lord's forgiveness and instruction. It voices honest distress at life's pressures and afflictions. It moves naturally to care for brothers and sisters who face these similar problems and need similar help. I guarantee, some or all of Psalm 25's realities are relevant to you today. *The promises of God in the Psalms—steadfast love, faithfulness, mercy, blessing, watchful care, refuge, and the like—speak directly. And they can also be filled out with New Testament details that show how every promise is tangibly "Yes" in Jesus.* Steadfast love and watchful care come in person. It *matters* that he is near. It *matters* that he's listening.

July 23

The troubles of my heart are enlarged;
bring me out of my distresses.
Consider my affliction and my trouble,
and forgive all my sins. —Psalm 25:17–18

Self-analysis cannot save us. It can become simply one more form of self-fascination. Others-analysis cannot save others. It can become simply one more form of judgmentalism.

True self-knowledge is a fine gift. *And true self-knowledge always leads us out of ourselves, and to our Father who, knowing us thoroughly, loves us utterly.* True self-knowledge does not wallow around inside. God intends to draw us out of self-preoccupation. Seeing the vertical dimension of the struggle with sin and death, we reach out more boldly to the One who is life and light.

It is helpful to name the mastering lust, fear, felt need, or expectation that hijacks God's place. Repentance becomes more intelligent. I can bring to the Father of mercies both my visible behavior and my inner motives. His love is magnified because I see my need for mercy more clearly. "For your name's sake, O LORD, pardon my guilt, for it is great" (Psalm 25:11). And he freely, willingly forgives his beloved children. When he thinks about me and about you, he remembers his own lovingkindness, and he answers our plea.

July 24

"For where your treasure is, there your heart will be also." —Matthew
6:21

Trust in him at all times, O people;
pour out your heart before him;
God is a refuge for us. —Psalm 62:8

Our motives are all active verbs that describe how we connect to the world around us: What are you seeking? What are you loving? What are you fearing? What are you trusting? Where are you taking refuge? What voices are you listening to? Where are you setting your hopes?

The answers to these questions describe characteristics of the whole person, who always orients toward either God or something else. They always propel us to view and treat other people either wisely or foolishly—so they are closely linked to actual behavior, emotions, and attitudes. When we take the Bible's God-relational verbs and turn them into questions, we are exposed for what we are. Such questions can help you to see how and why you are straying. Our answers to these questions describe the seedbed of our sins, how we curve in on ourselves and go blind to God and his will.

But such questions never intend to send you spiraling down on an inward journey. They don't intend to make you intrusively probe others for hidden dirt. They do invite all of us to come out of the dark and into the light of Christ. Seek him who is worthy. Trust him who gives freely. Love him who is lovely. Fear him before whom we stand. Take refuge in the one who truly is our shelter.

July 25

Do nothing from selfish ambition or conceit, but in humility count others more significant than yourselves. Let each of you look not only to his own interests, but also to the interests of others. —Philippians 2:3-4

Self-sacrifice brought Christ into the world and self-sacrifice will lead us his followers into the midst of people. Wherever people suffer, we will be there to comfort. Wherever people strive, we will be there to help. Wherever people fail, we will be there to uplift. Wherever they succeed, we will be there to rejoice. Self-sacrifice means not being indifferent to our times and our fellow human beings. It means absorption in them. It means entering into people's hopes and fears, longings and despairs. It means cultivating rich relationships that are others-focused.

We don't ever atone for anybody's sins, yet we are called to live out in our relationships what Christ did in atoning for our sins. This is the summary of Paul's discussion in Ephesians 4–5:1-2, "be imitators of God as beloved children, and walk in love as Christ loved us and gave himself up for us, a fragrant offering and a sacrifice to God." That means we are called to essentially lay down our lives for others in a secondary way. *We imitate Christ as we lay down our lives for the happiness of others, to alleviate the sufferings of others, to grieve their failures and heart-aches, and to rejoice in their successes and blessings.* That is the kind of fundamental sympathy we are called to.

July 26

Trust in the Lord with all your heart,
and do not lean on your own understanding.
In all your ways acknowledge him,
and he will make straight your paths. —Proverbs 3:5-6

There's so much going on in our lives. How do we sort it all out so we have clarity on what we're hearing, what we're seeing? We get disoriented. We are confused, we are baffled, we're overwhelmed when there are things going on in life, either sufferings or sins or chaos or ignorance. We grope in the dark—sometimes (often) feeling extremely confused.

One of the goals of a biblical dynamic of change is *reorientation*. It's like knowing what direction is east, south, west, north. It's knowing where you are, not being lost in the woods. You need to have a sense of where you are and where you're heading. Where am I in all this chaos, and where is it that I need to get to?

So as in all change, as in every psalm, we have this interaction between our sins and sorrows and things that happen to us and the things that erupt out of us. *We have this God who enters the stage of human need, who invades mercifully and powerfully to shield us, to strengthen us, to forgive us, to help us, to lead us, to care for us, to be a refuge for us.* When we trust him with our whole hearts, when we lean on him, he will make our paths straight. He will reorient us, not once, not twice, but every day, every time we ask.

July 27

You shall love the Lord your God with all your heart and with all your soul and with all your might. —Deuteronomy 6:5

A Prayer for Transformation

Our Father in heaven, we are so grateful that your people of all generations have been listeners from the heart to what you reveal about what it means to know you, how it is that we seek you, what it means to love you, to need you, to fall on our face before you, to tremble before you, to delight in you. And we pray that as we think today, tonight, and throughout the weeks to come about the way in which you meet us, you change us, and transform us, we ask you that you would give to us nothing less than your Holy Spirit himself, the one who enlivens us, awakens us, gives us ears to hear, who writes words of life upon our hearts and reveals who you are.

Show us our dire need, reveal your promises of mercy, and remind us that you do what you say and that your actions back up your words. *We pray that we would be men and women who enter into the good things that you offer, and we would be those men and women who give to others freely, humbly, caring for them, because of all the good things that you give to us.* We pray your blessing, your wisdom. Would you help us this very day by the power of your grace? Amen.

July 28

If then you have been raised with Christ, seek the things that are above, where Christ is, seated at the right hand of God. Set your minds on things that are above, not on things that are on earth. For you have died, and your life is hidden with Christ in God. —Colossians 3:1-3

People live in what the Bible would portray as a cacophony of voices—an absolute deluge from all sides. The world's bogus value system often dictates how we evaluate ourselves and each other. Every day we hear from different sides trying to dictate our value, based on our physical appearance, our wealth, our education, and more. Then there is the anxiety and pressure we feel from still other voices predicting all kinds of disasters that are right around the corner. There is a powerful interplay between the external voices and our internal voice. To the degree we set our minds on "the things that are on earth," we then live out of an earthly logic. Whether it's the logic of what we should aspire to, the logic of what we should fear, or the logic of what makes us superior or inferior, it's all based on setting our mind on what is on earth, not on what is in heaven.

But Paul calls us to a different logic—a heavenly logic that views all of life through the lens of Christ seated on the throne. Your life is hidden in him. You can view all the pressures and problems from a heavenly perspective. *Human beings live with an unfolding story and always come with a significant past. You, I, and everyone around us are always located in an unfolding story. That life history has a future trajectory anticipated. We will be raised with Christ—that's the heavenly logic that quiets all earthly voices.*

July 29

For you are my rock and my fortress;
and for your name's sake you lead me and guide me;
you take me out of the net they have hidden for me,
for you are my refuge.
Into your hand I commit my spirit;
you have redeemed me, O Lord, faithful God. . . .

my strength fails because of my iniquity,
and my bones waste away. . . .

Be strong, and let your heart take courage,
all you who wait for the Lord! —Psalm 31:3–5, 10b, 24

Relying on God's goodness and his mercy is essential to any honest and transformative kind of repentance process. It is important to always have something that you're focusing on outside of yourself that communicates the promises and the self-revelation of God in his graciousness, in his goodness. Notice how in Psalm 31's description of coming from danger into the safety of God's presence, there's a clear reliance and a trust in his God who is merciful. The end of repentance is gladness and thankfulness for real mercies. *Central to the change process is a continual going to your Redeemer and God who is sovereign and the Holy Spirit who makes it all personal.*

Accurate self-knowledge actually leads to two radical extraspections (looking outside of ourselves), which are faith and love. You are going to someone else who is the living God, and you are reaching out to other people in care. These two extraspections of faith move you from darkness to the light, and then God's love moves you out into your world courageously, constructively, mercifully, and candidly.

July 30

Let all that you do be done in love. —1 Corinthians 16:4

As we look at the world, how do we interpret our various difficult circumstances? How do we interpret the way we treat people? How do we interpret ourselves and how we react to others? The answers to those questions will help you see what your reality map is. For example, perhaps you struggle with talking to a particular relative about anything significant. Why would that be true for you? Or anyone? It's likely that your reality map tells you that it's because this person is so irascible and so feisty, right? *But in God's reality map, the reason we fail to talk with our family member may be that we do not love them. Perhaps we do not trust God in such a way that we are able to act in love toward them.* That's just picking one area of many in our lives where a change in the reality map means a change in how we understand each other's sinfulness and self-will and autonomy. We will only have a reason to move toward this person when our motivation changes.

Our reality map is our functional belief system. And our motivations have to do with what we want, what our intentions are, and what our fears are. Our reality map is what guides us as we move into relationships. Our reality map tells us what the world looks like and then describes how we intend to proceed into the world. But what would it be like if we gave up our reality map and lived in God's world? When we live in God's world, love is the overriding motivation for all we do.

July 31

"I the LORD search the heart
and test the mind." —Jeremiah 17:10a

There is always a God-relational thing going on in the human heart. For example, the world might notice that someone is very attuned to what other people think about him or her. But they don't see it for what it is: fear of man. Fear of man is actually an alternative to the fear of God. Similarly, we can all notice people that are proud. But we can't always see that pride is a way of exalting ourselves in the universe as if we were king—an alternative to the real King Jesus. That God-centeredness of the nature of motivation is one of the things that is unique in a biblical understanding. We respect the unsearchability of the heart, the fact that none of us sees it. We know that we don't see ourselves in the way that God sees us. There are layers of ignorance in us that will only be revealed on the last day. And we certainly can't see into other people's hearts. Because the issue of the heart, the issue of motive is a vertical dimension issue. *From a Christian point of view the issue of motive actually has to do with how you are relating to God. It's the Lord who searches the heart and tests our minds and our motives. Only in our relationship to him will we find clarity about our own hearts.*

August 1

Therefore, as you received Christ Jesus the Lord, so walk in him, rooted and built up in him and established in the faith, just as you were taught, abounding in thanksgiving. —Colossians 2:6-7

There is an essentially relational nature to the dynamic of biblical change—an essentially relational nature to the Christian life. Let me draw a couple of contrasts. One of the pieces of advice that you'll often hear about how to change is that you need to "behold Christ" or "behold the cross." But the idea of beholding is kind of passive, right? Most people don't understand what that means or how to do it. For most people, we need to see it ("behold") and then we need to seek it, right? And it's that relational seeking that is at the heart of change.

Here's another example that is even more commonly used: the language of "remember," like remember your identity in Christ. Remember that you are a child of the king, that you've been justified by faith. Remember that God works all things for good. Now, again, similar to "behold," there's nothing wrong with remembering. But the trouble is that the Bible doesn't take the tack of basing change simply on remembering something. Instead, change is a relational act. When you are struggling, you need to reach out of yourself and seek the one who is merciful and not try to just work up a mental framework, which is essentially a passive kind of act. *When you are feeling beset and overwhelmed by all of the forces of evil and face-plant into the abyss of your own sinfulness, you need to be presented with the God who is relevant as you are called to relationship with the God who is merciful. This is the place where the actual change process begins. This is how we are rooted in Christ and walk in him.*

August 2

Therefore be imitators of God, as beloved children. And walk in love,
as Christ loved us and gave himself up for us, a fragrant offering and
sacrifice to God. —Ephesians 5:1-2

All biblical change moves in both the vertical and the horizontal dimensions. The Spirit changes how we relate to people (the horizontal dimension) and how we relate to God (the vertical dimension). If you just stay horizontal, there will be a drift toward moralism. And if you just stay vertical, there will be a drift toward pietism. You can characterize whole movements within the church by whether they tend to be pietistic, and just go with the vertical dimension, or they tend to go moralistic and they just deal with horizontal. One of the things you realize as you grow in understanding is that in people there is an unbreakable connection between the vertical and horizontal— both in the negative and the positive sense. Your behavior and what rules you are inextricably linked. What you think, what you feel, and what you do always expresses what is mastering you in the vertical. What is your actual, functional god, is always coming out in every reaction.

On the good side, to the degree that you are seeking and finding and trusting the God who is Lord, you are able then to love people. You're able to move toward people constructively, with love for others and living faith in God. The horizontal expresses the vertical. The vertical is registered in the horizontal, and the two always work together.

August 3

Therefore, if anyone is in Christ, he is a new creation. The old has passed away; behold, the new has come. —2 Corinthians 5:17

For many people, there's a huge disconnect between all the "God talk" and all the Bible verses and where their life is actually lived. That can be discouraging. So where do you start as you talk with others? And as you think about your own relationship with God? Begin by examining the good things. Start with the evidences of grace in a person's life and with God's goodness that can already be seen in their life. List the ways that person has grown.

There's this tension in a genuine redemption: you are new, you are part of the new creation. You have been awakened to Christ. There are actual good works that God has prepared for you to walk in. And on the other hand, you've still got the old hanging around—that's the problem of indwelling sin, and that all our works are imperfect. That's one of those many places where there's a continual pattern from the old to the new via the mercy of Christ. It's always a from-to dynamic, and change always comes via mercies. It's always via the sheer redemptive goodness of Christ to you and to me. That is always the bridge. It's always the hope that we have.

Every day there's a place where the battle is joined. We'll be tempted to be asleep, tempted to be deaf and blind. And we need to awake, we need to see, we need to hear. And we need to turn toward the Lord and his mercies.

August 4

Put on then, as God's chosen ones, holy and beloved, compassionate hearts, kindness, humility, meekness, and patience, bearing with one another and, if one has a complaint against another, forgiving each other; as the Lord has forgiven you, so you also must forgive.
—Colossians 3:12–13

Putting on a new way of life is an incremental process. Part of the change process is learning, bit by bit, to ask forgiveness of the people you hurt. Did you know that most angry people don't ask for forgiveness? But you can put on humility and learn to ask for forgiveness more intelligently, not just saying, "Oh, I'm sorry," or "I'm sorry if you feel hurt," but instead you can learn to say things like, "It's wrong for me to speak to you that way. I'm sorry for hurting you. Please forgive me." This is a huge step of growth—to clean up your interpersonal relationships when you're dealing with the effects of an anger outburst.

Another increment of growth is learning to put on patience—for your buttons to not be pushed as easily. That's huge. There may still be ten things that push your buttons. Is it good that ten things push your buttons? No. Is it good that only ten things push your buttons, instead of fifty? Yes.

This idea of putting on incrementally captures something of the growth process for a Christian. That is the way our Lord works with us. There's a growing quickness to repent, appreciation for the grace of Christ, willingness to do the repair work in relationships. There is a lessening in the frequency and intensity of outbursts. And then you can even move on from there into some of the really hard things—like someone who used to struggle with a bad temper actually becoming a constructive peacemaker in problem situations. That's huge. And that, too, is another one of these increments forward. *We are in the hands of the Peacemaker. And he is committed to walk all the way through with us and make us in his image.*

August 5

Let all bitterness and wrath and anger and clamor and slander be
put away from you, along with all malice. Be kind to one another,
tenderhearted, forgiving one another, as God in Christ forgave you.
—Ephesians 4:31-32

Forgiveness is a conscious choice formed through knowing
God's mercy to you. It clearly recognizes that what happened
was wrong. It makes no excuses for what happened. And then
it lets it go.

Patience and forgiveness are the first two key aspects of the
constructive displeasure of mercy for a reason. As we respond
with patience and forgiveness to wrongs we have experienced,
we have gone a long way toward redeeming anger. But there is
more—we also need to respond to true wrongs with charity and
constructive conflict.

Charity moves toward the person who has done wrong with
undeserved kindness. But there is also a place for entering into
constructive conflict when wrongs have been done. *Mercy doesn't
stand idly by while others go in the wrong direction or when someone—oneself or another—is being mistreated. Mercy wades into
difficult situations and is willing to get involved. It's willing to raise
difficult issues, apply justice (when needed), and persevere to see good
come out of evil.* Constructive conflict continues the work that
patience, forgiveness, and charity have begun.

August 6

> "You have heard that it was said, 'You shall love your neighbor and hate your enemy.' But I say to you, Love your enemies and pray for those who persecute you, so that you may be sons of your Father who is in heaven. . . . For if you love those who love you, what reward do you have? Do not even the tax collectors do the same?" —Matthew 5:43–46

Philosophy of Life 101 for most people is: you scratch my back, I'll scratch yours. You do me wrong; I hold a grudge or get even. That's the easy way—and it's the recipe for disaster, estrangement, and war. Our Father doesn't operate by that philosophy. He teaches his children to love in a way that's hard, but good. It's the path to reconciliation and peace. He gives us three pictures.

First, notice the weather. "Our Father . . . makes his sun rise on the evil and on the good, and sends rain on the just and on the unjust" (Matthew 5:45). We need sun and rain in order to have food, and God doesn't discriminate in doing basic good. Can you do that too?

Second, notice how even bad people treat their friends right. "If you love those who love you, what reward do you have? Do not even the tax collectors do the same?" (Matthew 5:46). Can you take it a step up from bad people?

Third, notice how all people everywhere recognize a special bond between family members. "If you greet only your brothers, what more are you doing than others? Do not even the Gentiles do the same?" (Matthew 5:47). Can you take it a step up from the us-them loyalty that comes naturally to everyone?

Charity toward people who displease you is the "perfect" response—it's the way things ought to be.

August 7

Whoever walks with the wise becomes wise,
but the companion of fools will suffer harm. —Proverbs 13:20

Somehow germs seem more catching than good health, and a bad attitude travels faster than a good attitude. It would be an exaggeration to say the habit of patience and constructive anger is *easily* acquired from others! But it can happen. Did you ever know a parent or close friend, a teacher or coach, who was patient and generous with others, not easily set off, even in the face of apathy or selfishness? Did he or she save their anger for when there was a wrong that really mattered? Was anger expressed cleanly and constructively, as part of love for others that tackled wrongs? Wonderfully, some people express anger in ways that tackle the problem to solve it.

"He who walks with the wise grows wise" (Proverbs 13:20, author translation). There's nothing like a good role model to give you a vision for how it's possible to do life well. This is the type of person you can become, by God's grace. You can learn to walk with Jesus—the wisest person in the world and become more like him in how you respond when life goes wrong.

Blessed are the peacemakers. To respond constructively to trouble is a fine art, gained through long practice.

August 8

But you are a chosen people, a royal priesthood, a holy nation, God's special possession, that you may declare the praises of him who called you out of darkness into his wonderful light. —1 Peter 2:9 NIV

Christ is Lord and Master. He bought us with a price; we belong to him. Faith knows and embraces this core identity: "I am a *servant*, indentured for life."

The Lord is married to his people. He patiently nourishes and cherishes his wife, the living body of Christ. We need husbanding from someone faithful, kind, protective, and generous. Faith knows and embraces this core identity: "I *submit* to Jesus."

God searches every heart. We live before his eyes. Faith knows and embraces this core identity: "I am a *God-fearing* person."

Our God is good, mighty, and glorious. He is worthy of our trust, esteem, gladness, and gratitude. Faith knows and embraces this core identity: "I am a *worshiper*."

We could go on! The pattern is obvious. Every core aspect of our identity expresses some form of humility, need, submission, and dependency before the Lord.

Here is the pattern. Our core identity leads to the calling to act like God. Weakness leads to strength. Serving leads to mastery. Deaths lead to resurrections. It never works the other way around. *When your core identity is meek and lowly—like Jesus— then your calling develops into his image of purposeful, wise, courageous love.* You become like God.

August 9

"Blessed are the poor in spirit, for theirs is the kingdom of heaven. Blessed are those who mourn, for they shall be comforted. Blessed are the meek, for they shall inherit the earth. Blessed are those who hunger and thirst for righteousness, for they shall be satisfied." —Matthew 5:3-6

The right kind of strength comes from the right kind of weakness. The right kind of weakness is expressed in the first four beatitudes:

- *"The poor in spirit are blessed."* Jesus is described as one who, though he was rich, became poor—for you. He became utterly dependent, utterly needy. He died in the ultimate weakness and perishability of the human condition.

- *"Blessed are those who mourn."* Jesus is portrayed throughout his life as one who mourns (Isaiah 53:3). He mourns for your sake, he mourns the suffering that he must face, he mourns all the things that are wrong in this world, and he comes on a mission of mercy to make wrongs right.

- *"The meek are blessed."* Jesus describes himself as meek and lowly in heart. Meekness is not weakness in the negative sense. It's weakness in the positive sense. Jesus was under the hand and voice and will of Another, heeding the voice of his Father, fully trusting God's promises, fully obeying God's will.

Jesus is blessed because he *hungers and thirsts for righteousness.* He makes right what is wrong. He makes true what is false. And he remakes what is evil for the good of his people.

Our Lord is fruitful, and he is strong, but he is fruitful and strong on the foundation of this abiding sense of weakness and need. He warmly welcomes the weak and needy to the throne of his grace, that we might receive the mercy we need and the grace specific to whatever difficult situation we are in (Hebrews 4:16).

August 10

"Blessed are the merciful, for they shall receive mercy. Blessed are the
pure in heart, for they shall see God. Blessed are the peacemakers, for
they shall be called sons of God. Blessed are those who are persecuted
for righteousness' sake, for theirs is the kingdom of heaven."
—Matthew 5:7-10

We see fearlessness of public weakness in the life and words of
Jesus. What Jesus says to us in the Beatitudes captures what
he himself embodies. *When we think about how the image of Christ
is expressed in our lives, the Beatitudes show us how the right kind of
weakness leads directly to the right kind of strength, a strength grounded
and founded in need.*

Think about the qualities of strength that the last four beatitudes portray.

- Jesus says, *"Blessed are the merciful,"* describing a life characterized by a deep concern for the welfare of others—to
  be generous, open-hearted, and open-handed.

- Jesus says, *"The pure in heart are blessed,"* describing the ability to approach all people free from duplicitous motives, free
  of self-serving.

- Jesus says, *"Peacemakers are blessed. They're nothing less than
  the children of God."* Peacemaking is the ability to be candid,
  constructive, and caring—to pursue peace in a world that is
  full of war, dissension, conflicts, arguments, and avoiders.

- Jesus says, *"Those who are persecuted are blessed."* He calls
  us to joyful purposefulness, finding courage in affliction,
  finding perseverance in opposition.

These are wonderful traits. These are the traits of leadership and
loving fruitfulness in Jesus's life—and in ours as well.

August 11

If you turn at my reproof,
behold, I will pour out my spirit to you;
I will make my words known to you. —Proverbs 1:23

Consider how the Proverbs are written to provide an immediate flash of insight. What are you pursuing in life? What voices are you listening to? How are you talking with other people? How are you relating to sex, money, food, drink, rest, work? Can such topics ever not be relevant?! I flipped open Proverbs today and began reading chapter 17. I was arrested by the first line: "Better is a dry morsel with quiet than a house full of feasting with strife." I realized I'd been irritable that morning. I generated strife. So I honestly asked forgiveness. We gained a house full of quiet. So how will you bring your day into contact with some relevant beam of light? You could do worse than simply read in Proverbs until something strikes home. Then walk that one bit of wisdom out into the rest of your day.

It is impossible for your devotional life to be stale when you awaken to what is really happening in your life. God intersects, speaks into, and touches what is going on. But it takes stopping to notice. And then it leads to asking. The Sermon on the Mount (Matthew 5–7) is the keynote talk for Jesus's entire ministry. And the Beatitudes (Matthew 5:3–12) are the keynote of the keynote. Jesus places his first blessing on the "poor in spirit" for a reason. When you know your need for outside help, for gifts that only the Lord can give, then the kingdom of God is yours. The King will show up in your day today.

August 12

And everyone who thus hopes in him purifies himself as he is pure.
—1 John 3:3

Christianity opposes sexual immorality. For many people, that pretty much exhausts what the Bible has to say about sex. Granted, they've heard one thing rightly. Christianity does oppose sexual immorality as something inimical to life: "On account of these things the wrath of God is coming" (Colossians 3:6). But this one proposition doesn't come close to exhausting what Christianity has to say about sexual morality and immorality. The Bible makes at least three other major points about sex.

First, Christianity is utterly frank about sexual immorality. Scripture speaks openly, sometimes even graphically, of rape, homosexuality, pornographic fantasies, voyeurism, seduction, bestiality, incest, prostitution, and the like. God freely speaks of the sordid . . . as sordid. God freely speaks of how alluring the sordid can be—Proverbs 7 is classic—not to allure us but to protect us from that allure.

Second, Christianity revels in sexual fidelity. The Bible is frank about sexual joy within the circle of faithfulness, faithfulness first to God and second to one's husband or wife. God made sex. Sexual intimacy is intended to give great pleasure, to express love: generosity, kindness, gladness at giving.

Third, *Christianity is about forgiving the immoral and transforming them into the faithful. Christ bridges the chasm between the sordid and the glorious and invites us to cross over.* Christianity teaches a dynamic of transformation, the opposite of both determinism and moralizing.

August 13

Make me understand the way of your precepts,
and I will meditate on your wondrous works. —Psalm 119:27

What makes Scripture relevant in your life? One, God does it. He makes it relevant. He awakens you. Two, name your troubles. You know yourself, and you know where you need help. Three, think about what God says. *Meditate throughout your day. It's the Scripture I think about later in the day, that revisits me a second time, that actually makes a difference in my life.* It's not when I read something in the morning once, it's the second time it has a go-round in my life that it starts to get traction and ends up changing how I live.

Our Father, will you make these things so? We are dependents, we are like birds (Luke 12:22–31). We cannot store up your Spirit. We cannot store up the connect between us and who you are and what you say. We need you to help us and we need you to help us to do the hard thinking about your Word. We need you to help us be honest about where we struggle, where our troubles are. We need you to make us see that it is in the love of Christ that we have life. It is in your tenderness for us as a Father. It is in your life—giving to us yourself, the Spirit of life— that we have life.

We pray these things in confidence that Jesus Christ will lead us through thorny ways to the joyful end we are heading to. We pray this in the name of that Christ, Amen.

August 14

"It is the LORD who goes before you. He will be with you; he will not leave you or forsake you. Do not fear or be dismayed." —Deuteronomy 31:8

As we learn about the relevance of Scripture, we consider this: What are the big questions that haunt a person? This is more existential. At some level, all of us carry around these questions: What will happen to me? How will my life turn out? Will I be abandoned? Am I all alone? Is God really for me?

Scripture speaks straight to these questions. Psalm 1 is about how will your life turn out. Will you end up as chaff that is nothing, or are you a tree planted by streams of water, yielding its fruit in its season? Deuteronomy 31 speaks to the question of abandonment. "I'm with you, I'm for you, I won't abandon you." Romans 5 speaks straight to the heart of the inner anguish about whether we are loved, even in our failure. There is nothing that can separate us from the love of God in Christ Jesus our Lord (Romans 8:38–39).

The love of God pours straight into these deepest questions. *Scripture reaches us when our faith reaches out, and it gives us a home when our lives are, in a sense, homeless and bedraggled.* What are people asking deep down when you cut below the surface? You will always find that when you ask those right questions that the Word of the living God, the grace of the living God, the mercies of Jesus Christ, they are exactly tailored to human need.

August 15

Seek the Lord and his strength;
seek his presence continually! —Psalm 105:4

Martin Luther made the comment that from Psalm 119 he had learned there are three masters that had taught him everything he knew about God: prayer, meditation, and suffering. He said that from other sources he could learn other Bible knowledge, but these three elements are what led him to live gratefully, dependent on God, listening to and receiving his care, his wisdom, and his will.

Luther also said that affliction in particular is the touchstone to teach you how right, true, sweet, mighty, and comforting God's Word is. *It is in life experience that the Word actually comes to life and gains reality. There's something about facing hardship that makes real the things of the Bible and works to transform us into the image of Jesus.* Jesus entered into our world of difficulty in order to love people who also face struggle and difficulty.

Affliction is both the things that happen to us and the things that are inside us. We are essentially weak. We are weak because of our sinfulness and our mortality. One of the comprehensive words that embraces the totality of human struggle is temptation. We are led astray by allure from the outside and by affections from within. This is actually a paradoxical door to help. This drives us to look to the Lord for his strength, his power, his presence.

"Draw near to the throne of his grace that [you] may receive mercy and find grace to help in time of need" (Hebrews 4:16).

August 16

He put a new song in my mouth,
a song of praise to our God.
Many will see and fear,
and put their trust in the LORD. —Psalm 40:3

God's Word doesn't stop with us. It always goes out and connects to other people. It has this instinctive, intuitive dynamic. God's purposes are not a moral self-improvement project or to give you a sense of self-satisfaction and joy. His purpose is to create people who get out of themselves. As you see and experience for yourself how God and his words connect, it leads you out of yourself, to offer faith and love to others. We go outward to people in love, patience, forbearance, and generosity. *When the Bible comes to life in your life, it doesn't end with you.*

Psalm 40 is really interesting in this regard. David is retrospective about the Lord's deliverance in the past (vv. 1–3a). Then he immediately moves to other people; ministry to other people (v. 3b). It's your testimony too. This is what happened to you. You were in great trouble, and God met you. You've got a story to tell, and it's going to have an effect on other people because the gospel is not just a theory—the gospel is embodied in your life. It's a story of deliverance that you get to tell as you live within it.

August 17

Search me, God, and know my heart;
test me and know my anxious thoughts.
See if there is any offensive way in me,
and lead me in the way everlasting. —Psalm 139:23-24 NIV

How can you find and give help in dealing with anxiety? Some orienting realities will help you move forward honestly and fruitfully. First, identify what is going on within you. Is anxiety hiding under anger or a controlling nature? Are you squandering your life in aimless fun? Anxiety can show up in many ways. Second, remember that you are not alone and that the Lord is with you. You may have good reasons to feel afraid and anxious right now, but you have better reasons not to be afraid. Third, name your particular troubles, whether it is a medical diagnosis or financial difficulty or loneliness.

Once you have examined the dynamics of your struggle, have an honest conversation with God. Bring your troubles to the one who can actually help, so it's a conversational-relational solution. Ask him for help. After you have poured out your heart to God, the next step of faith is to faithfully do whatever needs doing today. Give yourself to today's task. *Of all the things you worry about, very few of them are in your control, and of those things that are in your control, not all of them are your responsibility today. What are you called to do today? Giving yourself to the small obediences is extremely liberating.*

Anxiety as it's remade, and as it is honestly faced, actually opens the door to your faith, and a door to loving God and others more deeply.

August 18

I have calmed and quieted my soul,
like a weaned child with its mother;
like a weaned child is my soul within me.

O Israel, hope in the Lord
from this time forth and forevermore. —Psalm 131:2-3

In Psalm 131 you have intimate access to the inner life of someone who has learned composure, and then he invites you to come
along. It is show-and-tell for how to become peaceful inside. He
has learned the only true and lasting composure, and he shares the
details of what the peace that passes understanding is like.

Amazingly, this man isn't noisy inside. Not obsessed or on
edge. The to-do list and pressures to achieve don't consume him.
Failure and despair don't haunt him. Anxiety isn't spinning him
into freefall. He's quiet.

Are you quiet inside? Is Psalm 131 your experience too? When
your answer is No, it naturally invites follow-up questions. What is
the "noise" going on inside you? Where does it come from? How do
you get busy and preoccupied? Why? Do you lose your composure?
When do you get worried, irritable, wearied, or hopeless?

Psalm 131 does not portray blissful, unruffled detachment, a
meditative state of higher consciousness. It's not stoic indifference,
becoming philosophical about life. It's not about having an easygoing
personality or having low expectations so you're easy to please. It's not
retreat from the troubles of life and the commotion of other people.

*The composure of Psalm 131 is learned—in relationship. Such
purposeful quiet is conscious, alert, and chosen. It is a form of self-mas-
tery by the grace of God. You are "discipled" into such composure. You
learn it from Someone.* Psalm 131 aims to become your words as a
chosen, anointed, loved, and blessed child.

August 19

O Lord, my heart is not lifted up;
my eyes are not raised too high;
I do not occupy myself with things
too great and too marvelous for me. —Psalm 131:1

Faith delivers you from your biggest problem, a proud self-will. Do you remember *Alice in Wonderland*, how Alice was either too big or too small? Because she was never quite the right size, she was continually disoriented. We all have that problem. We are the wrong size. We imagine ourselves to be independent and autonomous: proud hearts. We become engrossed in monstrous trivialities of our own devising. We pursue grandiosities and glories. We become afraid of our own shadows. We become noisy inside.

Our restless disorientation seems so natural. The static of anxiety, irritation, despondency, or ambition makes sense from within the logic of a proud heart.

If you are not proud, then quietness and composure make sense. When you pursue what you are called to pursue, it makes sense you'd have composure. You've discovered what you're made for. Paul once put it this way, "Flee youthful passions and pursue righteousness, faith, love, and peace, along with those who call on the Lord from a pure heart" (2 Timothy 2:22). When you go after the right things, you'll find what you're looking for. Quiet your noisy self to know the peace that passes understanding.

How does a proud heart become a humble heart? You do not wrestle yourself down by doing penance. You do not destroy the tumult of self-will by sheer will. You only wrestle yourself down by the promises of God's lovingkindness. You need the invasion of the Redeemer, the hand of the Shepherd. *We escape ourselves by being loved by Jesus Christ through the powerful presence of the Holy Spirit himself. From our side, we escape ourselves by learning a lifestyle of intelligent repentance, genuine faith, and specific obedience.*

August 20

"Therefore I tell you, do not be anxious about your life, what you will eat or what you will drink, nor about your body, what you will put on. Is not life more than food, and the body more than clothing? Look at the birds of the air: they neither sow nor reap nor gather into barns, and yet your heavenly Father feeds them. Are you not of more value than they?"
—Matthew 6:25-26

"Do not be anxious about your life." Why did Jesus say to not be anxious? He focused on really simple things: God cares for mere birds, and he feeds them. How much more for you? God clothes the lilies of the field that can do nothing. And you— God knows what you need. He gave you Jesus to rescue you from yourself.

The troubles of life can be magnified by our all-consuming fears. It feels very threatening when things happen that we cannot control, that are bigger than us. We feel our fragility and our vulnerability.

The experience of extreme fear is an isolating experience. You are all alone and you've got thoughts that have gone crazy and feelings that are horrible. In this struggle, you need to know there is another voice speaking into your situation: God's voice. He sympathizes with your weaknesses. He does not despise you. He's willing to enter your plight. You can approach the throne of grace with confidence that you will find mercy and help in time of need (Hebrews 4:15–16).

You may have good reasons for fear, but you have even better reasons for courage, faith, and love. We have hope, and that hope is Christ.

August 21

"And do not seek what you are to eat and what you are to drink, nor be worried. For all the nations of the world seek after these things, and your Father knows that you need them. Instead, seek his kingdom, and these things will be added to you." —Luke 12:29–31

Jesus lists reason after reason after reason why you should not be in the grip of fear and worry. He says, "Consider the ravens. They make no preparations and have no storage. Yet God feeds them. How much more valuable are you than birds?" "Which of you by worrying can add a single hour to his life span? If you can't do the littlest thing like this, why do you worry about the rest?"

Jesus addresses our driven, obsessed state of mind, the preoccupation with money and possessions. "Your Father knows that you need these things. But seek his kingdom. These things will be added to you."

"Don't worry" doesn't hang in space as a moral platitude! Jesus gives you solid reason after solid reason to live without fretting—even when you're facing the very things that are inherently uncertain and uncontrollable. There's so much more to who you are than what you have or don't have. His promise is far more than "God will take care of you." It is "God will clothe you in nothing less than his radiant glory!" *God is giving you a life that is radiant and indestructible and full of glory. Having given you so much, your Father calls you to the radical freedom of giving your life away.* Because you have been given, because you are being given, because you will be given a sure, certain, and wonderful thing, then give. It's his pleasure to give to you, so you can give too. Focus there.

August 22

Trust in him at all times, O people;
pour out your heart before him;
God is a refuge for us. —Psalm 62:8

Anxiety is a universal human experience, and you need to approach it with a plan. First, name the pressures. You always worry about *something*. What things tend to hook you? What "good reasons" do you have for anxiety? Second, identify how you express anxiety. For some people it's feelings of panic clutching their throat, or just a vague unease. For others, it's repetitive, obsessive thoughts, or even anger. Third, ask yourself, *Why* am I anxious? Worry always has its inner logic. If I've forgotten God, who or what has edged him out of my mind and started to rule in his place? Fourth, what better reason does Jesus give you not to worry? "If God feeds the crows, won't he provide for you?" (Luke 12:24, author's paraphrase) has been particularly meaningful to me.

Go to your Father. Talk to him. He cares about the things you worry about: your friends, health, money, children, etc. You can go to him with the things that concern you. You'll have to leave your worries with him. They are always outside of your control! You have good reasons to be concerned about such things, but you have better reasons to take them to Someone who loves you.

Finally, give. Do and say something constructive. Give to meet human need. In the darkest hole, when the world is most confused, there's always the next right thing to do. There's always some way to give yourself away. The problem might seem overwhelming. *You could worry, but instead you're called to do some small, itty-bitty thing. There's always some way to give. Be about the business of today. Leave tomorrow's uncertainties to your Father.*

August 23

Be still, my soul: the Lord is on thy side.
Bear patiently the cross of grief or pain.
Leave to thy God to order and provide;
In every change, He faithful will remain.
Be still, my soul: thy best, thy heav'nly Friend
Through thorny ways leads to a joyful end.
—Katharina von Schlegel, "Be Still, My Soul"

God works in and through suffering. In a season of significant suffering in my life, how did God work? First came the suffering itself. Amid cascading losses and troubles, all familiar habits and assumptions were thrown up in the air. My faith and love had to grow up—again.

A handful of wise, godly friends played a significant role. Some were going through analogous experiences. They understood. Other friends knew me well enough to translate their sympathy into helping me plan and to act within marked limitations. I needed both the tenderness and the realism. Both incarnate Jesus Christ.

The wisdom of saints whose race finished long ago played a significant role in how public worship sustained and instructed me. I had never realized how many hymns (like the Psalms) inhabit suffering. The hymns spoke to me: "The Lord is on your side, even in this. He is your best friend who will not bereave you. He rules this storm too. He will restore to you love's purest joys."

God met me with his words and his Spirit—through preaching, the Lord's Supper, the informal counsel of friends, and my own reflection on Scripture. As familiar words engaged current experience, they took on meanings and resonances I could not have imagined. My faith needed to find expression in new ways. Obedience had to take new forms. The living faith that embraces Christ is formed in the crucible of weakness. The strong love that cares well for others is formed in the crucible of struggle.

August 24

In the way of your testimonies I delight
as much as in all riches.
I will meditate on your precepts
and fix my eyes on your ways. —Psalm 119:14-15

The Bible's stories, histories, and prophecies, even many of the commands, teachings, promises, and prayers, take thoughtful work in order to reapply with current relevance. If you take them straight—as if they speak directly to you, about you, with your issues in view—you will misunderstand and misapply Scripture. For example, the angel's command to Joseph, "Take the child and his mother and flee to Egypt" (Matthew 2:13), is not a command to anyone today to buy a ticket for Cairo! Attempts to take the entire Bible as if it directly applies to you distort the Bible. It becomes an omni-relevant magic book teeming with private messages and meanings. God does not intend that his words function that way.

These passages do apply. But most of the Bible applies differently from the passages tilted toward immediate relevance. What you read applies by extension and analogy, not directly. In one sense, such passages apply exactly because they are not about you. They draw you out of the temptation to see God through the lens of self-preoccupation and felt need.

Understood rightly, all these other parts of Scripture give a changed perspective. They locate you on a bigger stage. They teach you to notice God and other people. They call you to understand yourself within a story—many stories—bigger than your personal history and immediate concerns.

God reveals himself and his purposes throughout Scripture. Wise application always starts there.

August 25

Hear my cry, O God,
listen to my prayer;
from the end of the earth I call to you
when my heart is faint.
Lead me to the rock
that is higher than I. —Psalm 61:1-2

Why do you pray? I suspect that you and I are probably alike. When we are honest, we say the reason we pray is that we need to pray. It is the door of life. And if we don't, we perish. If we don't, we are insane.

In order to explore how prayer goes right, it helps to identify ways that prayer goes wrong. Here are a few ways prayer drifts:

- Prayers can be vague and confusing.
- Prayers can function as a wish list.
- Prayers can be superstitious, a way to ensure bad things don't happen and good things do happen.
- Prayers can just be a religious or pious practice, a habit that separates the religious from the irreligious.
- Prayer can be a mantra that seeks to evoke good feelings, treating prayer as a psychological experience.
- Prayer can be a reflex—something we simply do before we "get down to business" or after something is completed.
- Prayer can be something we simply tack onto life.
- Prayer can be boilerplate—a simple repetition of stock religious phrases.

But prayer goes right when it is honest conversation with the Lord we need, trust, and love. Prayer is a spiritually needy person's communication with the God who hears. Whether or not you pray reveals what you believe about everything that really matters. When you pray, you live with a fundamental humility before God and others. This humility fits reality—everyday needs can only be met by God himself.

August 26

I cry out to God Most High,
to God who fulfills his purpose for me. —Psalm 57:2

It's fair to say that having a "quiet time" is a misnomer. We should more properly have a "noisy time"! By talking out loud you live the reality that you are talking with another person, not simply talking to yourself inside your own head. Of course silent prayers are not wrong (1 Samuel 1:13; Nehemiah 2:4) but they are the exception. Even in such silent prayers, the essentially verbal nature of prayer is still operative, though the speaking is subvocal. Words could be spoken out loud if the situation warranted or the state of mind allowed.

In Jesus's teaching and example, a praying individual seeks privacy so he or she can talk out loud with God. "Go to your room and shut the door" (Matthew 6:6). That's so you can talk straight, rather than being tempted to perform. Jesus "would withdraw to desolate places and pray" (Luke 5:16). Why? He was talking out loud. And when Jesus walked off into the olive grove that Thursday night in order to pray, his disciples could overhear his fervent, pointed words (Matthew 26:36–44).

You can do the same sort of thing. Close the door, take a walk, get in the car—and speak up. Of course, in group contexts throughout the Bible, in public gatherings, God's people naturally pray and sing aloud, just as they hear the Bible aloud. We naturally do the same in corporate worship, whether in liturgy, in led prayers, or in small-group prayer. And even moments of silent confession and intercession, though subvocal, remain essentially verbal in character and content.

Prayer is verbal because it is relational. It is a verbal connection with someone you know, need and love.

August 27

With my voice I cry out to the LORD;
with my voice I plead for mercy to the LORD. —Psalm 142:1

I 've known many people whose relationship with God was significantly transformed as they started to speak up with their Father. Previously, "prayer" fizzled out in the internal buzz of self-talk and distractions, worries and responsibilities. Previously, what they thought of as prayer involved certain religious feelings, a set of seemingly spiritual thoughts, or a vague sense of comfort, awe and dependence on a higher power. Prayer meandered and was virtually indistinguishable from thoughts. But as a person begins to talk aloud to the God who is there, who is not silent, who listens, and who acts, he or she begins to deal with him person-to-person. Speaking up is no gimmick or technique, but out-loud prayer becomes living evidence of an increasingly honest and significant relationship.

Of course, God tells us to be quiet. Be still. Slow down. Stop. Reflect. But the purpose is not to learn a technique for accessing an inner realm of silence where you transcend your sense of self and experience a god-beyond-words. *The true God quiets us so we notice him and notice what's going on around us and inside us. This true God is profoundly and essentially verbal, not silent (Genesis 1:9; John 1:1).* We take the time to hear his words of grace and truth. We consider Jesus.

Do be quiet, and for the right reasons—so you can notice and listen, so you can learn to think, feel, and talk the way the psalms think, feel, and talk. This living God is highly verbal and listens attentively. He made us in his image, highly verbal, meant to listen attentively.

August 28

Let no corrupting talk come out of your mouths, but only such as is good for building up, as fits the occasion, that it may give grace to those who hear. —Ephesians 4:29

Jesus says that God is actively listening to every word, even the most casual, unthinking things we say (Matthew 12:36). He takes note of what we are saying and weighs our words. Are your conversations empty, misleading, inappropriate, or judgmental? Or is the way you talk nourishing, constructive, timely, and grace-giving (Ephesians 4:29)?

Jesus never said a pointless word to other people. He was never just marking time or keeping things that matter at arm's length. He always engages the important matters. He never just describes, analyzes, and complains about what's wrong. His conversations always go somewhere helpful. Jesus speaks life-giving words: candid, constructive, relevant, and redemptive. And one of the constructive things Jesus talks about is helping us to assess the quality of what we talk about. "The mouth speaks out of the abundance of the heart"—either good or evil (Matthew 12:34).

The Holy Spirit helps us generate wise conversations. Scripture demonstrates how every conversation can go somewhere good. It even captures how, in some important moments, what must next be said is to be silent. Sometimes there are no more words to say. Perhaps you are grieving. Perhaps you are thinking or praying. Perhaps your quietness communicates how much you care. When Jesus was silent before his accusers, his silence was the most eloquent thing that could be said. *A meaningful silence expresses what is true, constructive, most appropriate, and grace-giving. And then you will find the right words at the right time.*

The Lord is committed to you and working in you. As he works in us, you, I, and all of us together can become much more honest and much more constructive!

August 29

Having given you so much, your Father calls you to the radical freedom of giving your life away. It's both a reason and an alternative. Everything before was *get*. We become anxious because we want to get. We don't want to lose what we've got. We become presumptuous, and kick back into a life of leisure, because we have gotten. Everything is get, got, gotten. But the end of Jesus's message in Luke 12 is all *give*. Because you have been given a sure thing, because there's nothing to really worry about, then give. It's his pleasure to give to you, so you can give too. When that sinks in, a marvelous transformation takes place. You have good reasons to let your worries go. We—who tend to be obsessed and anxious about money—become able to open our hands.

That doesn't mean you have to live exactly like Francis of Assisi—but to have Francis of Assisi's attitude. In that is the only true freedom and the only real happiness. *It's an attitude of trusting your Father and living a life that's worth something. You can give yourself away. You can use your gifts. Your life can be about give.*

August 30

For all that is in the world—the desires of the flesh and the desires of the
eyes and pride of life—is not from the Father but is from the world.
—1 John 2:16

I think that "idols of the heart" is a great metaphor (if we don't overuse it!). It captures the match between inward desire and outward objects of desire. People are always reaching out to worship something, anything—either God or the mini-gods. Sin causes the psyche to operate as if we were self-referential and encapsulated. But our souls are in fact God-relational and God-accountable. The sense of self-encapsulation with which we experience our desires simply describes our defection from reality.

If I go on an "idol-hunt" into myself, I become intensely introspective and self-analytical. Similarly, if I go on an "idol-hunt" into you, I try to read your mind, as if I could peer into your heart, as if I had the right to judge you. Idol-hunts of any kind forget that knowing ourselves and others is not an end in itself. Accurate knowledge of our need leads directly away from ourselves and into the mercies of God for us and for others.

Faith makes self-knowledge look to God and relate to him. Faith is not introspective. Love makes knowledge of others gener-ous-hearted and merciful. Love is not judgmental.

Faith and love draw us out of sin's enmeshing self-obsession (including enmeshment in obsessive introspection). So come forth. Our Savior gives us his own joy, and joy is an interpersonal emotion. He throws open the doors to the fresh air and bright light of a most kind grace.

August 31

Little children, keep yourselves from idols. —1 John 5:21

The relevance of massive chunks of Scripture hangs on our understanding of idolatry. But let me focus the question through a particular verse in the New Testament which long troubled me. The last line of 1 John woos, then commands us: "Beloved children, keep yourselves from idols" (v. 21). In a 105-verse treatise on living in vital fellowship with Jesus, the Son of God, how on earth does that unexpected command merit being the final word?

John's last line properly leaves us with that most basic question which God continually poses to each human heart. *Has something or someone besides Jesus the Christ taken title to your heart's trust, preoccupation, loyalty, service, fear, and delight? It is a question bearing on the immediate motivation for one's behavior, thoughts, and feelings.* In the Bible's conceptualization, the motivation question is the lordship question. Who or what "rules" my behavior, the Lord or a substitute? The undesirable answers to this question—answers which inform our understanding of the "idolatry" we are to avoid—are most graphically presented in 1 John 2:15–17; 3:7–10; 4:1–6; and 5:19.

In contrast, to "keep yourself from idols" is to live with a whole heart of faith in Jesus. It is to be controlled by all that lies behind the address "Beloved children" (see especially 1 John 3:1–3; 4:7–5:12). The alternative to Jesus, the swarm of alternatives, whether approached through the lens of flesh, world, or the Evil One, is idolatry.

September 1

You have kept count of my tossings;
put my tears in your bottle.
Are they not in your book? —Psalm 56:8

Grief is not wrong. It can be an honest expression of sorrow over the brokenness of this world. It can include a turning toward God for help and believing that our tears are counted and saved by the Good Shepherd who hears and sees our suffering (Psalm 56:8). It is part of being made in the image of God to grieve hard things. When Jesus was facing the cross, he was grieving. He said, "Let this cup pass from me" as he cried and sweated blood (Matthew 26:39).

On the cross Jesus quoted two psalms of great affliction, grief, and heartbreak. He cried out, "My God, my God why have you forsaken me?" (Psalm 22:1) and, as he breathed his last, "Into your hands I commit my spirit" (Psalm 31:5). Yet the direction his grief went was not hopelessness and despair. As a man who trusted God fully in the valley of death, hope and joy reverberates from his grief. Hebrews says that he went to the cross for "the joy set before him" (Hebrews 12:2). *Jesus knew God's Word and he trusted in his heavenly Father. So, just as he withstood Satan's temptations in the wilderness, he was also able to stand against Satan's temptation to despair.* On the cross he is utterly powerless. He is utterly dependent. He can't raise himself. He must depend on his Father. He's dependent on the Spirit of Life to rescue him from death. So he casts himself into God's care—and he died in faith. His death now opens the way for us to also face death by committing our spirits into our heavenly Father's hands.

September 2

We are afflicted in every way, but not crushed; perplexed, but not
driven to despair; persecuted, but not forsaken; struck down, but not
destroyed; always carrying in the body the death of Jesus, so that the
life of Jesus may also be manifested in our bodies.
—2 Corinthians 4:8–10

So often the initial reaction to painful suffering is "Why me?
Why this? Why now?" The real God comes for you, in the
flesh, in Christ, into suffering, on your behalf. He does not offer
advice and perspective from afar; he steps into your significant
suffering. He will see you through and work with you the whole
way. He will carry you even in the most difficult situations. This
reality changes the questions that rise up from your heart. That
inward-turning "Why me?" quiets down, lift its eyes, and begins
to look around.

You turn outward and a new and wonderful question forms.
"Why you? Why you, Lord of life? Why would you enter this
world of evils? Why would you go through loss, weakness, hardship, sorrow, and death? Why would you do this for me, of all
people? But you did this for the joy set before you. You did this
for love. You did this showing the glory of God in the face of
Jesus Christ."

As that deeper question sinks home, you become joyously
sane. *The universe is no longer supremely about you. Yet you are not
irrelevant. God's story makes you just the right size—neither too
big nor too small. Everything counts and everything matters, but
the scale changes to something that makes much more sense.* You
face hard things. But you have already received something better,
which can never be taken away. And that better something will
continue to work out the whole journey long.

September 3

"Ask, and it will be given to you; seek, and you will find; knock, and it will be opened to you. For everyone who asks receives, and the one who seeks finds, and to the one who knocks it will be opened."
—Matthew 7:7–8

How do you get the living hope that God offers you in Jesus? By asking. Ask God for help, and don't stop asking. You need him to fill you every day with the hope of the resurrection.

At the same time you are asking God for help, tell other people about your struggle with hopelessness. God uses his people to bring life, light, and hope. Getting in relationship with wise, caring people will protect you from despair and acting out of despair. Share your struggles with those who love you and ask them to pray for you. God will answer your cries and theirs.

Become part of a community of other Christians. Look for a church where Jesus is at the center of teaching and worship. Get in relationship with people who can help you, but don't stop with just getting help. Find people to love, serve, and give to. Even if your life has been stripped barren by lost relationships, God can and will fill your life with helpful and healing relationships.

September 4

Through him we have also obtained access by faith into this grace in which we stand, and we rejoice in hope of the glory of God. Not only that, but we rejoice in our sufferings, knowing that suffering produces endurance, and endurance produces character, and character produces hope, and hope does not put us to shame, because God's love has been poured into our hearts through the Holy Spirit who has been given to us. —Romans 5:2-5

S ome psalms suffer honestly: "O God, I am in anguish. Deliver me from my sufferings and my sins." Other psalms delight honestly: "O my God, you are good. I thank you, worship you, and adore you." Somehow, in the way God runs his universe, our willingness to enter into the experience of pain, disappointment, loneliness, hurt, and stress—being willing to face it and not bolt for some lesser pleasure—winds up being the door to the greatest pleasure of all. And with the best come the other true pleasures, felt deeply.

In 1 Peter 1, suffering is the context in which you experience "joy inexpressible and full of glory" (v. 8 NASB). In James 1, trial is the context of purpose, endurance, meaning, and joy. In Romans 5, we are told that we "rejoice in our suffering" (v. 3). In the midst of sorrows, anguish, misery, and pain we come to know that "the love of God has been poured out within our hearts through the Holy Spirit who was given to us" (v. 5 NASB). *Walking into suffering with eyes wide open, and not running after escapist pleasures, opens the door to knowing the love of God.*

September 5

Such were some of you; but you were washed, but you were sanctified,
but you were justified in the name of the Lord Jesus Christ and in the
Spirit of our God. —1 Corinthians 6:11

W hat mental image comes to mind when you hear the word
sanctify? I suspect that your associations, like mine, are easily muddled. Let's define terms to orient ourselves.

We are describing a growing-up process, a learning curve, a development of particular life skills. God has built a familiar, living illustration of this into our life cycle. Growth in Christ is similar to how a child's competence matures from helpless infancy into capable adulthood. But growing in Christ is also different. Competence never means independence; it means growing dependence. And our maturing takes place in a broader context. The unfolding present tense builds on a definitive past tense and builds toward a climactic future tense. Consider each of these briefly:

- *You are already sanctified. It is past tense.* By a decisive and defining act of God, you are his saint, just as you are his child, and you are righteous. This identity is given to you as a gift. In the Bible, the word *sanctification* is most often used with this past tense meaning, describing something that has already happened.

- *Your sanctification is now being worked out. This is your life in the present tense.* God continues working with you— on a scale of days, years, and decades over a lifetime—to remake you into the likeness of Jesus.

- *Your sanctification will be perfected. It has a future tense.* Faith will become sight. You will be saved when Christ comes for you and imbues you with his glory. You will live.

September 6

I lift up my eyes to the hills.
From where does my help come?
My help comes from the LORD,
who made heaven and earth. —Psalm 121:1–2

To be a *saint* and to become *sanctified* is simply to become more human and humane. Your faith becomes honest, simple, clear-minded, and purposeful—like the Psalms, like Jesus. You need God. You know God. You love God. You are thankful for all the good in your life, and even more thankful for the lifesaving realities embodied in Christ's love. There is nothing more honest than needing outside help every day. You size up the Lord, yourself, and other people more accurately. You better understand people's limitations and strengths—including your own. You're more realistic about life's afflictions and blessings. Greater sanctification means learning to love more thoughtfully, specifically, and helpfully—like the Proverbs, like Jesus. How other people are doing matters to you. You care. So you help practically, pray honestly, and speak constructively. You are more kind and more realistic, less cynical and less naïve.

In other words, to be holy and to grow in holiness means you are becoming a wiser, more engaged, more realistic human being. You deal better with your money, your sexuality, your emotions. You work hard; you stop and rest. You enjoy youthful vigor; you are willing to grow old and frail. You become a better friend and family member. You are a better listener. When you talk, your words bring more good sense, more gravitas, more joy, more reality. Your prayers bring together God's promises and human need. You worship from the heart, not by rote.

September 7

May the Lord make you increase and abound in love for one another and
for all, as we do for you, so that he may establish your hearts blameless
in holiness before our God and Father, at the coming of our Lord Jesus
with all his saints. —1 Thessalonians 3:12–13

True sanctification does not make you religiously obsessive, or self-righteous, or self-lacerating, or paranoid, or aloof from the storms of life. The Holy Spirit is wise in the ways of humankind. Jesus knows all about our sorrows and our sins, our joys, and our graces. Our Father loves us. So you live with clear-minded hope. You know the purpose of your life. You roll up your sleeves and get about doing what needs doing today. You do menial tasks willingly because they are important. You do things that others think are important without becoming self-important. You are more patient and more firm, more gentle and more honest with others. You are truly thankful for good things. You candidly face disappointment and pain, illness and dying.

Saint and sanctification, holiness and holy? These words describe the most paradoxical and desirable life a human being could ever aspire to live. There is nothing more practical. There is nothing more honest. There is nothing more God-given. There is nothing you could want more. *To be a saint, to be holy, means to be human. All these holiness and saintliness words simply describe becoming oriented to God and other people the way human beings are meant to be oriented.*

September 8

Thus says the LORD:
"Cursed is the man who trusts in man
and makes flesh his strength,
whose heart turns away from the LORD. —Jeremiah 17:5

Scripture describes life concretely. "Which way are you turning?" visualizes us making significant choices. We are never neutral, never static, never directionless. *We are always in gear, always in motion, always heading somewhere. That somewhere will either turn out very good or turn out very bad. If we are going bad, we can turn and reverse direction. The gospel of grace turns us around.*

But people also take a turn for the worse. The heart grows hard. The conscience becomes calloused. The lifestyle darkens. The Bible pays close attention to turning the wrong way. We have a built-in tendency to forsake God in favor of someone or something else. This passage in Jeremiah is one particularly vivid passage about taking a bad turn.

Trusting in yourself or other people, trusting in innate strength and ability means you actively turn away from trusting the Lord. There are consequences. Forsake the Giver of life, and you embrace the curse of death. You will be "written in the earth." You return to dust, rather than flourishing as a living tree planted beside streams of fresh water.

September 9

"Sanctify them in the truth; your word is truth." —John 17:17

False messages invite us to turn toward darkness. Lies are anti-Scriptures. They powerfully affect how we think about who God is, who we are, the purpose of life, the meaning of suffering, the source of redemption. Lies directly shape how we handle interpersonal conflict, failure, success, money, and everything else. False views become codified and organized into words to live by: a worldview, a popular philosophy of life, a cultural value, a view of God, an explanation of why we do what we do, a bit of advice, a political agenda. The Bible is not the only persuasive voice in the marketplace of ideas! Other pervasive cultural messages, whether informal or formal, are eager to shape our hearts.

Lord, deliver us from The Lie in its 10,000 disguises. Turn us to the truth.

False messages come humanly embodied. We are deluged by plausible, deceptive voices—and, in a visual culture, deluged with compelling, deceptive images. People tell us lies, we believe lies, we become people of those lies, we become liars. False values, false explanations, and false beliefs are woven into everyday conversations. When friends, parents, therapists, pastors, or popular opinion assert things that are not true and endorse things that are wrong, they express the voice of "the world."

Which way are you turning? Every one of us is a full participant in the epic action adventure between good and evil.

September 10

"Our Father in heaven,
hallowed be your name.
Your kingdom come,
your will be done,
on earth as it is in heaven.
Give us this day our daily bread,
and forgive us our debts,
as we also have forgiven our debtors.
And lead us not into temptation,
but deliver us from evil." —Matthew 6:9-13

Notice how the Lord teaches us to pray. The Bible rarely focuses on health, finances, travel mercies, doing well on a test, finding a job, or the salvation of unsaved relatives. These are legitimate things to pray for, because God cares for all of life. But he never intends that these topics dominate our prayer requests. They miss the real action of God's dealings with his beloved people. They skirt our real problems, and God's front-and-center concerns.

Notice the central concerns in the Psalms, in the Lord's Prayer, in the letters of Paul. *Biblical prayers ask God to show himself so we will know him. They name our troubles and seek refuge in him. They name our sins and seek mercy from him. They ask for the clarity of mind and strength of purpose to love others. They name our holy desires and commitments. They name our God, remember his promises, seek his will.*

When people start to identify where they really need God's help, they are entering the realm where both prayer and counseling live. We step into reality. If you are praying for matters with personal consequences, then you will have conversations of consequence.

September 11

For God alone, O my soul, wait in silence,
for my hope is from him.
He only is my rock and my salvation,
my fortress; I shall not be shaken. —Psalm 62:5–6

" God said . . . and it was so . . . In the beginning was the Word . . . and the Word was made flesh and dwelt among us." So we listen to God. We take the time to hear his words of grace and truth. We consider Jesus. And we pay attention to what's going on in our lives, seeing the world and ourselves in truer colors.

Becoming quiet to listen to God enables us to pray more intelligently and more candidly. We can think straight, and feel honestly, and choose well. There is great benefit in turning off the noise machines, the chatter, the music, the crowd noise, the talk—whether it's playing inside your head, or all around you, or both. Turning off the distractions is not actually *prayer* to the living God. It's not how to know Jesus deeply, or how to relate to our Father, or how to "experience" the Spirit. Be quiet so you can notice and listen, so you can find your voice. Your God speaks and listens attentively to you.

Our understanding and practice changes as we begin to talk aloud to the God who is here. He is not silent or inactive. He listens. He cares. He acts. We begin to deal with him person-to-person. God wants to catch your ear in order to awaken your voice. When you have your "quiet" time, or as you walk outdoors, or during your commute, may the decibel level appropriately rise to joyful noise and cries of need—and may you trust that God listens to the sound of your voice!

September 12

May all who seek you
rejoice and be glad in you!
May those who love your salvation
say evermore, "God is great!"
But I am poor and needy;
hasten to me, O God!
You are my help and my deliverer;
O LORD, do not delay! —Psalm 70:4–5

The two voices of faith—both the confidence and the need—also happen to be the two voices of the Psalter. The Psalms essentially break down into what we could call the minor key and the major key. The first ninety psalms are largely minor key. They are psalms of need, guilt, trouble, affliction, anguish, feeling overwhelmed. There are a few major key psalms scattered in, like Psalm 23, which mentions the dark side in the context of the Lord as our Good Shepherd. And then the last sixty psalms are largely major key: the royal psalms, the Psalms of Ascent, the great hallelujahs, with just a few minor key psalms just seeded in. *You could say that the flow of the entire Psalter expresses something of the essential nature of the Christian life—the sorrow and heartache and need and struggle and joy.*

The emotional modes—the voices of minor key and major key in the Psalms—also happened to be built into the sacrificial system. There are the sacrifices for sin and guilt, which express our need and our liability to destruction, and a plea for God to be merciful to us. Then there are the sacrifices that are expressions of gratitude: the peace offerings, the wave offerings, the thank offerings and so forth, which are expressions of gratitude and joy and worship and confidence. Taken together, the sacrificial system and the book of Psalms show us how to go to God with everything that is on our hearts.

September 13

Count it all joy, my brothers, when you meet trials of various kinds, for you know that the testing of your faith produces steadfastness. And let steadfastness have its full effect, that you may be perfect and complete, lacking in nothing. —James 1:2-4

James is a very savvy pastor. He knows how people work. Throughout the entire book, in the whole way he talks about how life works, we are given these orienting perspectives and then are shown how it works. And then by implication, we are invited to press into that general truth. We're invited to press our specifics that do map on to the general category. How on earth can I count it all joy when I meet various trials, unless there is a big circle around my entire life, unless there's a God who is actually purposefully working my good, my joy, my endurance of faith, my steadfastness, my wisdom rather than folly?

This passage contains a call that we would grow up into wisdom. We grow up into this wonderful grace that gets called endurance or steadfastness, which isn't just gird your loins and grit your teeth. It is a purposeful going forward in the midst of everything that we face in a broken, dying, hard, financially stressful, health stressful world. There is a purpose, there's something that is being done behind the scenes. And the reason that James can say, "count it all joy" is because there's that larger purposefulness in the hand of God.

We are going to find, when the heat hits us, we struggle and we show our foolishness. And there is this overwhelming sense through the book of James, that we serve a God who gives. A God who is generous—God the giver who helps us and meets us in our need.

September 14

O Lord, the hope of Israel,
all who forsake you shall be put to shame;
those who turn away from you shall be written in the earth,
for they have forsaken the Lord, the fountain of living water.

Heal me, O Lord, and I shall be healed;
save me, and I shall be saved,
for you are my praise. —Jeremiah 17:13–14

Sinful deeds lead to a parched life. "Like the partridge that gathers a brood she did not hatch, so is he who gets riches, but not by justice" (Jeremiah 17:11). There's a bit of contorted syntax there, but the passage is basically talking about manipulating to get money: deceiving, angling, giving less than you promise. All those things that are so characteristic of life in a fallen, broken world. There's a bit of a warning that follows: "In the midst of his days, they will leave him." His riches will leave him. Riches—ill-gotten gain—are not going to last.

In this chapter, Jeremiah cries out to God and beseeches him for mercy. Built into it is his conviction that God alone can heal him. Jeremiah is aware of his iniquity, of the depth of this darkness. *God alone can make it right. God alone can save him, and he will be saved. And the conclusion is, again, vertical dimension, "You are my praise" (17:14).*

In everyday life we can think about consequences as being either the good fruit that grows on the true fruit tree or the bad fruit (the thorns) of a parched life in the desert. The good fruit can only grow as we turn toward the true fruit tree, that is the cross, the Redeemer, the God-man. The fountain of life flows from Christ, the Redeemer.

September 15

"Blessed is the man who trusts in the Lord,
whose trust is the Lord.
He is like a tree planted by water,
that sends out its roots by the stream,
and does not fear when heat comes,
for its leaves remain green,
and is not anxious in the year of drought,
for it does not cease to bear fruit." —Jeremiah 17:7–8

We know from Jeremiah 17 that we are called to trust the living God, who is the fountain of living water. We are called to turn away from our idolatries and to trust only him (v. 7). So, conversations about the heart are asking, who is your god at this moment? Who do you love? Whose voice are you listening to? What do you want? Do you want the will of the Holy Spirit? Do you want the will of the Spirit? Or do you want the will of the flesh, the devil, of sinful human beings?

At all times, at the most fundamental level, we are all doing something with God. Every thought, word, deed, action, reaction, and choice are growing out of what we do with God. What we call the heart is meant to be a relational category. And what we call "fruit" and "thorns" is ultimately also about our relationship with God. Both good and bad thoughts and actions—thorns or sweet fruit—come out of the heart, they come out of what motivates you. *So your relationship to God gets expressed in how you deal in life—every emotional reaction you have, every thought pattern that hooks you, every choice you make. All of these things, at bottom, express the core of who or what you worship.* Change comes as what you worship shifts from your own desires to Christ, your Redeemer and Friend.

September 16

May the LORD give strength to his people!
May the LORD bless his people with peace! —Psalm 29:11

A Prayer for Living Faith and Living Love

Our great Lord, we do thank you that you have poured upon us pure promise. And we beseech you above all else to give us ears that we might hear the kind, powerful, merciful, hopeful things you say to us and let us see the ways that you are at work in this world that is broken. A world with rivers of sorrow, a world that has brokenness, a world where everyone of us, should we live so long, will end up aged and decrepit and dying. So we beseech you that you will give us courage. You will give us hope. You will give us strength. You'll give us wisdom and insight. You will give us nothing less than a living faith and a living love that is willing, able, empowered, grateful to serve you and serve the welfare of our brothers and sisters. And indeed Lord, the welfare of an entire world that is filled with woe, a world where sorrow seems infinite. We love you; we commit this day to you. We pray for your particular wisdom to us even now, in the name of the Savior of the world, Jesus Christ. Amen.

September 17

For we do not want you to be unaware, brothers, of the affliction we experienced in Asia. For we were so utterly burdened beyond our strength that we despaired of life itself. Indeed, we felt that we had received the sentence of death. But that was to make us rely not on ourselves but on God who raises the dead. —2 Corinthians 1:8–9

How does God in this particular passage break in? I want you to pay very close attention here. Notice how precisely 2 Corinthians reveals particular things about God. The actual turning point is a disarmingly simple little line in the middle of verse 9 where Paul in effect says, "I almost died in Asia suffering affliction, *in order that* something else good would happen." Paul is pointing directly to the sovereign, purposeful, intervening God, with whom there are no accidents. He doesn't just show up later. "In order that" is a paraphrase that captures Paul's sense that our sufferings are fundamentally meaningful. They are purposeful.

You wrestle with the issue of how the purposes of God work in things that seem broken, destructive, and hopeless. How could there be anything constructive in this? And yet, there is. And it happens in a way that is far deeper than meet the eye. The situation is terrible, but God is up to something good in suffering.

In some fundamental way, every destructive behavior arises out of self-trust, self-reliance. But God is up to better things in Paul's life and in your life. "In order that" is pointing to a transformation at the level of who a person is, at the level of their fundamental vertical dimension: "to make us rely not on ourselves but on God" (v. 9).

September 18

And he answered, "You shall love the Lord your God with all your heart
and with all your soul and with all your strength and with all your mind,
and your neighbor as yourself." —Luke 10:27

The single most influential factor in whether or not you're able to help another person is who you are—your own walk, your own faith, your own love for God. Second, genuine love for others is fundamental. Every person who walks into a relationship with any other person, at some level, is asking, "Are you trustworthy?" A second question is, "Can I be honest with you?" With someone you trust, you are willing to be honest about things that matter: dark things, bright things, happy things, hard things, struggles, guilts, sins, and joys. We can talk about the light and the deep, and we can talk about the happy and the sad. The final questions are about their own relationship with God: "Will I embrace the change purposes of Christ? Will I get a biblical agenda for my life?" Will I be a thorn bush or fruit tree? Will faith work through love or will lies and idolatry work through selfishness and fear?

Now think through these questions from the lens of your relationship with God. *Do you trust God? Is the quality of your conversation with God up to what it is with people? Our best human relationships can shine a mirror and say, "Now, the reason I trust that person is because he or she actually, in some tiny way, is like God. They're manifesting something of what the real God is like.* Thus, if I'm able to have this kind of head-on relationship of substance with that person, how much more with the real God who stands behind the person?"

September 19

Who can discern his errors?
Declare me innocent from hidden faults.
Keep back your servant also from presumptuous sins;
let them not have dominion over me!
Then I shall be blameless,
and innocent of great transgression. —Psalm 19:12–13

The average person believes that for something to count as sin, it must be consciously chosen. But our desires often deceive us, so we aren't even aware we're doing it. We're blind to ourselves. Think of some of the biblical metaphors: "drunken," "asleep," "like an unreasoning animal." Sin is like a madness in our hearts, things that we aren't even aware of.

A circumstance does not create the lustfulness of the heart. The situation becomes the place, but then our hearts generate particular, tailor-made cravings. Only a Christian's worldview says that our desires are about our relationship with God—either because we want the things God wants, or we want, contrary to God, my will to be done. You can't actually understand desire without understanding the God-relatedness of it.

It is so important that we have a robust sense of the unique significance of the heart from a Christian standpoint. There are all sorts of implications for practically understanding how the idea of "lusts of the flesh" tracks into people's deepest problems. When the Bible talks about the lusts of the flesh, it's giving us a way to understand ourselves at the most fundamental level as worshipers. When we worship something or someone besides the living God, that can be described as a "lust of the flesh," and it can result in a variety of sinful behavior. One particular act of wrong can come from many different possible desires. What rules you comes out and what comes out reveals what rules you.

September 20

Peter, an apostle of Jesus Christ,

To those who are elect exiles of the Dispersion in Pontus, Galatia,
Cappadocia, Asia, and Bithynia, according to the foreknowledge of
God the Father, in the sanctification of the Spirit, for obedience to
Jesus Christ and for sprinkling with his blood: May grace and peace be
multiplied to you. —1 Peter 1:1–2

A Prayer of Thanksgiving to the Triune God

Our Father, how great and good this salvation is.
Jesus Christ, how great and good, humble, merciful,
powerful is your work of saving us from all that is dark,
from sin and death, from the evils that beset us. We thank
you that you have promised your protecting care, that you
are Shepherd, you are Friend, you are Shield. You are the
one who is King. You are the one who is interposed his
own blood that we might live.

Holy Spirit, we thank you that you minister unto our hearts
individually and corporately, nothing less than the presence,
the love, the power, the truth of Jesus Christ and the Father.
We thank you that you come to dwell within us, and we
beseech you that as we continue to talk, think, wrestle,
interact, write, ponder, read, that you yourself, Holy Spirit,
will be the one who does nothing less than write the word
of truth, the word of life upon our hearts. That we would be
men and women who live in the light, who are empowered
by the God of power, who are shielded by the God who is
good to his beloved children. We thank you. We love you.
We beseech you that you will help us this very day to grow
before you by the grace of Jesus Christ. Amen.

September 21

Bear one another's burdens, and so fulfill the law of Christ.
—Galatians 6:2

One of the characteristics of wisdom in the Proverbs is that the wise person listens and invites correction—wants correction. Because who of us can see himself or herself perfectly? We all have a million flaws. We may be aware of some of them, but other people often see us better than we see ourselves. We need to develop a willingness to invite and to involve each other in the real, moral dramas of our lives. God created community for this reason—we need each other.

I can't think of how many good sermons I've heard on "one-anothering"—for you to forgive each other, for you to love each other, to do toward other people the thing that you want done toward you. And the main point of the exhortation is to encourage us to bear each other's burdens. But every one-anothering passage also implies a reciprocity. I'm to bear your burdens, and you need to let me know your burdens. I've got burdens too, and how can I seek help unless I share them?

One-anothering cuts both ways. And the giving of help is reciprocal to the asking for help. *Who can you reciprocally share burdens with today? You get to talking that way and the fellowship just starts to ignite. You start to create a community in which people are both asking and giving of aid, bearing each other's burdens, praying for each other about real stuff.* You are actually creating something that is a very sweet kind of good fruit.

September 22

Put on then, as God's chosen ones, holy and beloved, compassion
hearts, kindness, humility, meekness, and patience, bearing with one
another and, if one has a complaint against another, forgiving each
other; as the Lord has forgiven you, so you also must forgive. And
above all these put on love, which binds everything together in perfect
harmony. —Colossians 3:12–14

How do you create a truly Christian community? We move toward people. We create a climate of grace and relate to others with a large-hearted and generous spirit. We are not suspicious, narrow, self-preoccupied, critical, wary, quick to look for fault, opinionated, judgmental. Love is patient. Love is kind. These are fundamental characteristics of how we are to approach everyone. It's an attitude, a stance in life, an orientation.

Patience, endurance, forbearance, long-suffering, perseverance, and steadfastness are qualities that God hugely desires. They are communicable attributes of God himself. This is what he is like in dealing with a broken world.

Oh Father, give us a vision for a life that is fruitful and flourishing and, by your grace, sheds some light in a dark world, does good to other people, and lives purposefully and with reconciliation, kindness, repentance, humility, faith, joy, and gratitude as grace plays more and more of a part in who we are. We confess, Lord, that we get really stuck. We get into some ruts, we get blind and stubborn, and we beseech you that in your great, patient mercy that we would learn to treat others the way you treat us. Keep working with us, contending with us. Teach us to contend with ourselves in the right way. We thank you, most of all, that one day, all manner of thing will be well. In Christ's name, Amen.

September 23

If we are afflicted, it is for your comfort and salvation; and if we are comforted, it is for your comfort, which you experience when you patiently endure the same sufferings that we suffer. —2 Corinthians 1:6

Ultimately everything we learn, even a small increment of wisdom or comfort, becomes something to give away. You know, as we look at 2 Corinthians 1, everything you learn becomes the content you can use to reach out to another person in love. That's what Jesus Christ does, and that is what he is doing in his church—making us into people who move into each other's lives with constructive intent.

We need to understand that our fundamental call is to this redemptive engagement—bringing mercy and light into a world of darkness and sin. Why, if we've been given some excellent gift, would we not go outside the gates and try share it with others?

Lord, I do pray that each one of us, by the mercy of God, would become a wiser man or woman, that we would live more fruitfully, more quickly repent of our sins, more quickly cast our burdens on you, and more quickly have a hand to reach out to another person. Would you also teach us to pray more wisely, to rejoice more wholeheartedly, to suffer more honestly, to seek help more quickly from our brothers and sisters? And we beseech you to make that little part of the kingdom that we represent and have impact on a brighter place, more full of goodness, more full of the evident sparkling goodness of the living God. Amen.

September 24

The night is far gone; the day is at hand. So then let us cast off the
works of darkness and put on the armor of light.... But put on the Lord
Jesus Christ, and make no provision for the flesh, to gratify its desires.
—Romans 13:12, 14

For good, biblical, and practical reasons, Christians have always understood that we face a threefold moral enemy; the world, the flesh, and the devil. Over this unholy trinity hangs the specter of our last enemy—the shadow of death and death itself.

Even though the term doesn't appear in Scripture, here are four ways to understand spiritual warfare biblically.

First, spiritual warfare is a metaphor for standing on the Lord's side in the epic struggle between the Lord and his enemies. Second, spiritual warfare is a moral struggle. It is a conflict over who you are, what you believe, and how you live. Third, spiritual warfare is a synonym for the struggles of the Christian life. Fourth, it is a battle for lordship. At its core, it's the battle for who you will serve.

In whose image are you being made? *Will you resemble the Good Shepherd who lays down his life for his sheep? Or will you grow more and more like Satan, the liar and destroyer? This is a battle that encompasses all of life.* Not just for a few odd or bizarre moments, but in every moment of every day we are in a battle for who we will serve.

September 25

Finally, be strong in the Lord and in the strength of his might.
—Ephesians 6:10

U nderstanding how spiritual warfare intersects with common, everyday problems like anger, fear, and escapism starts with remembering that the whole world is in the power of the Evil One (1 John 5:19). The Evil One is a God-mimic. He wants us to be God-mimics too.

How does this play out when we are angry? If we are mimicking God instead of going to God, we become, like Satan, a false judge and an accuser (Revelation 12:10). James unpacks this dynamic in his letter (James 4:1–12). We become self-righteous, condemning, malicious, unfair.

What about fear? Here we see Satan mimicking God as a false prophet. My colleague Ed Welch describes anxiety as a voice that tells us lies about ourselves, our God, our world, and about our future. What do people hear in their minds when they are anxious? "You have ruined everything." "God doesn't love you." These are not the words God speaks in Scripture to his beloved children.

What about escapism and addiction? The common theme that runs through the wrong kind of pleasure-seeking is that we are looking for something besides God to make us happy, to make us feel good, to help us deal with the unpleasant realities of our lives. Satan is continually proposing self-salvation schemes to people that are designed to keep them from the real Savior.

So when we struggle with anger, fear, and escapism we see all of our enemies at work. This is a daunting trio. But our hope is embedded in what we learn in Ephesians 6: Be strong in the Lord (v. 10). Put on the whole armor of God, which will enable us to stand firm (vv. 11, 13). In all circumstances the shield of faith can extinguish all the flaming darts of the evil one (v. 16). Keep alert with perseverance in prayer and the Word of God (vv. 17–19).

September 26

What causes quarrels and what causes fights among you? Is it not this,
that your passions are at war within you? —James 4:1

Here are five questions to ask yourself, and one thing you need
to do, that will direct your honest meeting with God when
you struggle with anger:

1. *What is happening around me when I get angry?* Make a
list of the last five times you got angry. When did you get
angry at something that doesn't really matter in God's
world? When did you get angry because you had made
a good thing more important than God? And when did
you get angry because you were truly wronged?

2. *How do I act when I get angry?* Do you express your anger
in bitterness? In arguing? In slander? Were there any
times when anger actually was an expression of love, not
hate, and was expressed constructively?

3. *What were my expectations when I became angry?* This
question about your motives reveals what hijacked God's
place in your heart. Your answer will show you where you
need God's help the most.

4. *What message does God, in his Word, have for me that will
speak to my anger?* If you remember that this is God's kingdom and not yours, the way you deal with your anger will
be hugely affected. When you add to that an understanding of your real sins, then you will also see how God, in
Christ, is tenderhearted and forgiving to you.

5. *Ask God for help.* You must turn to God for help if your
wrong anger patterns are going to change. Turn to the God
who loves you and tell him all about what is making you
angry.

September 27

Know this, my beloved brothers: let every person be quick to hear, slow
to speak, slow to anger; for the anger of man does not produce the
righteousness of God. —James 1:19-20

Becoming like God means that, when you see a true wrong, you
will learn to respond in the way God does. When God sees a
true wrong, he responds constructively. He has done this toward us
by naming our wrongs clearly and then offering us the mercy and
grace we do not deserve. Here are some ways that God responds:

- *God is patient.* God is described in the Bible as "slow to
  anger" (Exodus 34:6). Learning to be "slow to anger"
  means living in a world that has things wrong in it and
  being willing to stay in difficult situations and relationships for the long haul. Why? Because although this wrong
  needs to be addressed, your call from God is to persevere
  in addressing it constructively, patiently, and kindly.

- *God is merciful.* Because God is merciful, he sent Jesus to
  die on the cross for you. His just anger was poured out on
  Jesus. As you experience God's mercy, you will learn to be
  merciful. Instead of angrily judging others, you will roll up
  your sleeves and help to right the wrongs you see.

- *God is forgiving.* God's forgiveness doesn't make what was
  wrong okay. He names what is wrong and deals with the
  wrong by paying the price himself. Forgiveness is a way to
  be displeased in a constructive way. Loving someone who's
  done wrong is the way to overcome that wrong.

- *God confronts in love.* Because God lovingly confronts, so
  can you. It is both constructive and loving for wrongdoers
  to face the consequences of their wrongs. Your anger can
  be constructively expressed as a clear reprimand and fair
  consequences.

September 28

All the ways of a man are pure in his own eyes,
but the LORD weighs the spirit. —Proverbs 16:2

The sinfulness or godliness of anger arises from the motive. People motivated by desire for God's glory, for personal conformity to Jesus's model and will, and for the well-being of others will be angry in one way. People motivated by the "desires of body and mind" (Ephesians 2:3), by pride and false beliefs, will be angry in a different way. *The simplest question to ask about what underlies anger is, "What do I really want?"* If you are honest, with God's help, you can recognize if you really crave to get even, or to hurt someone, or not to be inconvenienced, or to prove someone wrong, or to score points, or to be recognized and appreciated, or to humiliate, or to win, or to get your way. You are ruled by what the Bible terms "self." And, with God's help, you can also recognize if you really want the Lord of life to be honored in word, deed, attitude, and intention. The counsel of brothers and sisters can help us sort things through when we are blind to something and can't figure it out. Counsel can help us when we deceive ourselves about our motives, dressing up something unsavory as though it were God's will.

One of the delightful things about sorting out our own anger is that the link between root and fruit is so accessible. God is honored and gives grace in the struggle toward righteousness just as in the accomplishment of righteousness.

September 29

But God, being rich in mercy, because of the great love with which he
loved us, even when we were dead in our trespasses, made us alive
together with Christ—by grace you have been saved. . . . For we are
his workmanship, created in Christ Jesus for good works, which God
prepared beforehand, that we should walk in them. —Ephesians 2:4–5, 10

How you see and understand yourself is of central importance
to the Christian life. If we truly know God, we will come to
know ourselves. The issue that we call *low self-esteem* represents
a profound skewing in self-understanding. Low self-esteem is a
serious problem full of debilitating heartache, broken relationships, discouragement, sense of failure, an overwhelming sense of
not belonging. Self-evaluation is a much healthier term, because
it combines the picture you have of yourself with the assessment
you make of that picture. Is the way you know yourself actually
true? Do you understand yourself as you actually are? You can't
answer those questions accurately without going to what God
says about you.

An accurate self-evaluation must include the fact that you
are a creature of the living God, dependent on him, while also
seeing your sinfulness. In true self-knowledge, you also know
you've been loved at the price of the life of the Son of God, you
are saved by grace, and you are cared for by the heart of the One
who matters. You can then rightly understand both your gifts
and your limitations. *There is a dignity and a joy in knowing what
you have to offer and where you need help. True self-knowledge is
not an issue of good or bad self-esteem, but true or false assessment of
yourself. This is a door to sanity.* Are you understanding God, the
world, sin, and your growth in the right way?

September 30

For you have delivered me from death
and my feet from stumbling,
that I may walk before God
in the light of life. —Psalm 56:13 NIV

How are you changing? There's been some process of transformation in your life already. The darkness is not as dark; the light is getting lighter. Redemption is ongoing until the day we die.

There are fundamental similarities running through all of our stories as light dawns from deep darkness. The reason for these similarities is that there is the same Person at work, with the same fundamental purpose for each one of us, although the details may be completely different in Christ's particular way of working with you.

There are three simultaneous dynamics in every person's story. There are always situational evils—things that deceive you and heinous actions committed against you. There is always a challenging, tempting, disorienting situation. And the things that happen to us count.

There's also always something going on with you. There are internal evils, struggles, disturbing emotions, confusion, chosen sins, and disorientation to be reckoned with.

The third dynamic at play in each of our stories is that there's always an intervening Savior, a Redeemer on site. He says what he does, and he does what he says. His intervening hand and voice are on hand in each situation.

When these dynamics are knit together, it creates a fourth dynamic: what is changing in you. *The person in the situation (you) changes under the hand of the onsite Redeemer. Your story is not done: it is unfolding. You can have strength, purpose, forgiveness, and courage. You can walk before God in the light of life.*

October 1

"Blessed are the poor in spirit, for theirs is the kingdom of heaven.
Blessed are those who mourn, for they shall be comforted.
Blessed are the meek, for they shall inherit the earth.
Blessed are those who hunger and thirst for righteousness, for they shall
be satisfied." —Matthew 5:3-6

The Beatitudes envision a world that is hard. And they give us a blueprint for how to live in the midst of a world that has many hardships in it.

The poor in spirit are blessed because the kingdom of heaven is theirs. To be poor in spirit is to know you need help from someone outside yourself. You are fundamentally needy—you are not independent. You need help from outside yourself and you call to the One who can help you. That, in fact, is the key that opens the door to the very presence of the King of kings.

Those who mourn are blessed because they will be comforted. The losses that happen aren't the way they should be. This is a sorrowful world that needs comforting; it needs strengthening. It needs help, and the King is the only one who can bring that comfort.

The meek are blessed because they will inherit the earth. The meek are those who put their hope in God. The meek want God to tell them who he is and who they are and how they can live and what his promises are.

Those hungering and thirsting for righteousness are blessed because they shall be satisfied. There are many things we wish we could have and keep and treasure, but we only lose them. Hunger and thirst for the one thing that can never be lost. That is a gift of the One who will satisfy you, the One who will make all that is wrong right.

October 2

"Blessed are the merciful, for they shall receive mercy.
Blessed are the pure in heart, for they shall see God.
Blessed are the peacemakers, for they shall be called sons of God.
Blessed are those who are persecuted for righteousness' sake, for theirs is
the kingdom of heaven." —Matthew 5:7–10

The merciful are blessed because they will receive mercy again and again. Mercy deals with the problem of sin and the problem of suffering. The gospel is about both. Mercy is not only forgiveness; it's generosity and addressing the needs of all who are broken, needy, struggling, hurting, and confused. The merciful are given even more of the very thing they already have. Now they overflow with mercy and are able to give even more of it away.

The pure in heart are blessed because they will see God. Pure in heart fundamentally describes our motives and why we do things. It propels us forth into the world with the purposes of mercy, peacemaking, courage, and a willingness to be part of the solution.

The peacemakers are blessed because they will be called the sons of God. The world is full of heartache, war, conflict, hatred, lying, cliques, and competition. We are called to become men and women who are part of the making of peace, who are able to live content with who we are and with an eye and a heart for the need in the world around us.

Those persecuted for righteousness' sake are blessed because the kingdom of heaven is theirs. This is a calling to be willing to suffer, to lose, to bear pain, and to go toward what is hard. This is a call to courage.

The Beatitudes are about the reorientation of our lives and a transformation of our life purpose.

October 3

"Blessed are the poor in spirit, for theirs is the kingdom of heaven.
Blessed are those who mourn, for they shall be comforted.
Blessed are the meek, for they shall inherit the earth.
Blessed are those who hunger and thirst for righteousness,
for they shall be satisfied.
Blessed are the merciful, for they shall receive mercy.
Blessed are the pure in heart, for they shall see God.
Blessed are the peacemakers, for they shall be called sons of God.
Blessed are those who are persecuted for righteousness' sake, for theirs
is the kingdom of heaven." —Matthew 5:3-10

The eight promises in the Beatitudes are absolutely flooded with the love of God. They promise you a kingdom, comfort, and the earth as your inheritance. They promise satisfaction, mercy, eyes to see God, and that you will be called a child of God.

Within them are contained in seed form everything that the Bible is about—everything that Christ is doing and everything we need for our lives to be transformed into his image. *The Beatitudes are about the transformation of normal people into exceedingly unusual people who live for a different reason, who have a reason for their indestructible hope, in the face of all that is lost.*

Our Father in heaven, will you flood us with your love and awaken us to the reasons we have for courage? Will you grant to us the ability to have a deep care and concern for others? We ask you that we would bear each other on our hearts. We are your children. We are brothers and sisters, and you intend for us to be a blessing to each other. Let us live in the light of life through Jesus Christ our King. Amen.

October 4

But he said to me, "My grace is sufficient for you, for my power is made
perfect in weakness." Therefore I will boast all the more gladly of my
weaknesses, so that the power of Christ may rest upon me.
—2 Corinthians 12:9

There are seasons where progress in your spiritual growth goes very slowly. You wonder why you keep struggling with a temper, anxiety, or being clumsy in relationships. But often when we think about growth and transformation, we have an idealized image in our minds. I doubt that most of us picture honest struggles. It is not unusual for life to be difficult. We see things within ourselves that we wish would change, but we keep failing in some way. If sanctification means becoming like Christ, then the way we struggle is as much a part of our sanctification as some idealized image of what we hope that we would become.

There are also particular kinds of growth and strength that may be happening in our lives that we don't even see. Living in weakness doesn't necessarily feel like growth, but your heart may be becoming more generous to other people. You may have less of a sense of your rights and prerogatives, what you want to accomplish, or that you need to get credit. You have a growing sense that other people really matter. You can be gracious to them in their shortcomings and their heartaches. Now none of those things are splashy transformations. They're just good, quiet, strong, steady fruits of the Lord working in our lives.

If you add these two things together—realism about the ongoing struggle that makes you need the Lord and then contentment with quiet, unspectacular graces in your life, then sanctification can, in fact, go forward, even when you're going through a hard patch in life.

October 5

He who began a good work in you will carry it on to completion until the day of Christ Jesus. —Philippians 1:6 NIV

If you have baggage from a sinful past, you may be wondering how Christ can heal you. You feel shame or grief over past sin and you wonder if God could really love and accept you. In all hard human questions, the Bible shines, but it particularly shines here because where else in the world is mercy the response to a lot of really bad baggage?

There is a beautiful story of redemption woven throughout Scripture. The Bible is full of people with checkered pasts who were redeemed and restored by God. If you feel humbled and discouraged, understand that is already a work of God's mercy, and he will finish the work he has started in you.

There's a grace that deals with the past, a grace that deals in the present, and there's a grace that will deal with us in the future. Regarding the guilt of what was done in the past, the gospel speaks to us of a sin-bearer, the Lamb of God who takes away the sins of the world and erases them. When you think about why you still feel the stain, the promise of present grace applies—there is a promise of presence and power to help in the moment of struggle. He promises to give us the Holy Spirit. Regarding future grace, Christ will come back to finish what he's begun. God's grace and mercy are our foundation and hope at every point.

October 6

Blessed is the one whose transgression is forgiven,
whose sin is covered. —Psalm 32:1

You and I face a choice regarding our guilt and shame. On one hand, if we try to deal with it on our own, we are choosing to experience loss—separation from mercy and loving-kindness, being left alone with our troubles. On the other hand, if we turn to the Lord with our guilt and shame, we have access to all of the Lord's blessings.

All you need to do is ask for the exact help you need from the One who can help you. It's a personal transaction. Recognize that Jesus is the one who can solve what is most wrong. If you know your guilt, you can be forgiven. If you know your weakness, you can be strengthened. If you know your folly, you can be given wisdom. If you know your brokenness, you can be made whole. If you know you have failed, you can be planted by streams of living water and prosper in all you do. If you don't know these things about yourself, you can't be helped. If you don't know you are in trouble, you can't find peace with God. Those who humble themselves will be exalted—it's a wondrous paradox found in our relationship with our Lord. *The humility of knowing your need and asking for help and saying thank you and loving the One who helps you is what the Christian life is about.*

October 7

"My son, do not regard lightly the discipline of the Lord,
nor be weary when reproved by him.
For the Lord disciplines the one he loves,
and chastises every son whom he receives." —Hebrews 12:5–6

O ur life stories involve innumerable encounters with God. God is man's environment. We are continually dependent, continually colliding with him, continually under observation, continually needing and receiving mercies, continually disciplined. He interrupts us, protects us, leads us, afflicts us, encourages us.

Much of personal change is a matter of slow-forming habits—the accretion of new habits of thinking, habits of attitude, habits of response. Much of how we grow happens subliminally, just as a child grows. We grow up in innumerable daily choice points between good and evil. We receive subtle influences from modeling. We accumulate consequences of blessing or curse. We slowly learn to handle both felicities and frustrations with grace.

Our lives in Christ take a lifetime of "formation," of learning, unlearning, and relearning. Like any skill, wisdom includes definable, explicit things learned. Wisdom also involves tacit, implicit, caught-not-taught learning. There are ways that I have grown that I could never quantify, that I do not even see. God always retains the right to work in ways beyond our comprehension. And, because learning how to live is the most complex skill imaginable, the struggle will not cease until I have faced the last enemy and see the face of God.

Your entire Christian life is a series of variations and permutations of the process of sanctification. This is how you grow. This is how you live. This is how you minister to others, loving them well in their need. This is how you arrive in heaven, seeing Jesus face-to-face, and finding that you have been made like him.

October 8

For this light momentary affliction is preparing for us an eternal weight
of glory beyond all comparison. —2 Corinthians 4:17

God's ways with us do not work according to a formula. No single factor, no one truth, no protocol can capture how and why a person grows into Christ's image. Multiple factors always cooperate in progressive sanctification. But how do we keep our bearings amid a multitude of variables?

Though our lives involve innumerable variables, change occurs through the interplay of four factors: you are changed by *God*, by *the Word of truth*, by *wise people*, and by *suffering and struggle*. Each one contributes to how we change. They are present in differing degrees as our lives are re-scripted. Grace comes to fruition in a change of mind, in turning, hoping, taking refuge, trusting, loving, and obeying. The way a life unfolds is non-formulaic, yet variants on these four elements intertwine within every story of our discipleship. They appear everywhere in Scripture. The story of your life in Christ is also composed of these elements.

By definition, a person who changes takes action. You do something. You believe something. You ask for help, from a friend, from God, from both. You make different choices. You change your mind, your attitudes, your feelings, your goal in life, the way you treat others, your habits, your goals.

And you find, sooner or later, that God himself was working all along—within the hardships, amid the sins, by the friendships, through his Word, in you. The farther you walk on this road, the more you realize that God is the decisive actor and foundational factor in the drama.

October 9

May the God of hope fill you with all joy and peace in believing, so that by the power of the Holy Spirit you may abound in hope. —Romans 15:13

God himself changes you. He intervenes in your life, turning you from self-will to the kingdom of life. He raises you in Christ when you are dead in trespasses and sins. He restores hearing when you are deaf and gives sight when you are blind. All good fruit in our lives comes by the Holy Spirit's work. The Holy Spirit continues to do the things that Jesus does.

Second, *the Word of truth changes you.* God communicates messages to us—many messages. Scripture speaks with a true voice into a world churning with false voices. Scripture reveals innumerable features of God's person, purposes, will, promises, and actions. It clarifies every facet of human experience.

Third, *wise people change us.* Godly growth is most frequently mediated through the gifts and graces of brothers and sisters in Christ. At the most basic individual level, whoever walks with the wise becomes wise (Proverbs 13:20). The honesty and graciousness, humility and clarity, good sense and convictions of others have radiant, fruitful effects (James 3:17–18).

Fourth, *suffering, struggle, and troubles change us.* Difficulties make us need God. Hardships make Scripture and prayer come alive. The difficulties that we experience necessitate grace and awaken a sense of weakness—where the Spirit is working. People change because something is hard—not because everything goes well. Christ enters trouble, lives through trouble, is unafraid of trouble, and speaks and acts into trouble.

October 10

My soul clings to you;
your right hand upholds me. —Psalm 63:8

The Lord describes our relationship with him from many perspectives. Love him. Fear him. Walk in his ways. Entrust yourself to him. Believe his promises. Seek him. Do what he says. Serve him. Yet he knows that we tend to get stuck in ruts—I do anyway, and I'm pretty sure you do too. So he keeps coming at us from different directions. Here is one way the Bible puts it that we don't often hear mentioned: *cling* to him. Hold on tight. Be glued to him. Don't let him go. Hold fast.

What does it mean to cling to Christ by faith when you face something threatening: a cancer diagnosis, the sudden loss of a job, or other difficult news? Faith has two core activities: dire need, then utter joy. The order matters. First, we are weak and need his help. Second, knowing his care, we become strong and joyful. When cancer intrudes into your body and changes your life, or when you face crushing financial burdens, you are invited to become aware of your dire need for help. Many psalms cry out to God in need. We cling to Christ. We ask the Lord to save us from our real troubles, real sins, real sufferings, and real anguish.

October 11

"It is the LORD who goes before you. He will be with you; he will not leave
you or forsake you. Do not fear or be dismayed." —Deuteronomy 31:8

When facing crisis or times of fear, you may go to the one who loves you. You may bring your struggles and tell him all about them. Remember who he is. He cares. He is involved. He is a sure and certain presence. He will walk with you through pain. He will strengthen you and give you courage. He will deliver you from your fears. He is your refuge, a safe place amid danger. He will clarify your thinking. He will anchor your hopes in what can never be lost. He is merciful to you, and he will make you merciful. He will settle you in your true identity.

Many biblical truths will serve and bless you in your struggle, but the simple reality that "God is with you" overarches all. It is a summary of all God's blessings to you. *The promise of God's caring, committed, merciful presence through all of life in every circumstance is a primary strand of biblical DNA. This reality weaves through all of Scripture. It is woven into the life of every one of God's children.* Again and again God repeats to his people, "I will never leave you." In all kinds of ways, in all kinds of circumstances, "I will never forsake you." He reminds us, "Though you walk through the valley of the shadow of death, I will be with you. Though the mountains fall into the heart of the sea I will be with you. I will not leave you as an orphan. I will come to you" (Psalms 23:4; 46:2; John 14:18).

October 12

The LORD is my strength and my shield;
in him my heart trusts, and I am helped;
my heart exults,
and with my song I give thanks to him. —Psalm 28:7

What is your greatest struggle and need right now? Where will you face today's crucial choices? In that moment, in that situation, what will you do? How will you treat people? What will you believe? Where will you place (or misplace) your trust? What will you want? How will you react in that circumstance? These questions look for the significant, decisive choices in a person's everyday life: "When you face that situation, which way will you turn?"

Second, what does the Lord say that speaks directly into what you are facing? Who is he? What is he doing? What does he promise? What does he will? And what does he call you to believe, need, trust, hope, and obey? These questions explore a person's current perceptions of the God who is there. Is what God says and does immediately relevant or basically irrelevant?

Both questions help us to work on the things that count. The first question helps us grasp the environment (providentially arranged by the Vinedresser) in which growth (or hardening) takes place daily. It makes discipleship relevant. The second question helps us grasp what we do (or don't) understand about God and how he meets us. *Often we already know significant truth, but we don't know it in a way that changes our lives. Discipleship does the hard work of kneading what is true into how we actually live.*

October 13

Be merciful to me, O God, be merciful to me,
for in you my soul takes refuge;
in the shadow of your wings I will take refuge,
till the storms of destruction pass by.
I cry out to God Most High,
to God who fulfills his purpose for me.
He will send from heaven and save me;
he will put to shame him who tramples on me. *Selah*
God will send out his steadfast love and his faithfulness! —Psalm 57:1-3

Consider a simple example of how the Scripture above disciples us amid what we face. Has anyone ever faced a threatening situation more wonderfully and honestly?

Notice all the active verbs. They describe the God I honestly need. Are those you disciple learning such a straight-on relationship with this God?

So what are you facing today? Anything that threatens you? The psalm makes the experience of danger chillingly specific, but it leaves specific circumstances undefined. That invites disciples to insert their own details.

Notice further, amid this disturbing and difficult experience, the astonishing centerpiece of the psalm: *"Be exalted above the heavens, O God. Let your glory be above all the earth" (v. 5). It is a wonder. Here is the living faith toward which true discipleship aims. Pointedly placed right in the midst of troubles, this is a whole different way of seeing things and responding.* These sentences are the pivot around which everything in the psalm turns. You and I don't think this way very often. People who feel threatened usually react with fear, retaliation, or escapism. They forget the Exalted One. Discipleship aims to help such people remember.

October 14

"I am the true vine, and my Father is the vinedresser. Every branch in me that does not bear fruit he takes away, and every branch that does bear fruit he prunes, that it may bear more fruit." —John 15:1-2

I'll often say to someone, "The Vinedresser uses pruning shears, not a chain saw. He's not going to work on everything all at once. He's not going to make you face every kind of trouble right now. He's not going to teach you everything about himself. But something about who he is and what he says to you can make a decisive difference in some challenge you are facing right now." In discipling another, I am doing nothing more than pursuing the same line of questioning and reasoning that I need myself. God meets you—and me—exactly where we are.

The Word is alive with the love of God in Christ Jesus. He invades our darkness and his words vividly portray the human struggle. The wise will of God is realistic and relevant, as God shows himself operating in the midst of the worst and best of life and all the muddling in the middle. Scripture is timely, adapted to the varied conditions and experiences of real people, because God is a timely Redeemer.

October 15

Incline your ear, O LORD, and answer me,
for I am poor and needy. . . .

Be gracious to me, O Lord,
for to you do I cry all the day.
Gladden the soul of your servant,
for to you, O Lord, do I lift up my soul. —Psalm 86:1, 3–4

Right now you may be living in a world of despair. You can't see any solution to your problems. You're not looking forward to anything. The future seems empty.

But God's perspective on your life is very different. Your life is precious to him. He knows everything about you—even how many hairs are on your head. He loves you to such a degree that he sent his own Son to die for you (John 3:16).

Your Savior is not surprised or put off by your hopeless feelings. He wants you to bring your despair to him and cry for help right now, in the middle of your darkness and pain. Throughout history God's children have cried to him. He has helped them. Psalm 86 captures for us how David cried out his despair to God thousands of years ago: "In the day of my trouble I will call to you, for you will answer me" (v. 7).

Today is your day of trouble. Tell Jesus all your sorrows, all your troubles . . . Say out loud to God, "Hear my prayer O LORD; listen to my cry for mercy" (v. 6 NIV). On this day the living God promises to listen to you and help you. "You will seek me and find me, when you seek me with all your heart" (Jeremiah 29:13).

October 16

"You are the light of the world. A city set on a hill cannot be hidden. Nor do people light a lamp and put it under a basket, but on a stand, and it gives light to all in the house. In the same way, let your light shine before others, so that they may see your good works and give glory to your Father who is in heaven." —Matthew 5:14-16

A Prayer for Growing in Love for God and People

Our dear Father, we do not take for granted that the energies, opportunities, responsibilities, and even the breath we take is a gift of yours to us. I pray that we who tend to be so caught in the closet of our own self-generated perceptions would be, by your mercy, mastered in new ways by you, such that we start to wear other people on our heart. I pray we would de-center out of self-interest and center our lives on you. I pray that we, who have been so spectacularly loved by Christ, would in some measure, by the power of your Spirit become like him.

Lord, we can't anticipate all the contingencies that there will be, what trials or tragedies may come into our lives. But we beseech you that whatever you bring into our lives, that we would seek you, we would find you. We would grow in knowing you. We would love you. And that we would cooperate with your work in us, that through you we would increase the quantum of light that is in this world. And we pray these things in Jesus's name, Amen.

October 17

The LORD is my rock and my fortress and my deliverer,
my God, my rock, in whom I take refuge. —Psalm 18:2

There's always something profound underneath your actions and words, feelings and thoughts—an organizing pattern that drives you. There are many possible strands of motive: There is fear of man where we seek approval and honor from other people. There is pride that wants its own way above all else. But there is another important strand at the motive level—*the love of pleasure.* It's one of things Paul discusses in his letters to Timothy. Love of pleasure is given an overarching description, and our culture has a lot of ways to invite us into that. Pleasure says, "I love feeling good. I'll do anything to keep that feeling going and to forget my troubles."

But think about the fact that in the entire book of Psalms, the leading theme is that God is our refuge in the midst of trouble. You could say that most of the Psalms are actually the antidote to what drives people addictively. Life is hard, and I look for something to make me feel good, something to make me forget my troubles. The Psalms say, life's hard and there's a refuge. And it's not what you might decide to turn to. It's not heavy drinking, it's not watching four football games on Sunday, it's not scouring the internet for pornography. It's not exercising hard so that you get endorphins. When these things own you, they become the substitute for seeking and finding the refuge that would actually be life itself. Unbelief does not happen in a vacuum; it expresses itself in active false belief in the moment. Faith actively expresses itself too—in going to God, in claiming God as my rock, my fortress, my deliverer, my refuge.

October 18

"For each tree is known by its own fruit. For figs are not gathered from thornbushes, nor are grapes picked from a bramble bush. The good person out of the good treasure of his heart produces good, and the evil person out of his evil treasure produces evil, for out of the abundance of the heart his mouth speaks." —Luke 6:44-45

What is Jesus saying when he describes the person whose heart produces good as opposed to the person whose heart produces evil? *Jesus is saying that your situation is significant but it is not determinative of the quality of your moral response. It's what is inside you that determines how you will respond.*

Imagine that I have a glass full of water. When I hit the glass hard, water will come spilling out of it. Why is there water on the floor? It's not just because it was hit—that's only the external pressure. Water comes out of the cup because there was water in the cup. This illustrates an important biblical truth. When we get hit by life's hardships, what determines our response is what is inside of us. Do we have a good heart that trusts in Jesus? Or do we have an evil heart that trusts in ourselves?

At the end of the day, the human heart is searched by God, and people will reveal their character and their fundamental life choice, even through their diseases, disabilities, horrible nurture, cultural setting, and so forth. That's why we need a heart that is being transformed to be like Christ. The good news is that, because of God's mercy and grace, the gift of a new, good heart is ours for the asking.

October 19

But I say, walk by the Spirit, and you will not gratify the desires
of the flesh. —Galatians 5:16

Let's zero in on the issue of the heart. It is out of the heart that comes life. The wellspring of life and the wellspring of death both emerge out of the heart. I want you to have many different doors in to understanding this issue of the heart.

I want to zero in on one particular verb, which is the notion of desire—what we lust for, crave, demand, and believe we need. It all adds up to, "I want." Using the language of desires lets you get specific. Desires have an object. It was hugely helpful in my own sense of where I needed to repent to see, for example, that in a conflict I was desiring to be accurately understood and desiring vindication. I became frustrated and obsessed and pre-occupied if I didn't get what I wanted in a particular situation.

What is the desire that drives your anger? What do you want? What are your expectations? What are you after? Interpersonal conflict is driven by what we want and aren't getting. The Bible has a rich description of this linkage between the issue of the heart and our desires. You've got God-centered desires on one side of the equation, and on the other side, the desires of the flesh. *Desires of the flesh are opposed to God's rule over our lives. The fruit of the Spirit expresses submission to the desires of the Spirit.*

Romans 13:12–14 speaks to this struggle by telling us what to do next: "Let us cast off the works of darkness and put on the armor of light. . . . But put on the Lord Jesus Christ, and make no provision for the flesh, to gratify its desires."

October 20

Be not quick in your spirit to become angry,
for anger lodges in the heart of fools. —Ecclesiastes 7:9

One key to getting anger straight is to understand that when you are angry, *you* are doing something. Anger is not an "it." Anger is not just one part of you. Anger does not "happen" to you. You do anger.

Anger is a single complex system. It's something *you* do with all your heart, soul, mind, and body. You size something up in a flash, "I don't like that!" As your adrenaline surges, your body wakes up, heats up, tightens up. You feel intense emotions, which emote into your tone of voice, decibel level, body language, and facial expression. You think quickly, rehearsing what happened, imagining scenarios, evaluating, planning, and choosing. You go into action, choosing what to do and say (or not do and not say). Your desires and expectations are active. You want fairness, or to be proved right, or to be treated lovingly, or to get to your appointment on time, or to protect someone, or to get your way.

When anger goes astray, it says something about who is the center of the universe. When anger runs amok into temper, grousing, or bitterness, you don't just need a technique to calm yourself down. You don't just need other people to change. Your core motives must change. The god you worship (my will be done, my kingdom come . . . or else) must be overthrown.

The Most High God, his higher law, his loving mercies, and his higher purposes transform anger. Something miraculous happens when I no longer say, "My kingdom come, my will be done on earth." My motives no longer act in the God-usurping mode. *The mercy that humbles us begins to master us, and my universe returns to reality.*

October 21

Search me, O God, and know my heart!
Try me and know my thoughts!
And see if there be any grievous way in me,
and lead me in the way everlasting! —Psalm 139:23-24

Overthrowing the false god of your own will and way takes something much deeper than simply learning conflict-resolution skills, valuable as those are. It calls for more than altering how you talk to yourself, though that also will change. It takes more than finding some technique, recreation, or medication that works to calm you down. Sure, take a deep breath or count to ten. But motives are the goals around which you organize your life.

Motives are your core values and commitments, what you base your identity on. They shape and energize your emotions, thoughts, and actions. They determine how you treat people. They determine how you react to pain, loss, or threat (the provocations to anger). They determine how and why you get angry—and whether your anger is radiantly healthy or somehow diseased.

Motives are not only the fine china of plausible desires and honest hurt. They are also the steel and high explosives of all-consuming self-will. When anger goes bad, it's because motives operate in the godlike mode.

When God's larger purposes are in control, the poisonous evil of anger is neutralized. Anger becomes a servant of goodness. The anger becomes just, and the purposes become merciful to all who will turn and trust and become conformed to his image. He changes our motives.

October 22

Be angry and do not sin. —Ephesians 4:26a

Anger is the fighting emotion. Anger is the justice emotion. Anger is the deliver-the-oppressed-from-evil emotion. It stems from love for the needy. All of us come wired with a sense of justice. We can override it or pervert it.

Your sense of justice can be bent in many directions, for good or ill, but you cannot erase it. It's part of the original equipment in human nature. What's the term for this? "The image of God" is the shorthand way of describing the way we were all meant to be. You identify something wrong and harmful. It matters. You are created to get upset about it. You speak and act forcefully to address the problem. When human beings work this way, it's beautiful. It's constructive. Our anger is natural. It is a capacity given by creation in the image of the God who is just.

If only you and I got angry at the right time and in the right way. But, sadly, anger is "natural" in a second way. Creational good is entangled with and distorted by fallenness and innate evil that has become "second nature."

So to be human means you come created with a capacity for just anger. And to be human means you come fallen, with a bent toward bad anger. A lot of what makes anger so hard to sort out is our difficulty in figuring out and accounting for these two sides of human nature.

October 23

He does not deal with us according to our sins,
nor repay us according to our iniquities.
For as high as the heavens are above the earth,
so great is his steadfast love toward those who fear him;
as far as the east is from the west,
so far does he remove our transgressions from us. —Psalm 103:10–12

Forgiveness does not ignore what's wrong. It does not excuse what's wrong. It does not pretend that the person didn't really mean it. Instead, recognizing that a debt is owed, it forgives the debt.

What is the dynamic? Pay close attention to how Psalm 103:8–13 unfolds. It begins by remembering how God described himself to Moses when they met on Mount Sinai:

"The LORD is merciful and gracious, slow to anger [patient] and abounding in steadfast love" (v. 8).

These words express the genetic code of the Bible. This DNA comes in the flesh in Jesus Christ. This is who he is and what he is like. It is what it is like when you or I live out the image of God. A different life purpose makes all the difference. May it be said of you and of me, "He is merciful. She is gracious. He is patient. She abounds in steadfast love." Your anger experience changes as you are refashioned in this image.

"As far as the east is from the west, so far does he remove our transgressions from us" (v. 12).

His forgiveness is that wide—from one end of the universe to the other. To know such a Savior is to be in awe of him and to love him. *By receiving forgiveness in our need, we become able and willing to give forgiveness to others. Is it easy? No. One and done? Rarely. Entirely possible? Yes. Christ shows love to the loveless that they might lovely be.*

October 24

"Bear fruit in keeping with repentance." —Matthew 3:8

The Christian life is a lifelong "race of repentance,"* but we want to have arrived already. We don't like having to become different, but *repentance* is the Bible's word for "thorough, deep-seated, genuine change." It means turning from old ways to new. You wake up to find yourself living in God's universe, no longer sleepwalking through the universe of your desires and fears. A race of repentance calls for the ongoing reversal of our deepest instincts and opinions. You wake up again and again.

J. C. Ryle said that coming to vital Christian faith starts a lifelong quarrel inside a person: "You and sin must quarrel, if you and God are to be friends."** Imagine, I must quarrel with myself if I am to befriend God! To deal firmly with yourself is the hard way, the narrow way . . . and the only good way. Perhaps I should say it more strongly. To enter into war with yourself is the brutally wonderful, painstakingly delightful way. It sometimes feels like death, but always comes up life. The alternatives sometimes feel like life but always come up death.

Honest war with yourself comes paired with incomprehensible gifts. The peace of God passes all understanding, at the cost of all your fears! The love of God surpasses knowing, at the cost of every false love! Whatever you do, get this wisdom, this kingdom of God, this Christ! Nothing you could possibly desire compares. The cost is high: your very life. The reward is higher: no eye has seen, no ear has heard, no heart has conceived what God has prepared for those who love him.

---

* John Calvin's piercing phrase in *Institutes of the Christian Religion*, Book III 3:9, in John McNeil, ed., *Library of Christian Classics*, Vol. XX (Philadelphia: Westminster Press, 1960), 602.
** J. C. Ryle, *Holiness: Its Nature, Hindrances, Difficulties, and Roots* (London: James Clark, 1952), 70.

October 25

"I will not leave you as orphans; I will come to you. . . . Because I live, you also will live." —John 14:18-19

Therefore, preparing your minds for action, and being sober-minded, set your hope fully on the grace that will be brought to you at the revelation of Jesus Christ. —1 Peter 1:13

God's future grace to sinners demonstrates that he will come to us. How do you know that he will come for you, that he will make right all the wrongs that rise up within you? "We know that when he appears, we shall be like him, because we shall see him as he is" (1 John 3:2). The good news is not simply for the past and present. What Jesus will do reshapes what we do. For example, 1 Peter bases the transformational power of the Christian life now on what will happen in the future. "Set your hope completely on the grace to be brought to you at the revelation of Jesus Christ. As obedient children, do not be conformed to the former lusts which were yours in your ignorance" (1 Peter 1:13–14 NASB). How will you hang in over the long haul, growing wiser until the end? Future grace beckons you.

October 26

When the righteous cry for help, the Lord hears
and delivers them out of all their troubles.
The Lord is near to the brokenhearted
and saves the crushed in spirit. . . .

The Lord redeems the life of his servants;
none of those who take refuge in him will be condemned.
—Psalm 34:17–18, 22

God's past, present, and future grace to sufferers demonstrates that he hears the cry of the afflicted. Grace is not only a mercy to sinners, but a mercy to sufferers. Jesus dies for the wicked; he also defends the innocent, feeds the hungry, gives refuge to the broken, and heals the sick. How do you know that you are safe? "Moses said to God, 'Who am I, that I should go to Pharaoh?' . . . And [the Lord] said, 'I will be with you'" (Exodus 3:11–12). At the center of the Christian life is our need and God's protection. In the past, he showed such mercies, in part to give us hope today (1 Corinthians 10:11; Romans 15:4). Right now he helps, comforts, heals, and encourages. Someday he will act decisively to remove all heartache and bring joy to pass (Revelation 20:4). His mercies to the broken change the way you face whatever afflicts you.

October 27

Therefore be imitators of God, as beloved children. And walk in love,
as Christ loved us and gave himself up for us, a fragrant offering and
sacrifice to God. —Ephesians 5:1-2

God never tacks willpower and self-effort onto grace. His words are about all of life, not some religious sector. *What happens as the scope and relevance of your Bible expands? God's self-revelation becomes the environment you live in. His promises become the food you live on. God's commands become the life you live out.*

Many people think that emphasizing obedience to God's commands equates with moralism. But when God calls for our obedience and a holy life, does that mean he is ignoring or contradicting the grace of his own gospel? May it never be!

Free grace—past, present, and future—is effective grace. It intends to change us from our sins in the midst of our sufferings. The gracious Master, who learned obedience through what he suffered, remakes disciples who become like him. "In his image" is the formal phrase for becoming more honest, constructive, purposeful, and loving.

These are long journeys, but the direction of grace is toward obedience to God's law of love. None of these changes mean perfection until Jesus returns. You will always need mercies to be renewed every morning. But there is substantial healing amid the ongoing struggle. It isn't always dramatic. Small choices count. But the Spirit will produce his fruit in us, and biblical counseling serves such practical changes.

October 28

Therefore, if anyone is in Christ, he is a new creation. The old has passed away; behold, the new has come. —2 Corinthians 5:17

Truth awakens us to reality.

We must *know* the gravity of our condition as human beings. We tend to defect. We are false lovers. We are traitors—compulsively, blindly. We want the wrong things. We are doomed. We need rescue from ourselves, from what we bring on ourselves, from what others do to us. The twin evils of perversity and pain aren't a general theoretical problem. It's my specific problem, and yours, and the other person's too (Ecclesiastes 9:3).

Sin and suffering are what's wrong.

We must *know* the sheer goodness of what our Father has given us in Jesus Christ. To know Jesus in truth and love is to find the one thing worth finding, the one lasting happiness, the purpose of life.

His mercies make wrongs right.

We must know our calling as children of such a Father. Jesus announces his kingdom with the words, "Repent." That simply means, "Change." His grace and truth get about the business of changing us. We are called to live a new creation onto the stage of history, into the details of our lives. We are called to change and to change the world. We are called to build a wise community. We run a lifelong race of repentance and renewal, not just individually, but all together. Jesus intends to teach us how to live as "disciples" (changers, learners, students), so that we become his instruments of change in the lives of others.

October 29

Thus says the LORD:
"Cursed is the man who trusts in man
and makes flesh his strength,
whose heart turns away from the LORD.
He is like a shrub in the desert,and shall not see any good come.
He shall dwell in the parched places of the wilderness,
in an uninhabited salt land. —Jeremiah 17:5-6

This passage develops a wide-ranging metaphor for what life is like. It's a compelling visual picture of our basic core dilemma: "Cursed is the man who trusts in man and makes flesh his strength" (v. 5). In this context, the Lord is speaking to the fact that Israel is caught up in idolatry and false worship, and they're being allured by the worship patterns in their surrounding socio-cultural setting. In the face of threat, they are turning to Assyrians or Egyptians who have political military power. *In your life, that can apply to putting trust in others, putting trust in yourself, or putting trust in human abilities instead of placing all your trust in the Lord.*

What is the sad result? "He is like a shrub in the desert and shall not see any good come. He shall dwell in the parched places of the wilderness, in the uninhabited salt land" (v. 6). The English language can hardly capture how vivid a picture this is of absolute barrenness. It's a life that has nothing truly alive in it. Throughout this passage, there's a turning away from God and a turning toward trust in the arm of flesh and trust in idolatries. This is the graphic image that Jeremiah gives us for the nature of sin and where sin ends up. But words of hope are right around the corner. There is another way. We can turn to the Lord and live the blessed life under his care.

October 30

"Blessed is the man who trusts in the Lord,
whose trust is the Lord.
He is like a tree planted by water,
that sends out its roots by the stream,
and does not fear when heat comes,
for its leaves remain green,
and is not anxious in the year of drought,
for it does not cease to bear fruit." —Jeremiah 17:7–8

In comparison to yesterday's passage, the next part of Jeremiah 17 provides a dramatic contrast: *Blessed.* Being blessed is the consequence of a certain kind of life. "Blessed is the man who trusts in the Lord, whose trust is the Lord" (v. 7). Being blessed comes with this incredible promise: "He is like a tree planted by water, that sends out its roots by the stream, and does not fear when the heat comes, for its leaves remain green. And it is not anxious in the year of drought, for it does not cease to bear fruit" (v. 8). There is a reference to the situation: difficult, tough times, troubles. There's a year of drought—of heat, of things that are incredibly difficult.

But here we see a rich portrayal of the nature of faith—a living connection with the stream. In fact, the stream is actually God, isn't it? The water is God. *When you are connected to God, you are not afraid in the face of difficult situations. Your "leaves remain green"—you are fruitful in the year of drought.*

When you are in an extremely difficult, high-heat, high-threat situation, there is actually a way to be a fruit tree and not a cactus. There is a tight connection between the motivations of the human heart and the way a person lives. You get this vertical dimension—whom do you trust? That directly effects the horizontal dimension—the fruit of your life.

October 31

If then you have been raised with Christ, seek the things that are above,
where Christ is, seated at the right hand of God. Set your minds on
things that are above, not on things that are on earth. For you have died,
and your life is hidden with Christ in God. —Colossians 3:1-3

What does it mean to not bail on the hardships of life—on the heat—and instead to move toward problems and see them as opportunities for redemption? When you move toward a problem, you will be challenged to notice your relational style, the instinctive pattern of reactions by which you put your world together, the ways you view people, and how you use or abuse or avoid others. *As you move toward problems and people, God desires that you become able to relate to others with the kind of candor, openness, and genuine listening that reflects Jesus our Lord.* You are raised with Christ. Your life is hidden with Christ in God. You can become like Christ in a way that was never possible before.

But that tension, between the old and the new natures, still exists. You are in the process of transformation. It's always messy and complex, and it always takes time. One of the advantages of having a visual theology of the thorn bush and the fruit tree is that it forces you to reckon with how the heat—your suffering— is really important, but your sins are also really important. On the one hand, you see Christ at work in the good things you see in your life, particularly in taking to heart the promises of God or a significant Scripture. On the other hand, you see all the work that still needs to be done. But the promise remains: "Your life is hidden with Christ in God."

November 1

Repay no one evil for evil, but give thought to do what is honorable in the sight of all. If possible, so far as it depends on you, live peaceably with all. Beloved, never avenge yourselves, but leave it to the wrath of God, for it is written, "Vengeance is mine, I will repay, says the Lord."
—Romans 12:17–19

The Bible is realistic about life—there are hard things that happen to us, true wrongs are done to us, and they count. Look at how God describes what has happened when we are wronged. He calls it evil. After I name the evil done to me, then I can identify what's wrong in my response. This is my thorn bush, both root and fruit. There's a benefit to identifying what's wrong in my reactions and realizing that I am the one who wants what I want, and I am the one who does what I do. Nothing and no one makes me respond the way I do. Then confession is able to be very specific. I can name my sufferings and also confess my wrong responses.

The Psalms are full of the prayers of those who are dealing with being sinned against and their own response of bitterness and hostility. Like the psalmists, you too can name your sufferings and sins in one breath. God hears our sorrows and draws near to us despite our sins. *His gracious approach gives us the confidence to confess our sins and leave the evil done to us in his hands.*

November 2

The steadfast love of the Lord never ceases;
his mercies never come to an end;
they are new every morning;
great is your faithfulness. —Lamentations 3:22–23

The process of coming to see when and how we get off track and learning how to reorient ourselves to God is a great gift of wisdom. *We drift, but God teaches us to recalibrate our lives to his mercy. We awaken afresh to his strengthening and shielding care. The Lord's mercies are new every morning. So is our need.*

One of the things I love about the way the Bible portrays God's mercies is that they speak and act in two directions. He comes to us in our sorrows and troubles, vulnerability, and weakness. Because he is our refuge, we learn to name our troubles and bring our burdens to him (Psalm 28). Second, he comes to us in our sinfulness, drift, and blindness because he is wondrously unfair and does not deal with us as our sins deserve (Psalm 103). We learn to name our failings in confession.

I need a daily awakening. You need a daily awakening. He is my strength, and he wins the one victory that most counts. He is a help. He is a comfort, and he helps my soul. He is a guide and keeper and a pilot, and he hears my cry.

The fine china of Christians' lives are their sins, their sorrows, and the fact that the Savior maps directly into their needs. When you trust in Christ, there is a fundamental sense that there is a joy and a hope and a confidence that rests, not in I—the vulnerable and straying—but in the mercy of another.

November 3

Know this, my beloved brothers: let every person be quick to hear, slow to speak, slow to anger. —James 1:19

How do you come to know yourself or other people? In part, seek to know what people feel (not neglecting what people do, think, and so forth). *Learn to pay attention to experience and emotions. These are crucial components of who people are. They are signals that register what is happening to you and within you.*

The feeling of being overwhelmed, for example, often drives people to God, to self-evaluation, to seeking help. It has a cause you need to discover and has a "way of escape" you need to wrestle out because "God is faithful" (1 Corinthians 10:13). Is the feeling important? It sure is. It is the point of entry, where words of truth and deeds of love will often make contact with a person.

Wise living involves alertness to experience and emotion. The goal of such self-awareness is not introspective self-preoccupation. Such awareness is rather a matter of integrity and honesty. It is meant to lead you to those twin radical "extraspections": faith and love.

Two of the most helpful kinds of questions to ask yourself or another are these:

1. What joys, highlights, delights, purposes, or glad anticipations fill you as you think of the past, present, or future?

2. What sorrows, burdens, guilt, frustrations, hardships, struggles, preoccupations, or fears press upon you as you think of the past, present, or future?

These are "feeling-toned" questions that invite people to become honest. Such questions also set the stage for more specific love, counsel, encouragement, confrontation, and intercession or praise to God. They are starting points, not stopping points.

November 4

Our culture besieges us with voices that comment on what we look like, what we ought to look like, and the blessings and curses that presumably attend success or failure. Our mass media culture silently beguiles us with images of the same. We are taught "good and evil" regarding our appearance by what we hear and see. If you want to expose the lies in order to bring liberating truth, learn to dig out that mosaic of false faiths and felt needs that drives people into bondage. Enculturating lies usurp the functions of God's truth.

The Word of God speaks extensively to such issues of "enculturation," of slavery to the falsely prophetic images and voices generated by the world and its systems of distorted value and stigma. In several places Scripture singles out the issue of beauty in a pointed way. Proverbs 31:10–31 portrays the true beauty of fearing, trusting, and loving the Lord our Redeemer. It comments on charm's deceitfulness and beauty's emptiness. The true and enduring beauty of character, peaceableness, wisdom, trust, and love breathe forth from those proverbs. First Peter 3:1–6 similarly redefines beauty. It contrasts the cultural image ("external adornment") with the true and imperishable image of God in the heart.

True beauty is fearless; it can never be ravaged by time or affliction; it can never be made insecure. The Word of God abounds with wonderful passages intended to renew minds and hearts, causing us to serve and aim for a different image.

November 5

And he said to his disciples, "Therefore I tell you, do not be anxious about your life, what you will eat, nor about your body, what you will put on." —Luke 12:22

There are lots of things to worry about. In fact, this is one of those topics where I know the shoe fits you! We all put our own spin on the temptation to worry. Money is as good an issue as any to get at what people most fear and at how they view Jesus. *How will we pay for college? Are we going to get a job? How are we going to afford kids?* Then there's the 401K or the unexpected dentist bill. There's *always* something to worry about.

What you see in common with all the things we worry about—every single thing—is that they are *uncertain.* Jesus explains our worries, however, not by pointing to how uncertain life is, but by pointing to something *in us. We lose sight of God because what we want (and worry about) is the only thing we see.* When faith is dying out, greed and worry come to life. When anxious greed comes to life, it kills off faith. A worrier is storing "treasure" in the wrong place.

Jesus gets very tender: "Your Father knows you need these things. . . . Don't be afraid, little flock, because your Father has chosen gladly to give . . ." (Luke 12:30, 32 NASB). You can throw your weight on this. Jesus makes it as personal, intimate, and generous as possible. He knows your situation. He knows your personality. Cast your cares on him, because he cares for you (1 Peter 5:7).

November 6

For it is God who works in you, both to will and to work for his good pleasure. —Philippians 2:13

What do you crave, want, pursue, wish, long for, hope to get, feel you need, or passionately desire? God has an interpretation of this that cuts to the marrow of who you are and what you live for. He sees our hearts as an embattled kingdom ruled either by one kind of desire or by another kind. On the one hand, what lusts of the flesh hijack your heart from God's rule? On the other hand, what holy passions express your love for God? Our desires are not a given, but a fundamental choice.

God must show us how to properly interpret our wants, because we are compulsive misinterpreters: we don't want the true interpretation. Our desires are often idolatrous cravings to get good gifts (overthrowing or ignoring the Giver). Sometimes they are intense desires for the Giver himself as supremely more important than whatever good gifts we might gain or lose from his hand. To examine desires is one of the most fruitful ways to come at the topic of motivation. Which will triumph, the natural deviancy of the lusts of the flesh or the restored sanity of the desires of the Spirit? Christ's apostles have the greatest confidence that only the resources of the gospel of grace and truth possess sufficient depth and power to change us in the ways we most need changing. *The mercies of God work to forgive and then to change what is deeply evil, but even more deeply curable by God's hand and voice. The inworking power of grace qualitatively transforms our very desires. We can be fundamentally rewired by the merciful presence of the Messiah.*

November 7

For the word of God is alive and active. Sharper than any double-edged sword, it penetrates even to dividing soul and spirit, joints and marrow; it judges the thoughts and attitudes of the heart. —Hebrews 4:12

Lusts of the flesh (cravings or pleasures) is a summary term for what is wrong with us in God's eyes. In sin, people turn from God to serve what they want. By grace, people turn to God from their cravings.

The New Testament writers use this term as a comprehensive category for the human dilemma. It will pay us to think carefully about its manifold meanings. First John 2:16 contrasts the love of the Father with "all that is in the world—the lust of the flesh and the lust of the eyes and the boastful pride of life" (NIV). In each of these passages, behavior intimately connects to motive, and motive to behavior.

Specific ruling desires—lusts, cravings, or pleasures—create bad fruit. Inordinate desires explain and organize diverse bad behavior and mental processes: words, actions, emotions, attitudes, etc.

Are preferences, wishes, desires, longings, hopes, and expectations always sinful then? Of course not. The moral issue always turns on whether the desire takes on a ruling status. If it does, it will produce visible sins: anger, grumbling, immorality, and despair. The things people desire are delightful as blessings received from God, but terrible as rulers. They make good goods but bad gods. They beguile, promising blessing, but delivering sin and death.

In the light of self-knowledge before God's face, the gospel offers many promises: mercy, help, and the Shepherd's care in progressive sanctification. Repentance, faith, and obedience become vigorous and intelligent when we see both our inner cravings and our outward sins in light of God's mercies.

November 8

Teach me your way, LORD, that I may rely on your faithfulness; give me an undivided heart, that I may fear your name. —Psalm 86:11 NIV

Can you change what you want? Yes and Amen! This is central to the work of the Holy Spirit. You will always desire, love, trust, believe, fear, obey, value, and serve something. You are motivated when you feel desire. God does not anesthetize us; he redirects our desires. The Holy Spirit works to change the configuration and status of our desires, as he leads us with an intimate hand. He tells you to be ruled by other, different desires. God promises to change what you really want! God insists that he be first, and all lesser loves be radically subordinate.

God challenges the things that everybody, everywhere eagerly pursues (Matthew 6:32). Consider our characteristic passions: desires of the body: health, food, clothing, sexual pleasure, and rest. Desires of the mind: happiness, being loved, meaning, respect, success, and control. Can these cravings really be changed? The Bible says yes and points us to the promises of God: to indwell us with power, to write truth on our hearts, and to pour out his love in our hearts.

The evil in our desires does not lie in what we want, but in the fact that we want it too much. Our desires for good things seize the throne, becoming idols that replace the King. God refuses to serve our instinctive longings but commands us to be ruled by other longings. *What God commands, he provides the power to accomplish: he works in us both the willing and the doing of his good pleasure (Philippians 2:12–13).*

November 9

"I will sprinkle clean water on you, and you shall be clean from all your uncleannesses, and from all your idols I will cleanse you. And I will give you a new heart, and a new spirit I will put within you. And I will remove the heart of stone from your flesh and give you a heart of flesh."
—Ezekiel 36:25-26

Jesus is in the rehab business. When he takes a broken thing into his hands, it begins to work again. That's so of an individual. It's so of a relationship. It's so of a church.

Obviously, this does not mean instant, complete change right now, in the twinkling of an eye. It's a lifelong process—until the day when we see Jesus. Then he will wrap it all up in a twinkling (1 John 3:1–3; Revelation 20–21).

It's less obvious that we don't become as good as new. We don't go back to just the way things were before. Instead, we are *qualitatively changed* in this process of repair. We are not restored, brought back to a previous condition, but we are *redeemed*, turned into something new, something better and different than we ever were.

The breaking and remaking leave marks on us—just as scars remain on Jesus's hands, just as Jesus never loses fundamental sympathy for the human plight with all its weakness. We come out different in the process. *We are marked—and so become able to comfort others whatever their troubles, as we have been comforted in our troubles.* So the very best gifts of God arise against the backdrop of your darkest need.

November 10

For by the grace given me I say to every one of you: Do not think of yourself more highly than you ought, but rather think of yourself with sober judgment, in accordance with the faith God has distributed to each of you. —Romans 12:3 NIV

Change calls for self-knowledge. But we have a hard time with self-knowledge. Here are four tendencies that sabotage this process.

First, pride spins webs of self-delusion. My perspective and my way of doing things seem intuitively plausible—if not the sum of all righteousness! To know myself as I truly am, I must come to know myself through the eyes of someone outside of myself—the God who searches and weighs every heart.

Second, we busy and distract ourselves. We often don't take the time to stop, look, listen, and consider. Our responsibilities and worries consume us. Entertainment offers us a wide choice of narcotics. Either way, we live mindlessly. We're either too numb or too wired to live an examined life.

Third, some of us are activistic. We live mindfully—but what's on our minds is the compelling press of opportunities, needs, problems to solve. There is so much to be done! Restless activism gets a lot done, but it never produces heartfelt patience or the ability to wisely enter another person's struggles.

Fourth, some of us are introspective. We live mindfully—but what's on our minds is the fascinating flood of experiences, feelings, insights, moods, interactions. The insights are mostly self-referential. Morbid introspection does not lead out into faith and love.

Biblical change, however, makes you into a man or woman who sparkles with patience, kindness, and clarity. You're not self-deluded and self-absorbed. You're both active and self-knowing, but neither activistic nor introspective. True self-knowledge makes you radically *extraspective* toward God in faith, toward others in love.

November 11

Not that I have already obtained this or am already perfect, but I press
on to make it my own, because Christ Jesus has made me his own.
Brothers, I do not consider that I have made it my own. But one thing I
do: forgetting what lies behind and straining forward to what lies ahead,
I press on toward the goal for the prize of the upward call of God in
Christ Jesus. —Philippians 3:12–14

The kinds of things that I struggle with are analogous to the kinds of things that you struggle with. The ways that Jesus meets me are analogous to the ways he meets you. Analogous, but not identical. God seems to love variety. You and I do not reduce to a category. Our Father is raising children, and every child I've ever known is unique. You cannot live someone else's story.

How on earth did I change? I was changed because God intervened personally. I was changed because words of Scripture invited me into Christ. I was changed because a friend was faithful and honest. I was changed because of failure, guilt, suffering, and disillusionment. I changed because I turned from sin to Christ.

How did God work? God spoke and acted into my harried, anxious experience. He addressed me pointedly, repeatedly, and patiently over days, months, and years. A suite of complementary truths slowly took root, blossomed, and bore fruit.

Your life, too, is lived (and re-scripted) in the details—just like all the people in Scripture. *Your Savior and Shepherd meets you in the particulars of your need for saving and shepherding.* He saves and sanctifies in specifics, not in theological generalities. Every person's life is a little bit or even a whole lot different from other people, and God meets you right there with his gracious, sanctifying purposes.

November 12

Be angry, and do not sin. —Psalm 4:4a

When we talk about anger, we are really talking about the problem of evil. There are evils that are worth reacting to. But the problem lies in how we react to those things that are wrong. Unraveling and fixing anger is a long and messy process. As you read Scripture, you'll see the issue of anger is always on the table.

The DNA at the heart of anger, whether good anger or bad, is that something displeases you, it matters, and it's wrong. But there is too much wrong with how our anger comes out. It's too destructive, whether it's irritation, bitterness, or outright violence.

Jesus gets angry in Scripture. Unbelief matters to him, and he stands against it. When people stand in the way of him serving and helping children, peasant women, and the sick, he gets mad. He gets mad when the worship of the one true and living God becomes a sideshow of buying and selling. Because he cares so much, he gets upset at the things that are wrong. You can learn to respond to true wrongs the way Jesus does.

Here is how Scripture tells us to handle our anger: be slow to anger (James 1:19)—not hot-tempered. It says not to let the sun go down on your anger (Ephesians 4:26)—be quick to resolve things. *Instead of feeding your anger or trying to get rid of it all together, there is a third way forward: constructive displeasure. Get differently angry. Instead of overreacting, seek to react appropriately and constructively.*

November 13

Beloved, never avenge yourselves, but leave it to the wrath of God, for it
is written, "Vengeance is mine, I will repay, says the Lord."
—Romans 12:19

He will send from heaven and save me;
he will put to shame him who tramples on me.
God will send out his steadfast love and his faithfulness! —Psalm 57:3

I wish we'd hear more sermons on how the wrath of God is something to set our hope on. Part of understanding that God is our refuge and defender is knowing that God's wrath goes to bat for us. He will set you free from the very things that cause the deepest pain and suffering—he will deal with the wrongs of this life, both the wrongs done to you and the wrongs committed by you.

Concerning the wrongs done to you, God says through passages like Romans 12:19, "Don't get even. I will repay. I'll take care of it. I'll fix it." You don't have to be about the business of making things all right. Instead, you can be about the business of loving.

Concerning your own sin, God is committed to keep contending with you. He contends with your sins, he contends with your unbelief, and he keeps telling you about himself to rattle you out of your slump. It's the most loyal opposition you could ever imagine. *He is willing to oppose you in order to make you into his wonderful image. His wonderful displeasure is our hope.*

November 14

Refrain from anger, and forsake wrath!
Fret not yourself; it tends only to evil. —Psalm 37:8

When considering the problem of anger, what pushes your buttons? It could be something minor or something really big. How do you react? Do you scream or brood, attack or withdraw? It takes some courage to stop and acknowledge what happened and how you responded.

What are your buttons? The Bible is exceedingly rich in wanting us to understand the character of those buttons, because they always have to do with how you and God are getting along. In order to get stuck in bitterness, for example, you must forget who God is. This doesn't mean that you don't, in theory, believe in him and that this is his world, but functionally you are erasing his existence.

As you live out a lifetime of honest processing, expect to see patterns to your anger. You may get really uptight about money issues. Your anger may come from not being noticed and not getting the credit you deserve. Perhaps it comes from being inconvenienced.

It is into this world of buttons, button-pushers, and reactions that the living God speaks and acts. This world has a twofold source of evil—the evil that comes at us and the evil that comes from within us. God steps into that world of double evil and intends to give us a proper sense of perspective to understand our sufferings, provocations, and sins. *As you discover your reasons for anger, this opens the door to an honest relationship with God where you acknowledge your need for mercy and help.* In a culture where reacting and anger come easily, let's rebel against what comes easy and do what is hard—whatever small obedience God puts in front of you.

November 15

For I consider that the sufferings of this present time are not worth comparing with the glory that is to be revealed to us. —Romans 8:18

Anger at God is profitably examined by asking, "What do you want and believe?" You will invariably find that your heart is controlled by particular cravings and lies that have been substituted for the living and true God. For example, if I crave marriage and believe God will reward my devotion to him with a wife, my heart sets itself up for anger at God. Anger will come when the desire is not satisfied and the belief proves unwarranted.

Nowhere in the Bible do we find a shred of evidence that God ever truly betrays us. The Bible discusses suffering constantly, but it always shows us that any apparent "betrayal" by God must be seen in the context of his larger purposes.

Certainly suffering hurts—by definition. Anger toward tyrants and the arch-tyrant is heartily warranted. And groaning (to God, in faith and hope) about our sufferings is heartily warranted. But God has never promised freedom from tears, mourning, crying, and pain—or from the evils that cause them—until the great day when life and joy triumph forever over death and misery. The interweaving of God's glory and our well-being is far bigger than people imagine. Have God-ragers believed false promises or overlaid their own expectations upon God? Have they then become angry at a "disappointing" God, even confusing his actions and motives with Satan's and with evil people who imitate the devil's cruelty?

To really believe in God's sovereignty is to gain an unshakable foundation for trust in the midst of even hellish torments, let alone the milder pains.

November 16

Be not far from me,
for trouble is near,
and there is none to help. —Psalm 22:11

Losses are a particular kind of hardship or pain. Some good thing—something you really value, love, and deeply enjoy—proves to be fragile. It proves to be temporary. And then even unrecoverable. You valued it, but you have it no longer. And that hurts.

The Bible gives you the exact help you need when you face the loss of every good thing. These good, temporary things will in fact pass away, and the Bible is realistic about that. But the God of the Bible is also committed to enter into and speak into our pain and meet us in these realities.

What choice will you make next? Which path are you on in the face of these inescapable realities of loss? Are you going to believe that your pain is pointless, and your life is empty, or are you going to find a hope that is indestructible?

Those who fear God, who keep his commandments, who understand his grace, who receive his mercies, know he has loved us and entered our plight. He has been tempted like we are. He has suffered what we have suffered. The foundation of our hope is in Jesus who actually lost his life as a man and experienced grief and heartache and anguish. Psalm 22 became his prayer. It can be your prayer as well.

November 17

The Lord is my strength and my shield;
in him my heart trusts, and I am helped;
my heart exults,
and with my song I give thanks to him.
—Psalm 28:7

Facing a severe trial such as a dire diagnosis, there are many ways to lose the spiritual battle, reverting to the darkness of flesh, world, and devil. Will we go blind to God, becoming absorbed in the immediate threat? Will we worry, feeling an undercurrent of anxiety or even stark fear? Will we obsess about medical intervention? Will we go into denial? Will we get irritable with each other, exacerbating the tension by bickering? There are many ways to revert to the darkened understanding that expresses alienation from the life of God (Ephesians 4:17–18).

We could revert, or we could face our troubles the way Ephesians and Psalms face trouble. In this situation, Psalm 28 takes us in hand. It is one of many psalms in which human need finds God's strength and shielding care. This psalm walks us through our battle with the world, flesh, and devil during a difficult time. The first few lines give voice to a sense of utter need and great vulnerability in the face of threat. Need cries out to one able and willing to help. In the next few lines, David grapples with the specific evils animating this plea for mercy. We need to take up the shield of faith "in all circumstances." Psalm 28:3–5 flags human enemies. But the same pattern of faith applies when we face other grievous circumstances where we need God's strength and shield.

This psalm moves quickly across the emotional register, arriving at joyful peace and trust far more quickly than we tend to. Scripture is giving us a template, not a timetable. David is showing us the direction in which to walk.

November 18

But to all who did receive him, who believed in his name, he gave the
right to become children of God. —John 1:12

When you come to God through trusting in Jesus, he gives you a new identity. You become part of the family of God. You are his dearly loved child. Listen to what the apostle John says about your identity: "How great is the love the Father has lavished on us, that we should be called children of God! And that is what we are!" (1 John 3:1 NIV). You have a perfect Father in heaven who loves you and wants to fill your life with the good gift of himself (Luke 11:13).

Experiencing Jesus's presence and love will give you the courage to see that the story of your life is bigger than your suffering. The difficult things that happen to you are not the last word on who you are and where your life is going. They are a significant part of your story, but they are not *the most* significant part of your story. This is only one part of the new story of your life that Jesus is writing.

The Gospel of John closes with this verse: "Jesus did many other things as well. If every one of them were written down, I suppose that even the whole world would not have room for the books that would be written" (John 21:25 NIV). Your life is one of those books that John was talking about. You're continuing the story of what "Jesus did." Jesus showed up and did something—he redeemed you and is still redeeming you so you can love, forgive, and do good to those around you.

November 19

Finally, be strong in the Lord and in the strength of his might. Put on the
whole armor of God, that you may be able to stand against the schemes
of the devil. —Ephesians 6:10–11

It is important that we rightly envision spiritual warfare as mounting an offense, not playing defense. Popular teaching makes associations about the protective aspect of individual weapons of spiritual warfare. But the Bible uses this imagery to portray the Lord overthrowing the powers-that-be in a darkened world. Christ comes bringing mercy to the humble and mayhem to the haughty. Paul is not describing how to maintain a defensive posture.

Spiritual warfare is what happens when he enlists us in his cause and equips us to join his battle. It's about light invading darkness. Often when people envision spiritual warfare, they think, "I'm under attack" and that is true. Satan does have his wily ways and he is out to get us. But we are also God's invading army, and we are on the attack. We are bringing light into a dark world. The children of light, the army of light, the servants of light are on the offensive.

In 2 Corinthians, Paul references all of his hardships, but then talks about how he has the "weapons of righteousness for the right hand and for the left" (2 Corinthians 6:7 NIV). Paul is going to war. The war is not just coming to him. *But what are the weapons he fights with? They are humility, love, truth, courage, faithfulness, goodness, and wisdom. These are unusual weapons. We fight like Jesus did when he came to this dark world. He is the Lord of light and he calls us to bring the light of his love into this dark world.*

November 20

Now may the God of peace himself sanctify you completely, and may
your whole spirit and soul and body be kept blameless at the coming of
our Lord Jesus Christ. He who calls you is faithful; he will surely do it.
—1 Thessalonians 5:23–24

Scripture portrays sanctification (growth in holiness and Christ-
likeness) in a range of colors and shades. But how do people actually change? We are saved from outside ourselves, and we are saved
from ourselves. But the burning question remains: how are disciples
made? It is a practical theology question, a ministry question, a life-
lived question. Could the sole key to sanctification be to continually
revisit how our broken relationship with God was reconciled by the
work of Jesus? A vast Bible, centuries of pastoral experience, and innumerable testimonies bear joint witness that there is a lot more to it.

Here is my core premise: *Ministry "unbalances" truth for the
sake of relevance; theology "rebalances" truth for the sake of comprehensiveness.**

What I mean is this: You can't say everything all at once—and
you shouldn't try. Say one relevant thing at a time. This is because
the Gospels capture a series of ministry moments in which Jesus
gives people what they need and can handle. By saying one thing,
not everything, he is always challenging, always life-rearranging,
always nourishing those who are listening.

The second half of the core premise is equally important. *The
task of theological reflection is to abstract, generalize, and "rebalance"
truth for the sake of comprehensiveness.* Balance—whether topical
(systematic theology) or narrative (biblical theology)—protects us
from exaggerating, ignoring, or overgeneralizing. Every Christian
doctrine and every part of the story matters. This has implications
for maturing our faith and love. Jesus claims our loyalty, commands
our attention, elicits our humility. He exposes us, delights us, masters us. We love this Jesus, and he compels us to grow in him.

---

* I am indebted to Rev. James Petty for this way of putting it.

November 21

Bless those who persecute you; bless and do not curse them. . . . Do not be overcome by evil, but overcome evil with good. —Romans 12:14, 21

The experience of being wronged is a door to understanding the sanctification process. Being wronged by another creates a major crucible experience. The heat is on high. There are two possible responses to being wronged. On the one hand, many people respond with some of the most flagrant sins that are possible: hatred, murder, criminality, and vengeance. But, out of that same crucible, there can come the most beautiful, brightest graces of which a human being is capable. There, in the crucible of being wronged, you can see the fragrance of the gospel, appearing in people's lives. You see mercy, forgiveness, courage, endurance, and the ability to persevere in hope in the midst of terrible pain and loss.

To be sinned against is expected in a fallen world. It always happens. We are sinners who live among sinners, and we will be wronged. Those who are evildoers, users, misusers, abusers, the violent, the hostile, the treacherous—God's anger is toward them. *In Romans 12, we are promised that God will right all wrongs and will destroy all that is evil. This is the hope of his children who are suffering and is at the core of why I do not need to be the vengeance-taker.* I do not need to be the vigilante. I do not need to get my pound of flesh, because there's one whom I trust to deal more than fairly, sometimes mercifully, with evil. Starting with this truth opens the door to responding to deep wrong with a clear-eyed mercy that gives off the lasting fragrance of heaven.

November 22

No, in all these things we are more than conquerors through him who loved us. —Romans 8:37

There's something about the experience of evil which can actually purify our faith, because it can force us to set our hopes on the only place our hopes should be set—Christ himself. Then we can counsel, comfort, and encourage other people in whatever they're facing, because of the way we have received comfort in the particular things that we face. Whether we are facing a relatively mild evil or something heinous, any step, no matter how small, toward the light of God's love can be shared with others.

The second half of Romans 8 speaks of how, in the context of suffering, we gain a settled hope. Our character is formed, and the love of God is poured out into our hearts through the Holy Spirit who has been given to us. It's counterintuitive, but in the context of being wronged, I can learn that God is for me, and who can be against me? The result: a settling of our hope and the transformation of our lives. Over time, there's a purposeful goodness that comes out of the furnace of affliction. *Given the passage of time and the pursuit of a living God, people are actually able to say, "God did work all things for good in my life, even through something very, very hard that I would never wish to go through again."*

November 23

*Though I walk in the midst of trouble,
you preserve my life;
you stretch out your hand against the wrath of my enemies,
and your right hand delivers me.* —Psalm 138:7

A sufferer's primal need is to hear God talking and to experience him purposefully at work. *When you hear, take to heart, and know that he is with you, everything changes, even when nothing has changed in your situation.* Left to yourself, you blindly react. Your troubles obsess you, distract you, depress you. You grasp at straws. God seems invisible, silent, far away. Threat and pain and loss cry out long and loud. Faith seems inarticulate. Sorrow and confusion broadcast on all the channels. It's hard to remember anything else, hard to put into words what is actually happening, hard to feel any of the force of who Jesus Christ is.

This struggle is not surprising. I suspect we've all felt that way sometimes. Words that someone else finds meaningful and thinks might be helpful are just words, empty sounds with no meaning.

But God works to reverse the downward spiral into deafness and despair. The Holy Spirit works powerfully and intimately in this age of new creation to communicate God's words, presence, and love into our hearts. Sufferers awaken to hear their Father's voice and to see their Savior's hand in the midst of significant suffering.

You need to hear what God says, and to experience that he does what he says. You need to feel the weight and significance of what he is about. Though you walk through the valley of the shadow of death, you need fear no evil. He is with you. Goodness and mercy will follow you. This *is* what he is doing. God's voice speaks deeper that what hurts, brighter than what is dark, more enduring than what is lost, truer than what has happened.

November 24

Oh give thanks to the Lord, for he is good;
for his steadfast love endures forever! —1 Chronicles 16:34

A Thanksgiving Prayer

Father in heaven, we thank you that you have poured out many kindnesses upon us—all the blessings of this life, our creation, preservation, and above all, your inestimable love in the redemption of the world through our Lord Jesus Christ. *We thank you today for the means of grace, for the hope of glory, for the many kindnesses, the good things that you have done in forgiving our sins, in healing our diseases, in redeeming us from the pit, in crowning us with steadfast love and mercy so that we would soar as on eagles' wings.*

We thank you, our Lord, that you utterly understand our plight. You know that we are but dust. You know that we are vulnerable. We are weak, mortal, prone to sin, prone to blindness, easily baffled. We thank you for invading our lives with light and life. You've come to make us new. You strengthen us for the battle. You give us the grace we need in our time of need. You shield us, you grow us, you do not give up on us, and you will complete what you have begun. We are grateful and we pray that you would look even this very day on us one and all. That we, as your children would grow in wisdom in favor with God and man. We would learn to love you more steadily, to hold in our hearts the struggles of other people, that we would be people of genuine kindness. People who are patient, people able to endure, people able to forgive by the mercies of Christ himself. And we do pray in the name of this great Messiah. Amen.

November 25

Therefore, as you received Christ Jesus the Lord, so walk in him, rooted and built up in him and established in the faith, just as you were taught, abounding in thanksgiving. —Colossians 2:6-7

"Thank you."

Simple to say, profoundly significant. And strangely hard to do. When we don't say, "Thank you," it's extremely revealing. Of all the valid things that might be said about the ignorance and waywardness of our hearts, Paul singles out ingratitude for special mention: "They didn't thank God" (Romans 1:21). It's as if "You never said thank you" is the transgression that clinches the case against us.

Thankfulness is a jewel in the crown of life. Colossians is a short letter but being thankful pops up seven times. "Thank you" is one of humility's core instincts.

Why wouldn't I say thank you? Perhaps I don't feel thankful. I feel entitled. I don't recognize who's giving me every good thing. I don't want to need help or depend on anyone. I want to take all the credit for myself, thank you very much, and no thanks to you. But when I awaken to who gives me good gifts, I'm grateful.

And gratitude is a primary expression of sanity. First Corinthians 4:7 teaches us to say, What do I have that is not a gift?! James 1:17 teaches us to see that every good gift is from above, coming down from our Father.

So what are you thankful for? Think about that.

November 26

The aim of our charge is love that issues from a pure heart and a good conscience and a sincere faith. —1 Timothy 1:5

Recently, this familiar sentence has been my daily companion in the Holy Spirit's discipling work. Here, Paul describes the goal of all ministry. This is what holiness looks like. This is what sanctification aims to become. This transformation of both behavior and motive is entirely rooted in sure promises of ongoing blessing.

Paul charges me to consider others because I am awake to God. Sanctification means pointedly, freely, genuinely loving other people. *Lord, help me to stop, to care, to notice, to listen, to express candid appreciation, to share my life.* And he helps. This goal has marked my conscious intentions when I've participated in meetings, when I've chatted with coworkers, when I've conversed in face-to-face counseling, when I've come home. These words have helped me to treat others well. Being indifferent, or opinionated, or avoidant, or preoccupied comes easy. But it is a bit of holiness when I am happy to see someone, when I ask a question and mean it, when I listen attentively, when I genuinely affirm, when I push back candidly and constructively.

Caring for others (horizontal sanctification) arises from reorientation to God (vertical sanctification). I have been consciously reflecting and seeking the three ways this command describes our reorientation to God. *A pure heart.* Father, make me less divided by competing loyalties and agendas, by unruly desires and anxieties. *A good conscience.* Lord, attune my conscience so that I weigh all things the way you weigh them. Imbue my conscience with Christ's merciful, redeeming purposes. *A sincere faith.* Holy Spirit, make me trust you in need, in gratitude, in joy, in dependence.

When we ask anything according to his will, he hears us, and we will be sanctified.

November 27

This I know, that God is for me. —Psalm 56:9b

Learning how God is for you and with you is foundational for every Christian. And there are so many different ways he shows it! Even the fact that he disciplines, reproves, and chastises us (Hebrews 12:5–14) demonstrates his fatherly love and hands-on commitment to pursue our welfare and sanctification. God gets our attention when life doesn't go well, or when the conscience rightly stings. He keeps working with us—using both comfort and reproof in their proper place—so that we learn to "strive for peace with everyone, and for the holiness without which no one will see the Lord." Does that contradict the incalculable flood of fatherly mercies expressed in Psalm 103? No. *His chastisement is one more purposeful mercy, and the Christian life dwells within all the riches of mercy.*

It is not surprising that God's way of working touches the most intimate, vulnerable acts of relationship with him. When I feel the sting of conscience, and directly confess and repent of my sins, I do not usually remind myself of justification by the work of Christ. What powerfully helps me is how Psalm 25:11 brings together a candid sense of need with the immediacy of God's person and promises: "For your name's sake, pardon my iniquities for they are very great."

But I dare not extrapolate my exact experience of God's mercies to everyone else. One pattern of Christ's working (even a pattern common to many people) should not overshadow all the other patterns. Scripture and the Holy Spirit play a 47-string concert harp, using all ten fingers, and sounding all the notes of human experience. Wise ministry, like growth in wisdom, means learning to play on all the strings, not harping on one note.

November 28

All Scripture is breathed out by God and profitable for teaching, for
reproof, for correction, and for training in righteousness, that the man of
God may be complete, equipped for every good work.
—2 Timothy 3:16–17

*G*od speaks to all of us together in public ministry of Word and
prayer. So we participate in worship. We listen well to
faithful preaching and teaching. We humbly receive our Lord's
Supper. We intercede together to our Father who gives good
gifts. Psalm 23 becomes a proclamation and corporate prayer:
"Lord, you are our shepherd. When we walk in dark places, we
fear no evil because you are with us!"

God speaks to each of us in private ministry of Word and prayer.
So each of us reads and reflects on Scripture. You meditate and
take truth to heart. You journal your insights, concerns, troubles, sins, prayers, joys, gratitude. You seek the Lord personally.
You take thought for how you trust, how you confess, how you
live wisely this day.

*God speaks to you (and through you) in interpersonal ministries
of Word and prayer.* You can seek honest friendships. You can ask
for help and ask how you can help. You can listen well. You give
help. You engage in the give and take of a small group. You seek
for yourself or offer someone else a season of counseling. You
seek or offer ongoing mentoring. You are intentional about life-
on-life caring for one another.

November 29

For whatever was written in former days was written for our instruction,
that through endurance and through the encouragement of the
Scriptures we might have hope. —Romans 15:4

It is a marvel how personally the Bible applies. The words pointedly address the concerns of long-ago people in faraway places, facing problems that no longer exist. They had no difficulty seeing the application. What they read was personal application. But nothing in the Bible is written directly to you or about what you face. We are reading someone else's mail. Yet the Bible repeatedly affirms that these words are also written for us (Romans 15:4). The Spirit reapplies Scripture in a timely way now.

Furthermore, the Bible is about God, not you. The essential subject matter is the triune Redeemer Lord, culminating in Jesus Christ. When Jesus "opened their minds to understand the Scriptures" (Luke 24:45), he showed how everything written—creation, promises, commands, history, sacrificial system, psalms, proverbs—reveals him. We are reading someone else's biography. Yet that very story demonstrates how he includes us within his story. Jesus is the Word of God applied—all wisdom embodied. As his disciples, we learn to similarly apply the Bible, growing up into his image. The Spirit rescripts our lives by teaching us who God is and what he is doing.

Personal application proves wise when you reckon with these marvels. *The Bible was written to others—but speaks to you. The Bible is about God—but draws you in. Your challenge is always to reapply Scripture afresh, because God's purpose is always to rescript your life.*

November 30

Your words were found, and I ate them,
and your words became to me a joy
and the delight of my heart. —Jeremiah 15:16a

Let me say two things about how to read Scripture. First, I encourage you to sit with the text and seek God and ponder. Perhaps on a first read it's either strange or feels irrelevant or just doesn't seem to connect. Sit with it for a while. God's Word is about life and people and a Redeemer and how it all connects. So sit with that and ask God himself to help you understand it. That will often bear fruit, and you'll be completely surprised by how a passage can become electrifying.

Second, feel free to go somewhere else in Scripture. Most of us have certain go-to passages, and they are there for a reason. Without fail I can get traction from Psalms 23, 40, and 103, as well as Philippians 4 and 2 Corinthians 1. *There are certain passages of Scripture that are so universally applicable to our daily lives that I can be unashamed to abandon my reading plan and go somewhere familiar, because I know I need the Bread of Life.* I'm perfectly willing to shift gears. We're not wed to a reading plan—a reading plan is a tool helping me to access the living God who speaks.

With that being said, after twenty years of reading Scripture at the chunk level, rather than the verse level, I find I'm different in ways that are hard to quantify. There's a cumulative effect to the way God works. So go read those harder chapters, even if afterward you go read something else. Both the long sections and the familiar verses will help you to know God and understand his ways.

December 1

The LORD is merciful and gracious,
slow to anger and abounding in steadfast love . . .

As a father shows compassion to his children,
so the LORD shows compassion to those who fear him. —Psalm 103:8, 13

Psalm 103 has a unique charm. It tends to make the head of the list as a favorite Scripture passage for a lot of people. One reason is that there is tremendous comfort in the expression of how our Father loves us. He has compassion on his children. This psalm has permeated my soul because I've gone back to it again and again throughout my life. As I have read and reread it over and over again it's become rich food for my life. Notice how it covers all the terrain of our lives, addressing all of the things that make life hard. It's a broad enough category to pour your life experience into it. God's love is so strong that it sustains us and overcomes our fragility. God's goodness is what adorns our lives and makes our life sparkle.

All of the major themes in the first chapter of Ephesians are in Psalm 103: sonship, adoption, sin, death, steadfast love, and mercy. *In Ephesians we understand how God forgives our iniquity, redeems our life from the pit, and surrounds us with steadfast love and mercy because of Jesus. In Psalm 103 we see how these themes connect to daily human experience and the hard things we struggle with.* It will do your heart good to climb back into Psalm 103 once you understand what Jesus has done for us.

December 2

But God, being rich in mercy, because of the great love with which he loved us, even when we were dead in our trespasses, made us alive together with Christ—by grace you have been saved . . . so that in the coming ages he might show the immeasurable riches of his grace in kindness toward us in Christ Jesus. —Ephesians 2:4–5, 7

N o one can truly change who does not know and rely on gifts from the hand of the Lord. Since Christ is both Giver and Gift, attempts to change without grace are barren of the very purpose, power, and Person that change is about. Self-manufactured changes do not dislodge almighty me from the center of my tiny self-manufactured universe. Still in the futility of my mind and the hardness of my heart, I only act a bit different. Successful living without grace describes mere self-reformation. Christless, grace-less attempts at change conclude either with the praise of your own glory or with your shame.

But in mercy, God purposes to give us himself. Ephesians 1 marvels at the glory of the grace that gives us glory in Christ. Ephesians 2 marvels at the sheer goodness of God and God's grace, what a friend of mind calls "God's thermonuclear goodness." His goodness is of an all-consuming intensity, like the nuclear furnace of the sun. In his presence, we, the dead in sin, children of just wrath, would be incinerated by goodness. But Christ's incalculable grace multiplies goodness times forgiveness times kindness times mercy. Christ carries us into the fiery sun of the living God. Ephesians 3 pleads with God that we would understand such a love as this. *Grace turns you upside down: the self-righteous and destructive become the grateful and constructive.*

December 3

Now there are also many other things that Jesus did. Were every one of
them to be written, I suppose that the world itself could not contain the
books that would be written. —John 21:25

John's Gospel largely consists of scenes selected from Jesus's encounters and conversations with various followers, foes, and undecideds. The common denominator is Jesus and his saving, sifting, sanctifying purposes. John takes time to zoom in, slowing everything down, lingering on a snippet of conversation or a situational detail. Watch Jesus interact, person by person, situation by situation. Listen to the questions he asks and how he answers questioners. He finds a point of engagement. He helps, rattles, invites, irritates, teaches, argues, clarifies, perplexes, saves, warns, and encourages. As Jesus crosses paths with people, he reveals people for who they are. In response to him, people change, either making a turn for the better or taking a turn for the worse.

As John's Gospel recreates different interactions between Jesus and his contemporaries, we learn a great deal about the kinds of interactions that recur throughout our lives, too. Jesus aims to catch your ear and sanctify you. He goes about the work of initial sanctification—life-giving faith. He also goes about the work of progressive sanctification—a lifetime of growing up in both faith and love. John repeatedly zooms in on interpersonal moments. And Jesus not only reveals himself in these moments of engagement, he also reveals the person he is engaging. We learn what both parties are facing, saying, and doing. *Truth comes to life at the intersection of Jesus's life and your life.*

It is noteworthy that Jesus never ministers by rote. There is no distilled formula. No abstract generalizations. Because situations and people come unscripted, fluid, and unpredictable, Jesus engages each person and situation in a personalized way. It is no truism to say that Jesus really does meet you where you are. Always.

December 4

Then Jesus told his disciples, "If anyone would come after me, let him deny himself and take up his cross and follow me. For whoever would save his life will lose it, but whoever loses his life for my sake will find it."
—Matthew 16:24–25

Jesus is a man on a mission. He is on the move, up to something. Life is not about you; it is about him. Did you ever see the retainers, groupies, or bodyguards for a rock group, sports star, or president? Their glory, their purpose, their happiness, their call is subordinate and derivative from the big person they serve. What does a secretary, a soldier, or an employee do? They serve the well-being and agenda of the boss, the officer, the owner. Jesus is this boss. He comes doing good to get you out of your presumption and your misery.

He claims you. He calls you to leave behind everything else you live for. What are you primarily about? Your toys? Your comforts? Your friends? Your money? Your career? Winning arguments? He's come to turn you away from something to give you someone so much greater—himself, the Lord of the universe.

He claims you. He calls you to follow him. Glorify him. Trust him. Love him. Die to what entangles you. *Let every emotion—of gratitude, of just outrage, of trusting encouragement—find its fulfillment and truest expression in Jesus Christ, the King of creation and re-creation. Let your every act, from driving, to paying taxes, to caring for your family members, find its organizing center in what will give glory to God.* He's come to turn you from something to who you are meant to be—a glad worshiper of the living God.

December 5

For this is the will of God, your sanctification. —1 Thessalonians 4:3a

When the risen Jesus gave final instructions to his disciples, he commissioned them to make more disciples (Matthew 28:18–20). In other words, they were to serve the processes of *sanctification*: the birth and growth of new people with a new way of life. We often hear Jesus's words as a call for personal evangelism, church planting, and world missions, with conversion as the desired result. *But conversion is the first step in a long salvation. It is the birth that leads to a lifetime of growing up into Jesus's image. Sanctification is discipleship into his way of life.*

What is his way of life? Jesus is the man of faith who lives within the psalms, depending on mercies. He is the man of wisdom who lives out the proverbs, fearing the Lord. He is the man of righteousness who simply loves God and neighbors. He is the man of redeeming mercies. He is the servant of the Lord who lays down his life for others. And Jesus called his followers to do everything that helps others to follow him.

The actual unfolding of progressive sanctification is no theoretical topic. All Christians already have at least some firsthand experience. Every Christian can say: "This was key in helping me when I struggled with that in those circumstances." The stories are so varied!

But firsthand experience also presents a danger. It is easy to extrapolate your own experience into a general rule: "This must be the key for everyone." Both Scripture and personal testimony teach us that there is no single formula for the kinds of problems that call for sanctification. There is no single formula for the kinds of change that sanctification produces. There is no single formula for the truths and other factors that produce change. Multiple stories help because they make you realize that not everyone is like you.

December 6

"Blessed are the poor in spirit, for theirs is the kingdom of heaven."
—Matthew 5:3

The first beatitude on essential poverty, need, and weakness comes first for a reason: we need what God gives. We need our Father to give the Holy Spirit to us, so that Christ dwells in our hearts by faith, and so that the love of God is poured out within us right when the heat is on. Augustine summarized the immediacy of grace this way: "Give what you command and command what you will." Some part of the good news of the Lord's redemptive purposes, will, and promise is absolutely necessary—right now.

The Bible models how ministry and life focus on one thing at a time. A good theology book rightly asks, Who is God? and goes on to fill 400 pages with truths. But Psalm 121 cries out, "Where does my help come from?", and seizes on one necessary thing: "The Lord keeps me."

In the Bible's vivid picture, we "turn" to our Father, Savior, and Comforter. He works in us toward one goal: change. The central dynamic of the Christian life has this FROM . . . TO . . . movement. *When God calls, you listen. When he promises, you trust and talk back to him in your need. When he loves, you love. When he commands, you obey. You aim your life in a new direction by the power of the Holy Spirit.* In every case, you turn. These are the purposes of the whole Bible, the whole mission of our Redeemer.

December 7

For as we share abundantly in Christ's sufferings, so through Christ we share abundantly in comfort too. —2 Corinthians 1:5

What is the way by which Paul (and we) gain wisdom to effectively and wisely help other people? It is mind-blowing when you think about where Paul starts as he writes his second letter to the Corinthians. He immediately starts to talk about his own troubles. Paul goes to the hardest things that happened, right down to the fact that he almost died, he was almost killed. Paul is going to explain how he learned wisdom, and not only wisdom, but joy, and the ability to have a persevering faith and endurance that hangs in there through all kinds of troubles.

As he begins talking about his own troubles, the language he chooses to use in 2 Corinthians 1:4–7 is interesting—he uses two words over and over again: suffering and affliction. Maybe the best way to put those words on the street would be to say, the word *affliction* literally means you are squeezed. You are under pressure. There is trouble, big trouble that just weighs heavily on you, it constricts you, it constrains you, it hassles you. Then there is suffering. Suffering literally means you hurt. You hurt and you're squeezed. You're under extreme pressure and in pain.

This is the way you get wisdom to help others—through turning to God in your suffering and affliction, and thus sharing both in Christ's affliction and his comfort.

December 8

If we are afflicted, it is for your comfort and salvation; and if we are
comforted, it is for your comfort, which you experience when you
patiently endure the same sufferings that we suffer. —2 Corinthians 1:6

If you get wisdom to help others through suffering, it's going
to be through the right kind of suffering, because the wrong
kind of suffering, or, more accurately, the mishandling of suffering, is also the way we show ourselves to be the biggest fools on
the planet—evil, selfish, self-pitying, self-righteous, vindictive,
escapist, and so forth. It is only through suffering that you learn
things that are absolutely necessary for you to help any other
person. And Paul camps there. He's going to get there through
his discussion of the suffering and the hardship that he went
through.

The wisdom of the flesh is what people do instinctively—
how we intuitively, as fallen human beings, respond to pressure
and pain. What tends to come out? When we suffer, it's natural
to grumble, complain, moan, and groan. Grumbling expresses,
"My kingdom come, my will be done in heaven as it better be
done on earth." There are so many kinds of things that the flesh
intuitively does in the context of suffering and pain. But what
do they all lead to, in terms of consequences? The wisdom of
the flesh at minimum, sabotages the possibility of a constructive
effect to the suffering you encounter.

*God is up to something in your suffering—something good. He
always wants to move us from trusting in ourselves, to trusting him.
He's working to shift our allegiance from ourselves to him.*

December 9

But that was to make us rely not on ourselves but on God who raises
the dead. —2 Corinthians 1:9b

Paul identifies suffering and affliction as God's means to shift our fundamental trust from ourselves to God. He wants our deepest allegiance to be to God. That is the path of life and hope. Notice he is calling us to trust in the God *who raises the dead*. Of all the things that could be said about God, Paul picks out the one thing those facing a death sentence most need to know. He is the God who raises the dead. That is a spectacularly relevant promise that utterly fits the need of the moment.

It may not be that the metaphor of trust is the one that most nails you. There are many different ways of talking about our hearts, both where we go astray and where we are found again. You could also ask yourself: What do I love? What do I listen to? What do I serve? Where do I set my hopes? Where do I take refuge?

Trust is just one of the active verbs that relates us to God— trust in God versus trust in myself, my money, my ability to control, my pleasure, my wife and family, etc.

How do we become wise? How do we learn to help other people? As you study this passage, you realize that we learn to help other people by being helped. *We become wise counselors by being counseled wisely, effectively, lovingly, ultimately by God himself.*

December 10

At its core, anger is very simple. It expresses, "I'm against that." It is an active stance you take to oppose something that you assess as both important and wrong. You notice something, size it up, and say, "*That matters . . . and it's not right.*" Anger expresses the energy of your reaction to something you find offensive and wish to eliminate.

All this is to say that anger always makes a value judgment. Anger is always a moral matter. It has rightly been called "the moral emotion" because it makes a statement about what matters. Human beings make moral judgments, therefore human beings do anger. Period. Like God, you come wired to size things up, to feel displeasure at wrong, and to act in order to do something about it.

But anger isn't the only reaction that proclaims what you value. In fact, every time you open your mouth (or don't open your mouth) you are broadcasting your values to others. This is what is meant, for example, when Jesus said that "every careless word" will be evaluated and that "out of the abundance of the heart his mouth speaks" (Matthew 12:36; Luke 6:45). Every word you say—including small talk—tells something important about you. What you choose to talk about (or never think of saying) broadcasts what matters to you. Your emotional reactions and your choices always proclaim your values. Stir in a bit of emotion—because you care, because something that matters is going wrong—and you can get the reaction we call anger. *Every time you get angry (or don't get angry) you broadcast what matters to you.*

345

December 11

We have fallen into sin. That's why our anger gets so messed up, so twisted, perverted, and misused. We play at being God and try to run the world, punishing evildoers on our own terms. We get mad at things that aren't evil (it's just that our almighty will was crossed). Then we ignore things that really are evil—our own temper and bitterness, for starters—remaining indifferent to suffering and oppression. Finally, when we do manage to get angry at a real evil, we blow it so out of proportion that we "return evil for evil." We become like the things we criticize so that even anger legitimately aroused gets expressed destructively.

That's not the end of the story, though. You and I are redeemable. By the grace of God we are utterly redeemable. Whatever is perverse and insulting to God, worthy of his anger, can be forgiven and changed. Our evaluative capacity—the conscience—can be rewired. *We can and will learn to perceive good and evil in a different way, the way things really are. This restores us gradually to sanity, to the image of Christ.*

Our responses can be changed. Hair-trigger irascibility becomes slow-to-anger. Hostility turns to active love for enemies. Long-standing bitterness softens into the ability to forgive our debtors. The God who is totally for us and who loves us too much to leave us in our sin—the all-powerful God of the universe—is in the business of the long, slow fixing. He is at work transforming his children so that our anger will be reflected in loving action.

December 12

Do not speak evil against one another, brothers. The one who speaks against a brother or judges his brother, speaks evil against the law and judges the law. But if you judge the law, you are not a doer of the law but a judge. There is only one lawgiver and judge, he who is able to save and to destroy. But who are you to judge your neighbor? —James 4:11-12

Who are you when you judge? None other than a God wannabe. We judge others—criticize, nitpick, nag, attack, condemn—because we literally usurp God's throne. In this we become devils to each other, acting as accusers. When you and I fight, our minds become filled with accusations: your wrongs and my rights preoccupy me. We play the self-righteous judge in the mini-kingdoms we establish: "You are so stupid. You've gotten in my way. You don't get it."

In an argument, you offend me by crossing my will. I respond by pointedly confessing your offenses to you! At the same time, I explain to you how all my failings are really your fault. If only you were different, I wouldn't be the way I am. You do the same to me, pointedly confessing my sins to me and excusing your own. Nowhere in the heat of conflict does anyone confess his own sins, except as a way to buy time for a counterattack: "Yeah, I was wrong to do that, but . . ."

The log remains firmly planted in the eye (Matthew 7:1–5) as each party plays lawgiver and judge. But there is one Lawgiver and Judge, he who is able to save and to destroy. Who are you that you judge your neighbor? *Here we see that a far more profound conflict burns at the heart of interpersonal conflict. Presumption, pride, demand, and self-will stand at odds with the one true God.*

December 13

What causes quarrels and what causes fights among you? Is it not this,
that your passions are at war within you? —James 4:1

James has this wonderful way of taking the veil off of the
human heart. What causes evil practice? Bad zeal. There's
something you want that takes over your heart. You become
zealous for the wrong thing. You lust, you crave, you want, and
you don't get, and the result is anger and interpersonal conflict.
You desire and don't have, so you fight with others.

Scripture goes right to the heart in probing for what is really
going wrong. My world is a place where my pleasures and what I
want reigns supreme. It's a place where I'm zealous about myself,
my ambition, and my self-affirmation.

Against this backdrop, James 4:6 is probably one of the most
astonishing one-liners in the entire Bible. Leading up to it is
a searing analysis of the human heart that lays us bare before
God. And then, you have this: "But he gives more grace." That
is astonishing. As dark as our hearts can be, he gives more grace.
He really cares. And his jealousy over us is meant to give us
confidence that he does love us. Even his anger is ultimately our
friend. It's warning us because he cares. That's one side of a true,
pure, proper jealousy. The other side is a desire for responsive
love. *God desires that just as his intense love has been given to us,
we give back to him our loyalty, intensity, focus, and undistracted
devotion. He wants us to be his alone and love him utterly in return.*

December 14

But he gives more grace. Therefore it says, "God opposes the proud but gives grace to the humble." —James 4:6

Grace is woven into the entire Bible from Genesis to Revelation—you could call it part of the DNA of the Scripture. You see it in the gracious blessing in Numbers 6:24–26: The LORD bless you and keep you, make his face shine on you, be gracious to you, turn his face toward you, give you peace.

Grace is one of the core promises of God. When you look at the unfolding story of Scripture, you see grace everywhere. Take for example, the story of King David. God's grace to David meant that God blessed him, kept him, shone his face on him, and brought him peace. You might say that the shorthand for grace in the life of David is that God was with him. The grace of God being with his people fasts-forwards into the Psalms, through the rest of the Old Testament, and into the New Testament.

This promise, "He gives more grace," is the entire basis of your relationship with God. It is the heartbeat of your prayer life. The promise of grace anchors the way that an honest psalm-like prayer says, "Oh Lord, my life is very hard now. Bless me, keep me, don't abandon me. You've promised to keep me. Make your face shine upon me. Be gracious to me. Turn toward me. Give me peace and not trouble. Have mercy upon me." The entirety of your relationship to God is predicated on this grace. It is what you trust, it is what you plead, it is what you sing, it is what you delight in it, and it is what you're thankful for.

December 15

But I say, walk by the Spirit, and you will not gratify the desires of the flesh. For the desires of the flesh are against the Spirit, and the desires of the Spirit are against the flesh, for these are opposed to each other, to keep you from doing the things you want to do. —Galatians 5:16-17

Anger goes wrong when we want a good thing more than we want God. It's not wrong to want your husband to love and listen to you. It's not wrong to want your children to respect and obey you. It's not wrong to want your boss to be honest with you. It's not wrong to want a warm meal and a hot cup of coffee, or to get to your appointment rather than getting stuck in traffic. But when fulfilling your desires, even for a good thing, becomes more important than anything else, that's when it changes to a "desire of the flesh." You want it too much. When you don't get what you want, demand, believe you need, and think you deserve, your anger flares up.

James, in the letter he wrote to the early church, said this about where our wrong anger comes from: "What causes fights and quarrels among you? Don't they come from your desires that battle within you? You want something but don't get it. You kill and covet, but you cannot have what you want. You quarrel and fight . . ." (James 4:1–2).

Wrong anger creates a big problem between you and God. Anger going wrong testifies to our pride. This insight into anger is hugely freeing and very sobering. *When you see yourself as a sinner, instead of focusing on how everyone around you is wrong, then God's grace and mercy is available to you.*

December 16

Do not be conformed to this world, but be transformed by the renewal of your mind. —Romans 12:2a

When you trust in Jesus, the Holy Spirit begins to transform what you want. The Spirit reconfigures our moral universe. You no longer want human approval more than anything, though of course you still get stuck there. But there's been a fundamental change. Take for example a man who has always lived for control. In Christ he can say, "I don't want to try control my world. It makes me angry, depressed, hostile, fearful. There is One who is in control, and I want to learn to take refuge in him."

Francis of Assisi prayed, "Grant that I would not so much seek to be understood as to understand, that I would not so much seek to be loved as to love." His prayer captures that fundamental upside-downness of life in Christ. *The redemption of us in Christ changes what we basically want, even though we still struggle with renegade desires that would take us a different direction.*

Lord, we do ask you that we, as your children, would understand the mind of God. We would be strengthened by the power of God; we would live the life that you call us to. Lord, this is the fine china of our lives and I pray that none of us would be untouched. I pray that you would sustain us, strengthen us, illumine us. In the places, Lord, where we are sloppy or dull or blind, give us eyes to see. In the places we are rigid or narrow, soften us. Grow us together in the image of our Savior. We pray in his name, Amen.

December 17

"Observe the Sabbath day, to keep it holy, as the Lord your God commanded you. . . . You shall remember that you were a slave in the land of Egypt, and the Lord your God brought you out from there with a mighty hand and an outstretched arm. Therefore the Lord your God commanded you to keep the Sabbath day." —Deuteronomy 5:12, 15

Why should we rest? In the first take of this commandment (Exodus 20), we hear how the Creator made all things—and then stopped to rest, enjoying all that he'd made good, so very good. Don't forget exactly how you got here. Faith awakens and remembers. We serve this Maker by working well and resting well. But in the second take (Deuteronomy 5), we hear how the Redeemer freed his beloved from the meaningless sweat of slave labor and carried those he had rescued into a place of rest and peace. Don't forget exactly how you got here. Faith awakens and remembers. We serve this Savior by working well and resting well, and also by giving others who toil—even work animals—the pleasures of rest.

Amazing. *To get hard work and sweet pleasure right is to image forth the One who made you. To get hard work and sweet pleasure right is to image forth the One who saved you. These two complementary truths draw out and sustain your faith.* They turn off the motors of restless busyness and restless amusement. Reasons outside of yourself give you the inner reason that makes obedience a most sweet wisdom. The sabbath was made for man, not man for the sabbath. You lay down burdens and cares. You enter into rest and pleasure because the God who made you his own does the same.

December 18

And so, from the day we heard, we have not ceased to pray for you,
asking that you may be filled with the knowledge of his will in all
spiritual wisdom and understanding, so as to walk in a manner worthy
of the Lord, fully pleasing to him: bearing fruit in every good work and
increasing in the knowledge of God. —Colossians 1:9–10

As you pray for others, pray intelligent prayers that braid together the real God and the real person in the real-life situation. If you are alert to both the Redeemer and the real needs of the needy, you won't ever pray rote prayers. You won't just pray for situations to go well—for health, success, a spouse, or children. You'll pray for the person that God is either sanctifying or is calling to conversion amid that situation. If there are people you care for and you carry their welfare on your heart, your prayers will be warmly personal, inclusive, and caring. You intercede for them before the God who is here and on whom we learn to depend. Your prayers will be concrete and immediate.

During the first dozen years of my Christian life, *my pastor's way of praying for people had a profound effect on me. He would never close a conversation by saying, "I'll be praying for you about this." Instead, he would say, "Let's ask God right now to help you."* That made a huge impression. Yes, he also prayed later on, but in the moment, those specific and relevant prayers communicated that God is here, he cares about what is going on with me, and he is up to something in my life. I learned who God is, and I learned about God's call in my life.

Live like David and Paul lived, thoughtful and talkative before the face of God.

December 19

*I write these things to you who believe in the name of the Son of God,
that you may know that you have eternal life.* —1 John 5:13

Stories are the interesting part of life. That's how God made us. We bear the image of a person whose own story plays out in all that has been made and all that happens. No surprise, that's how his Bible works too.

Think of the Bible as a richly annotated story. God clothes the big themes with events, action, named people, and complications. He doesn't simply summarize truth or provide us with an outline of topics with a list of key points and subpoints. But his purposes in writing are pastoral, not literary. He wants to change how you understand life. He wants to change how you live. So the story comes with extensive annotations. Imagine that the left margin of the page is crammed with explanatory notes, with propositions pointing out what's going on in the story, making the interpretive and thematic keys explicit. Imagine that the right margin is crammed with principles, telling us specific implications for how we should respond.* That rich page contains story, worldview, and application rolled into one.

The Bible contains the exact ingredients that our lives need. God intends that we see and hear—witness—what he's all about and what we're about. God has no interest in simply entertaining or inspiring. He has no interest in simply providing information or telling people what to do. Instead, he does and says everything needed to win us out of our self-fascination. He does and says what moves us to need him and love him.

---

* I am indebted to Paul Tripp for this insight.

December 20

Critics are God's instruments. None of us likes to be criticized. But critics keep us sane—or, by our reactions, prove us temporarily or permanently insane. Whether a critic's manner is gracious or malicious, the very experience of being criticized reveals you:

Self-satisfaction. I easily stagnate and drift off to sleep. You think that you solved the problems of the day (or the world) yesterday. Maybe you did. Then today the problems change, but you'd rather rest on your laurels. When someone poses a searching question to me, or directs a criticism at me— and I'm willing to hear and consider—it keeps me from etching in stone my last best insight or last best achievement.

Self-justification. I easily become arrogant, deaf, and self-righteous. Yesterday's faithful obedience (or what I thought was such) becomes today's prop for the kingdom of self. I forget that I remain a needy recipient of the lifelong process of redemption. Give me critics who open their mouths about what their eyes see and ears hear, and give me a non-defensive attitude toward what they say.

Self-protection (of the have-an-easy-life variety). To be criticized is not pleasant, so to avoid, duck, and hide can look very inviting. Real people and real problems are hard to deal with. *But I need to listen consciously to critics, even to invite criticism. This will help me live in the world that God controls, the world in which Christ keeps on working to redeem. Christ uses critics to guard our souls from self-destructive tendencies.*

December 21

Not only that, but we rejoice in our sufferings, knowing that suffering produces endurance, and endurance produces character, and character produces hope, and hope does not put us to shame, because God's love has been poured into our hearts through the Holy Spirit who has been given to us. —Romans 5:3–5

Grace teaches you courage. When God says, "Fear not," his aim is not that you would just calm down and experience a relative absence of fear. He does not say, "Don't be afraid. Everything will turn out okay. So you can relax." Instead he says, "Don't be afraid. I am with you. So be strong and courageous." Do you hear the difference? The deep waters have not gone away. Troubles still pressure you. The opposite of fear is courage, not unruffled serenity. Fearlessness is courageous in the face of fearsome things. It carries on constructively in the midst of stress that doesn't feel good at all. Courage means more than freedom from anxious feelings. Endurance is a purposeful "abiding under" what is hard and painful, and considering others even when you don't feel good.

There are countless ways to simply lessen anxiety. But none of them will make you fearless in the face of trouble. None of them creates that resilient fruit of the Spirit called "endurance," which comes up repeatedly when the New Testament talks about God's purposes in suffering. None of them gives you high joy in knowing that your entire life is a holy experiment as God's hands shape you into the image of his Son. None of them changes the way you suffer by embedding in it a deeper meaning.

In fact, fearless endurance is for the purpose of wise love. God is making you like Jesus in the hardships of real life.

December 22

Blessed be the God and Father of our Lord Jesus Christ, the Father of
mercies and God of all comfort, who comforts us in all our affliction.
—2 Corinthians 1:3–4a

Here are eight complementary ways 2 Corinthians describes what proves comforting when we go through trials, difficulty, and suffering.

1. *God comforts us by how he communicates his care in words.* In essence, he says "I love you" in many different ways.

2. *God comforts us by what he does.* He demonstrates "I love you" by actions: what he did, what he is doing, what he will do. He kept, keeps, and will keep his promises. His love is not a sentiment, an idea, a good intention, or a theological theory. It is tangible reality.

3. *God comforts us by his loving presence.* The one who says he loves you, the one who shows his love by actions, the one who best loves you—he sticks with you. Your Savior never leaves your side. He will never abandon you.

4. *God comforts us by how other people communicate their care in words.* In various ways, we are heartened when another person says and demonstrates "I love you," and "You matter to me," and "I'm proud of you and confident about you."

5. *God comforts us by what other people do for us.* Like God, people show their love not only by their words but by their actions.

6. *God comforts us by the loving presence of other people.* All the mercies of God are intended to bring his people near to enjoy peace with each other.

7. *God comforts us when we witness how other people respond to him.* Seeing someone else's responsiveness nourishes our joy.

8. *God comforts us as we see a growing stability of faith in ourselves.* He anchors our hope, in part, because we see ourselves growing.

This road is hard but good. It is the only road leading to life and joy.

December 23

Joy to the world, the Lord is come!
Let earth receive her King!
Let ev'ry heart prepare Him room,
and heav'n and nature sing,
and heav'n and nature sing,
and heav'n, and heav'n and nature sing

No more let sins and sorrows grow,
nor thorns infest the ground;
He comes to make His blessings flow
far as the curse is found,
far as the curse is found,
far as, far as the curse is found.
—Isaac Watts, "Joy to the World"

In the wonderful Christmas hymn "Joy to the World," Isaac Watts reminds us in the first line that, "the Lord *is* come." That's an odd tense. It has a present progressive, present perfect sense that basically means the Lord came and he's still here. He's still at work. So this is a great song for any time of the year. It is about the glory and mercy of Jesus Christ. It puts in perspective our twofold struggle with our sins and our sufferings. Christ, our King, comes to make his blessings flow as far as the curse is found. Obviously we live in the in-between period, where curses can still be found, but this hymn is absolutely filled with this joyous awareness of where it's all going. That perspective is key in helping us see past our tunnel vision that introspects in on our hurts and hardships and sins. All three of those have a tendency to make us turn in on ourselves. "Joy to the World" turns us out of ourselves. The Savior reigns, the Lord is come, he's the King of the whole Earth. The final stanza is just full of the love of God. The dominant note throughout is a call to living faith, a call to joy, a call to worship, a call to gladness. *It's a great hymn to encourage us to not get stuck in tunnel vision about ourselves and our world.*

December 24

And the Word became flesh and dwelt among us, and we have seen his glory, glory as of the only Son from the Father, full of grace and truth.
—John 1:14

The real gospel is the good news of the Word made flesh, the sin-bearing Savior, the resurrected Lord: "I am the living One, and I was dead, and behold, I am alive forevermore" (Revelation 1:18 NASB). This Christ turns the world upside down. One prime effect of the Holy Spirit's inworking presence and power is the rewiring of our sense of felt needs. *Because the fear of the Lord is the beginning of wisdom, we keenly feel a different set of needs when God comes into view and when we understand that we stand or fall in his gaze. My instinctual cravings are replaced (sometimes quickly, always gradually) by the growing awareness of true, life-and-death needs:*

- I need mercy above all else.
- I want to learn wisdom and unlearn willful self-preoccupation.
- I need to learn to love both God and neighbor.
- I long for God's name to be honored, for his kingdom to come, for his will to be done on earth.
- I need God's mighty and intimate help in order to will and to do those things that last unto eternal life, rather than squandering my life on vanities.
- I want to learn how to endure hardship and suffering in hope, having my faith simplified, deepened, and purified.
- I need to learn, to listen, to worship, to delight, to trust, to give thanks, to cry out, to take refuge, to obey, to serve, to hope.

Make it so, Father of mercies. Make it so, Redeemer of all that is dark and broken.

December 25

O come, O come, Emmanuel, and ransom captive Israel,
that mourns in lonely exile here until the Son of God appear.
Rejoice! Rejoice! Emmanuel shall come to thee, O Israel.
—"O Come, O Come, Emmanuel," 9th-century Latin hymn

The hymn "O Come, O Come, Emmanuel" is lasting. Its origins go back some 1500 years. Believers have been singing this for a long time! And we still sing it today and sing it appropriately at Christmas. It stays fresh. Why?

We are asking God to come in person. This cry gives voice to our greatest need. We need the Emmanuel whom Isaiah promises (7:14). Left to ourselves we die—captives, sorrowing, alone, refugees. But God's presence with us will bring life. So we call each other to join in rejoicing. He promises to come to his people.

Each of the stanzas embodies this same basic structure. *We call on one of the characteristics of the Messiah, as Isaiah portrays him. We express some aspect of our human struggle. We ask the Lord to intervene. We rejoice. We promise each other that he will come. It is a beautiful and significant pattern.*

Emmanuel embodies the Spirit of wisdom and understanding—Isaiah 11:2–3. We need him to guide us in the way. Emmanuel is the dawning sun—Isaiah 9:2. We need the Light of the World to drive away all that is dark. Emmanuel is the key who opens the door of life and shuts the door of death—Isaiah 22:22. We need that one door to open wide. Emmanuel is the Lord himself, reigning, speaking, and saving—Isaiah 33:22. We need his authority, power, words, and presence.

We've asked the Lord Jesus to come. Now we rejoice, rejoice, rejoice, rejoice—because he's going to do it. Emmanuel is going to come as he promised.

December 26

Beloved, we are God's children now, and what we will be has not yet appeared; but we know that when he appears we shall be like him, because we shall see him as he is. And everyone who thus hopes in him purifies himself as he is pure. —1 John 3:2-3

What is our direction? What is our destination? You might want to do an experiment with people. Ask them, "Who are you most looking forward to seeing when you get to heaven?" It's so interesting that almost no one says, "I'm looking forward to seeing Jesus." You do know Jesus is the one that we're going to see, right? And when we see him, we'll be like him. He who has this hope purifies himself as Jesus is pure (1 John 3:3). That's where the dynamic of change happens—in the light of the destination. We will see him. We will become like him; his name will be on our forehead. This is the vision of our destination.

Where are you heading, what is your direction, and what are you going to be?

When it comes to the dynamics of biblical change, it's a matter of direction. Where are you going? Don't be discouraged by your destination's distance from you; instead, use it to stay oriented to where you're heading. No matter how far away it is.

I'll never forget one of the things that my first pastor, Jack Miller, said. He used to often say that the glory of God in your life is not some absolute standard of achievement. Like, here's the ideal Christian, here's the ideal Christian family, here's the ideal church. *Instead, the measure of Christ's glory is the difference between what you would be by nature and what you are because of Christ.*

December 27

Repay no one evil for evil . . . Beloved, never avenge yourselves, but leave it to the wrath of God, for it is written, "Vengeance is mine, I will repay, says the Lord." . . . Do not be overcome by evil, but overcome evil with good. —Romans 12:17a, 19, 21

The reason we do wrong things in response to the huge wrong things done to us is that we are living for ourselves, not for Jesus. But the love of God in Christ transforms us. One mark of that transformation is that our eyes are opened to our need for a Savior. We see that Jesus died for our self-centeredness and our unbelief. We see how great our need is for God's mercy. *When you understand and know God's mercy, you will be able to grant mercy and forgiveness.* This may not happen overnight. But as you continue to pour out your heart to God and ask him for mercy, he will change you. Your trust in God will grow. Your ability to love others will grow. Your life will no longer be defined by the wrong done to you, but by God's love and mercy to you.

Why don't you have to return evil for evil? Because something bigger is going on. God will make things right.

You may be walking a difficult path. But you are not alone as you walk. Your faithful Savior is with you, and he will also send people to walk with you. Look for people to share your story with who understand that terrible things do happen, yet we have a wonderful God who invades those things with steadfast love and faithfulness. Look for someone who will take seriously the evil that happened to you, who will be compassionate, and who will have a vision of how God can redeem you and your past.

December 28

Let all bitterness and wrath and anger and clamor and slander be put away from you, along with all malice. —Ephesians 4:31

Perhaps it makes you feel hopeless to admit that some experiences will never go away. Hear me rightly. I don't mean that the poison and darkness of the experience will always haunt you. You won't get over it, but you do not need to be forever defined by what happened. You won't forget what happened, but there is a way out of the raptor's claws. I hope to walk with you part of the way out of despair and offer you realistic hope. It won't erase what happened—that would be to live a falsehood. But realistic hope runs deeper than any hurt. It can take the same experience and offer a different script, a different outcome, a different meaning. Deep hurt so easily gets infected—by mistrust, or fear, or rage, or callousness, or avoidance, or addiction. Hurt even gets infected by just trying to keep yourself busy and distracted. It turns inward. It turns self-destructive. *But hurt and loss can become transmuted into a deeper good—still fierce, still sorrowing, but now clean. Not only clean, but hopeful. Not only hopeful, but fruitful. Not only fruitful, but wise. Not only wise, but even loving.*

You won't forget. But you do not need to endlessly revisit what happened. You do not need to be imprisoned in the complexities and dead ends of your instinctive reactions.

December 29

"Remember the Sabbath day, to keep it holy. Six days you shall labor, and do all your work, but the seventh day is a Sabbath to the Lord your God. —Exodus 20:8–10a

The deepest and most significant reference point for our problems is always moral. We are made to love God and neighbor. The restlessness and drivenness pervasive in our lives and culture does not love anyone. It is a failure of love that misuses your time, your choices, your activities, your 24/7/365. In other words, the obsessions that sicken both our labors and our pleasures occur within the sphere of the fourth commandment: Exodus 20:8–11; Deuteronomy 5:12–15.

The Sabbath commandment exposes the arrhythmias of work and rest and bids to restore rhythm. The fourth commandment orients you with respect to God. He alone brings into focus the complex issues of work and rest. He alone fundamentally changes why you do what you do. He reveals (and alters) the meaning you attach to the basic activities of your life. The arrhythmias are revelatory—of what you live for that is not God. As you come to love him who loves you, he remakes you—sane.

But that specific commandment has surprising ramifications. It orients us to a way of seeing many other interconnected specifics. It crystallizes the relationship between all your toils and all your pleasures, revealing life-shaping attitudes. Like all the commandments, it opens a window. *And like all the commandments, it holds out a destination: meaningful work and meaningful rest, sparkling with intelligent faith, love, and purpose.*

December 30

You make known to me the path of life;
in your presence there is fullness of joy;
at your right hand are pleasures forevermore. —Psalm 16:11

We live in a culture whose icons and ambitions arise from the realms of entertainment, amusement, recreation, athletics, vacation, adventure, excitement, fashion, eroticism, convenience, technology, and whatever else feels good. We choose from an endless array of enticing distractions, things to watch, things to buy, things to do. Desire is the most high god. Limits are the only sin. Every possible pleasure becomes a niche market.

What do we make of this? We could sniff and rant, shaking the dust off our sandals. But for starters, let's consider that the Lord made our capacity for pleasure as part of his image: very good. And Eden is a "paradise": literally, a pleasure garden. And let's consider that in dealing with anything twisted and perverted by sin, God never sniffs and rants. *He doesn't erase pleasure, or say that it is irrelevant or suspect or downright bad. He redeems pleasure. Grace and truth take the perversity out and restore the felicity. Only what's wrong must go. Then pleasure becomes simple again, and it's a pleasure.* Christian truth cuts against the grain of a culture by offering something *better*. It is the sane alternative both to self-indulgence and to fussy religiosity.

December 31

For I know that nothing good dwells in me, that is, in my flesh. For I have the desire to do what is right, but not the ability to carry it out. . . . For I delight in the law of God, in my inner being, but I see in my members another law waging war against the law of my mind and making me captive to the law of sin that dwells in my members. Wretched man that I am! Who will deliver me from this body of death? Thanks be to God through Jesus Christ our Lord! —Romans 7:18, 22-25a

What sins do you still wrestle with? Forgetting God and proceeding as if life centers on you? Obsessive religious scrupulosity that starves your humanity? Defensive and self-assertive pride? Laziness or drivenness, or an oscillation between both? Irritability, judgmentalism, and complaining? Immoral impulses and fantasies? Obsessive concern with money, food, or entertainment? Fear of what others think about you? Envy of good things that someone else enjoys? Shading truth into half-truths to manufacture your image? Speaking empty or even destructive words, rather than nourishing, constructive, and graceful wisdom?

I can identify with each one, and I suspect you can too. *Our Father loves us with mercies new every morning and more numerous than the hairs on your heads.* He is good and he does good. He has chosen to love us. And we really do love him—as street children he has rescued and adopted. He says,

"You are mine. So take heart.
I will complete what I have begun."

Source Index

January 1. "The Right Kind of Weakness," *Journal of Biblical Counseling* 33, no. 2 (2019): 3.

January 2. CCEF 2016 Regional Conference: Everyday Worship: How God Brings the Bible to Life, Session 2: "Learning to Ask the Right Questions."

January 3. *Life Beyond Your Parents' Mistakes: The Transforming Power of God's Love* (Greensboro, NC: New Growth Press, 2010), 18 and 13—in that order.

January 4. *I Just Want to Die: Replacing Suicidal Thoughts with Hope* (Greensboro, NC: New Growth Press, 2010), 18.

January 5. *Breaking the Addictive Cycle: Deadly Obsessions or Simple Pleasures?* (Greensboro, NC: New Growth Press, 2010), 25–27.

January 6. *Breaking the Addictive Cycle*, 29–30.

January 7. CCEF 2016 Regional Conference: Everyday Worship: How God Brings the Bible to Life, Session 2: "Learning to Ask the Right Questions."

January 8. *Speaking Truth in Love: Counsel in Community* (Greensboro, NC: New Growth Press, 2005), 123.

January 9. "Slow Growth," *Journal of Biblical Counseling* 32, no. 3 (2018): 5–7.

January 10. *Speaking Truth in Love: Counsel in Community* (Greensboro, NC: New Growth Press, 2005), 14–15, 17.

January 11. *Good and Angry: Redeeming Anger, Irritation, Complaining, and Bitterness* (Greensboro, NC: New Growth Press, 2016), 164–65.

January 12. *Good and Angry*, 138–139.

January 13. *Good and Angry*, 94–95.

January 14. *Safe and Sound: Standing Firm in Spiritual Battles* (Greensboro, NC: New Growth Press, 2019), 42.

January 15. *Overcoming Anxiety: Relief for Worried People* (Greensboro, NC: New Growth Press, 2010), 8–9.

January 16. *When Cancer Interrupts* (Greensboro, NC: New Growth Press, 2015), 16–17.

January 17. *Speaking Truth in Love: Counsel in Community* (Greensboro, NC: New Growth Press, 2005), 42.

January 18. *Speaking Truth in Love*, 83–85.

January 19. CCEF 2016 Regional Conference: Everyday Worship: How God Brings the Bible to Life, Session 4: "Other People Make a Difference."

January 20. *Facing Death with Hope: Living for What Lasts* (Greensboro, NC: New Growth Press, 2008), 7–8.

January 21. *I Just Want to Die: Replacing Suicidal Thoughts with Hope* (Greensboro, NC: New Growth Press, 2010), 10–11.

January 22. "Let's Celebrate This Golden Anniversary," *Journal of Biblical Counseling* 32, no. 2 (2018): 3–4.

January 23. "The God of All Comfort," *Journal of Biblical Counseling* 31, no. 3 (2017): 3–4, 6.

January 24. "How Does Sanctification Work?" Part 3, *Journal of Biblical Counseling* 31, no. 1 (2017): 9–10.

January 25. "How Does Sanctification Work?" 25, 27.

January 26. "What Can You Do When God Seems Far Away?" *Journal of Biblical Counseling* 30, no. 3 (2016): 4.

January 27. CCEF 2016 Regional Conference: Everyday Worship: How God Brings the Bible to Life, Session 3: "Martin Luther's 3 Masters."

January 28. *Safe and Sound: Standing Firm in Spiritual Battles* (Greensboro, NC: 2019), 21–22.

January 29.   *Good and Angry: Redeeming Anger, Irritation, Complaining, and Bitterness* (Greensboro, NC: New Growth Press, 2016), 23–25.

January 30.   *Good and Angry*, 57–58.

January 31.   *Good and Angry*, 190–191.

February 1.   *Overcoming Anxiety: Relief for Worried People* (Greensboro, NC: New Growth Press, 2012), 10–11.

February 2.   "An Invitation to Speak Up!" *Journal of Biblical Counseling* 29, no. 3 (2015): 2–4.

February 3.   "What Is Your Calling?" *Journal of Biblical Counseling* 28, no. 3 (2014): 82.

February 4.   "'I'll Never Get over It'—Helped for the Aggrieved," *Journal of Biblical Counseling* 28, no. 1 (2014): 11–12.

February 5.   "In It for Good," *Journal of Biblical Counseling* 26, no. 2 (2012): 2.

February 6.   Taken from *God's Grace in Your Suffering* (Wheaton, IL: Crossway, 2018), 35–36. Copyright ©2018. Used by permission of Crossway, a publishing ministry of Good News Publishers, Wheaton, IL 60187, www.crossway.org.

February 7.   CCEF 2011 "Dynamics of Biblical Change" video course (filmed at Westminster Theological Seminary), Lecture 3.

February 8.   "Dynamics of Biblical Change," Lecture 4.

February 9.   "Dynamics of Biblical Change," Lecture 10.

February 10. *Good and Angry: Redeeming Anger, Irritation, Complaining, and Bitterness* (Greensboro, NC: New Growth Press, 2016), 191.

February 11. *Good and Angry*, 146–148.

February 12. *Safe and Sound: Standing Firm in Spiritual Battles* (Greensboro, NC: New Growth Press, 2019), 44–45.

February 13. *Safe and Sound*, 51.

February 14. *Good and Angry: Redeeming Anger, Irritation, Complaining, and Bitterness* (Greensboro, NC: New Growth Press, 2016), 53–54.

February 15. CCEF 2016 Regional Conference: Everyday Worship: How God Brings the Bible to Life, Session 1: "What Makes Words Relevant?"

February 16. *Overcoming Anxiety: Relief for Worried People* (Greensboro, NC: New Growth Press, 2012), 19–20.

February 17. "What Do You Feel?" *Journal of Biblical Counseling* 10, no. 4 (1992): 50–51, 53–54.

February 18. *Speaking Truth in Love: Counsel in Community* (Greensboro, NC: New Growth Press, 2005), 118–19.

February 19. *I Just Want to Die: Replacing Suicidal Thoughts with Hope* (Greensboro, NC: New Growth Press, 2010), 12–14.

February 20. "A Man's Identity," *Journal of Biblical Counseling* 34, no. 1 (2020): 79–80.

February 21. "How Does Sanctification Work?" Part 3, *Journal of Biblical Counseling* 31, no. 1 (2017): 10–12.

February 22. "How Does Sanctification Work?" 28–29.

February 23. "Getting Oriented," *Journal of Biblical Counseling* 30, no. 1 (2016): 2–3.

February 24. "What Is Your Calling?" *Journal of Biblical Counseling* 28, no. 3 (2014): 82–83, 85–86.

February 25. "The Personal God," *Journal of Biblical Counseling* 28, no. 2 (2014): 3.

February 26. "'I'll Never Get over It'—Helped for the Aggrieved," *Journal of Biblical Counseling* 28, no. 1 (2014):17.

February 27. "Resisting Idols of the Heart and Vanity Fair," *Journal of Biblical Counseling* 27, no. 3 (2013): 37–38.

February 28. *Safe and Sound: Standing Firm in Spiritual Battles* (Greensboro, NC: New Growth Press, 2019), 53–54.

February 29. *Good and Angry: Redeeming Anger, Irritation, Complaining, and Bitterness* (Greensboro, NC: New Growth Press, 2016), 71–72.

March 1. CCEF 2015 National Conference: Side by Side: How God Helps Us Help Each Other, Session 6: "Why We Pray and How We Pray."

March 2. CCEF 2015 National Conference: "Why We Pray and How We Pray."

March 3. "To Take the Soul to Task," *Journal of Biblical Counseling* 12, no. 3 (1994): 1.

March 4. CCEF 2011 "Dynamics of Biblical Change" video course (filmed at Westminster Theological Seminary), Lecture 5.

March 5. CCEF 2017 National Conference: Family: Embracing the Blessing, Facing the Brokenness, General Session 1: "Familial by Design."

March 6. CCEF 2011 "Dynamics of Biblical Change" video course (filmed at Westminster Theological Seminary), Lecture 6.

March 7. "Talk Incessantly? Listen Intently!" *Journal of Biblical Counseling* 15, no. 3 (1997): 2–4.

March 8. CCEF 2011 "Dynamics of Biblical Change" video course (filmed at Westminster Theological Seminary), Lecture 13.

March 9. *Safe and Sound: Standing Firm in Spiritual Battles* (Greensboro, NC: New Growth Press, 2019), 49–50.

March 10. *Controlling Anger: Responding Constructively When Life Goes Wrong* (Greensboro, NC: New Growth Press, 2012), 16–17.

March 11. *Controlling Anger,* 11–12.

March 12.   *Renewing Marital Intimacy: Closing the Gap Between You and Your Spouse* (Greensboro, NC: New Growth Press, 2008), 9–10.

March 13.   *Grieving a Suicide: Help for the Aftershock* (Greensboro, NC: New Growth Press, 2010), 12–13.

March 14.   *Grieving a Suicide*, 5–7.

March 15.   *I'm Exhausted: What to Do When You're Always Tired* (Greensboro, NC: New Growth Press, 2010), 13–14.

March 16.   CCEF 2011 "Dynamics of Biblical Change" video course (filmed at Westminster Theological Seminary), Lecture 17.

March 17.   "Dynamics of Biblical Change," Lecture 16.

March 18.   "Dynamics of Biblical Change," Lecture 16.

March 19.   "Dynamics of Biblical Change," Lecture 14.

March 20.   "Dynamics of Biblical Change," Lecture 13.

March 21.   "Dynamics of Biblical Change," Lecture 1.

March 22.   "How Does Scripture Change You?" *Journal of Biblical Counseling* 26, no. 2 (2012): 26.

March 23.   "'I'll Never Get over It'—Helped for the Aggrieved," *Journal of Biblical Counseling* 28, no. 1 (2014): 17–18.

March 24.   "The Personal God," *Journal of Biblical Counseling* 28, no. 2 (2014): 2–3.

March 25.   "An Invitation to Speak Up!" *Journal of Biblical Counseling* 29, no. 3 (2015): 4–5.

March 26.   "How Does Sanctification Work?" Part 3, *Journal of Biblical Counseling* 31, no. 1 (2017): 30.

March 27.   "How Does Sanctification Work?" 12–13.

March 28.   "The God of All Comfort," *Journal of Biblical Counseling* 31, no. 3 (2017): 6–7.

March 29.	"A Man's Identity," *Journal of Biblical Counseling* 34, no. 1 (2020): 79.
March 30.	*I Just Want to Die: Replacing Suicidal Thoughts with Hope* (Greensboro, NC: New Growth Press, 2010), 22–23.
March 31.	*Safe and Sound: Standing Firm in Spiritual Battles* (Greensboro, NC: New Growth Press, 2019), 77–79.
April 1.	CCEF 2015 National Conference: Side by Side: How God Helps Us Help Each Other, Session 6: "Why We Pray and How We Pray."
April 2.	CCEF 2017 National Conference: Family: Embracing the Blessing, Facing the Brokenness, Session 1: "Familial by Design."
April 3.	CCEF 2015 Regional Conference: Anxiety: How God Cares for Stressed People, Session 4: "Where Do We Go from Here?"
April 4.	"Who Is God?" *Journal of Biblical Counseling* 17, no. 2 (1999): 23.
April 5.	"Counsel the Word," *Journal of Biblical Counseling* 11, no. 2 (1993): 3–4.
April 6.	*Controlling Anger: Responding Constructively When Life Goes Wrong* (Greensboro, NC: New Growth Press, 2012), 7–8, 10.
April 7.	*Controlling Anger*, 3–4.
April 8.	"What If Your Father Didn't Love You?" *Journal of Biblical Counseling* 12, no. 1 (1993): 5–6.
April 9.	CCEF 2007 National Conference: Running Scared, Breakout Session: "Facing Death."
April 10.	"Pray Beyond the Sick List," *Journal of Biblical Counseling* 23, no.1 (2005): 2–5.
April 11.	Taken from *God's Grace in Your Suffering* (Wheaton, IL: Crossway, 2018), 38–39. Copyright ©2018. Used by

permission of Crossway, a publishing ministry of Good News Publishers, Wheaton, IL 60187, www.crossway.org.

April 12.   Taken from *Seeing with New Eyes* (Philipsburg, NJ: P&R Publishers, 2003), 44–45. ISBN 9780875526089. Used with permission from P&R Publishing Company, P.O. Box 817, Philipsburg, NJ, 08865.

April 13.   "Reading Scripture with David Powlison," CCEF *On the Go* podcast, April 11, 2018, https://www.ccef.org/podcast/reading-scripture/.

April 14.   "A Personal Liturgy of Confession," *Journal of Biblical Counseling* 29, no. 2 (2015): 47–49.

April 15.   *Overcoming Anxiety: Relief for Worried People* (Greensboro, NC: New Growth Press, 2012), 12–13.

April 16.   *Safe and Sound: Standing Firm in Spiritual Battles* (Greensboro, NC: New Growth Press, 2019), 26–27.

April 17.   *Safe and Sound*, 28.

April 18.   CCEF 2011 "Dynamics of Biblical Change" video course (filmed at Westminster Theological Seminary), Lecture 1.

April 19.   "Dynamics of Biblical Change," Lecture 3.

April 20.   "Dynamics of Biblical Change," Lecture 4.

April 21.   "In It for Good," *Journal of Biblical Counseling* 26, no. 2 (2012): 2–3.

April 22.   "Intimacy with God," *Journal of Biblical Counseling* 16, no. 2 (1998): 2–3.

April 23.   *Good and Angry: Redeeming Anger, Irritation, Complaining, and Bitterness* (Greensboro, NC: New Growth Press, 2016), 125.

April 24.   *Good and Angry*, 89–90.

April 25.   *Overcoming Anxiety: Relief for Worried People* (Greensboro, NC: New Growth Press, 2012), 15–16.

April 26.	"How *Does* Sanctification Work?" Part 3, *Journal of Biblical Counseling* 31, no. 1 (2017): 16–17.
April 27.	"How *Does* Sanctification Work?" 22–23.
April 28.	CCEF 2015 Regional Conference: Anxiety: How God Cares for Stressed People, "Six Ways to Help an Anxious Person."
April 29.	CCEF 2013 National Conference: Not Alone: The Relational Core of Life and Counseling, General Session 1: "All Relationships Are Intentional."
April 30.	CCEF 2013 National Conference: "All Relationships Are Intentional."
May 1.	CCEF 2008 National Conference: The Addict in Us All, General Session 2: "Escape to Reality."
May 2.	"X-ray Questions: Drawing Out the Whys and Wherefores of Human Behavior," *Journal of Biblical Counseling* 18, no. 1 (1999): 2–3.
May 3.	CCEF 2003 National Conference: Hope for the Suffering, Breakout Session: "Psalm 119: God and Your Hardships."
May 4.	CCEF 2005 National Conference: Redeeming Anger in a World Gone Mad, General Session: "Redemption: A Merciful Anger."
May 5.	CCEF 2007 National Conference: Running Scared, Breakout Session: "Facing Death."
May 6.	"A 'Moderate' Makeover," *Journal of Biblical Counseling* 26, no. 3 (2012): 2–3.
May 7.	"Why Do We Pray?" CCEF blog, January 13, 2017, https://www.ccef.org/why-do-we-pray/.
May 8.	"Straight Talk," CCEF blog, March 28, 2016, https://www.ccef.org/straight-talk/.

May 9. "When Suffering Won't Go Away, Parts 1–3," CCEF *Help and Hope* podcast, September 2–4, 2016, https://www.ccef.org/podcast/when-suffering-wont-go-away-part-1/; https://www.ccef.org/podcast/when-suffering-wont-go-away-part-2/; https://www.ccef.org/podcast/when-suffering-wont-go-away-part-3/.

May 10. "Anger Part 1: Understanding Anger," *Journal of Biblical Counseling* 14, no. 1 (1995): 53.

May 11. "Getting to the Heart of Conflict: Anger, Part 3," *Journal of Biblical Counseling* 16, no. 1 (1997): 42.

May 12. "The Fear of Christ is the Beginning of Wisdom," *Journal of Biblical Counseling* 17, no. 2 (1999): 50.

May 13. "What If Your Father Didn't Love You?" *Journal of Biblical Counseling* 12, no. 1 (1993): 1–3.

May 14. "Queries and Controversies," *Journal of Biblical Counseling* 12, no. 3 (1993): 45.

May 15. "How the Bible Gets Personal," *Journal of Biblical Counseling* 29, no. 2 (2015): 4–6.

May 16. "An Open Letter to the Suffering Christian," CCEF blog, March 21, 2018, https://www.ccef.org/open-letter-suffering-christian/. Originally published in Crossway article, "An Open Letter to the Suffering Christian." Published and used by permission of Crossway, a publishing ministry of Good News Publishers, Wheaton, IL, 60187, www.crossway.org.

May 17. "An Open Letter to Those Who Are Apathetic about Their Sanctification." CCEF blog, June 12, 2017, https://www.ccef.org/open-letter-apathetic-sanctification/.

May 18. "Anger Part 1: Understanding Anger," *Journal of Biblical Counseling* 14, no. 1 (1995): 41.

May 19. "Getting to the Heart of Conflict: Anger, Part 3," *Journal of Biblical Counseling* 16, no. 1 (1997): 32–34.

May 20.	"Getting to the Heart of Conflict: Anger, Part 3," 34–37.
May 21.	CCEF 2015, Regional Conference: Anxiety: How God Cares for Stressed People, Session 2: "Practical Steps toward Change."
May 22.	CCEF 2012 National Conference: Guilt & Shame, Breakout Session: "Low Self-Esteem."
May 23.	CCEF 2012 National Conference: "Low Self-Esteem."
May 24.	CCEF 2009 National Conference: Sex Matters, General Session 3: "Jesus Our Redeemer."
May 25.	"X-ray Questions: Drawing Out the Whys and Wherefores of Human Behavior," *Journal of Biblical Counseling* 18, no. 1 (1999): 3, 8.
May 26.	"X-ray Questions," 4, 7.
May 27.	CCEF 2008 National Conference: The Addict in Us All, Breakout Session: "Addicted to Religion."
May 28.	"Think Globally, Act Locally," *Journal of Biblical Counseling* 22, no. 1 (1999): 2–3.
May 29.	"Think Globally, Act Locally," 3–4.
May 30.	"How *Does* Sanctification Work? Part 1," *Journal of Biblical Counseling* 27, no. 1 (2013): 61.
May 31.	*Controlling Anger: Responding Constructively When Life Goes Wrong* (Greensboro, NC: New Growth Press, 2012), 20–21, 23.
June 1.	CCEF 2011 "Dynamics of Biblical Change" video course (filmed at Westminster Theological Seminary), Lecture 11.
June 2.	"Dynamics of Biblical Change," Lecture 7.
June 3.	"Dynamics of Biblical Change," Lecture 6.
June 4.	"Dynamics of Biblical Change," Lecture 6.
June 5.	"Dynamics of Biblical Change," Lecture 9.

June 6.   "Dynamics of Biblical Change," Lecture 13.

June 7.   "Dynamics of Biblical Change," Lecture 17.

June 8.   "Dynamics of Biblical Change," Lecture 19.

June 9.   *I'm Exhausted: What to Do When You're Always Tired* (Greensboro, NC: New Growth Press, 2010), 8–9.

June 10.   *I'm Exhausted*, 17–18.

June 11.   *Recovering from Child Abuse: Healing and Hope for Victims* (Greensboro, NC: New Growth Press, 2008), 21–24.

June 12.   *Grieving a Suicide: Help for the Aftershock* (Greensboro, NC: New Growth Press, 2010), 8–10.

June 13.   "Anger Part 1: Understanding Anger," *Journal of Biblical Counseling* 14, no. 1, (1995): 42.

June 14.   "Intimacy with God," *Journal of Biblical Counseling* 16, no. 2 (1998): 4.

June 15.   CCEF 2016, Regional Conference: Everyday Worship: How God Brings the Bible to Life, Session 1: "What Makes Words Relevant?"

June 16.   CCEF 2016 Regional Conference: Session 3: "Martin Luther's 3 Masters."

June 17.   Taken from *Seeing with New Eyes: Counseling and the Human Condition through the Lens of Scripture* (Philipsburg, NJ: P&R Publishers, 2003), 46–47. ISBN 9780875526089. Used with permission from P&R Publishing Company, P.O. Box 817, Philipsburg, NJ, 08865.

June 18.   *Good and Angry: Redeeming Anger, Irritation, Complaining, and Bitterness* (Greensboro, NC: New Growth Press, 2016), 194 –95.

June 19.   *Good and Angry*, 73–74.

June 20.   *Good and Angry*, 77–78.

June 21.   *Good and Angry*, 84–85.

June 22.   *When Cancer Interrupts* (Greensboro, NC: New Growth Press, 2015), 11–13.

June 23.   *Overcoming Anxiety: Relief for Worried People* (Greensboro, NC: New Growth Press, 2012), 11–12.

June 24.   *Overcoming Anxiety*, 13–15.

June 25.   *Speaking Truth in Love: Counsel in Community* (Greensboro, NC: New Growth Press, 2005), 42–43.

June 26.   *Speaking Truth in Love*, 33–34.

June 27.   *Speaking Truth in Love*, 35.

June 28.   *Speaking Truth in Love*, 57–58.

June 29.   CCEF 2011 "Dynamics of Biblical Change" video course (filmed at Westminster Theological Seminary), Lecture 17.

June 30.   "Dynamics of Biblical Change," Lecture 19.

July 1.   *Safe and Sound: Standing Firm in Spiritual Battles* (Greensboro, NC: New Growth Press, 2019), 29–30.

July 2.   *Safe and Sound*, 30–31.

July 3.   *Safe and Sound*, 32–33.

July 4.   *Safe and Sound*, 33–34.

July 5.   *Safe and Sound*, 36–37.

July 6.   CCEF 2016 Regional Conference: Everyday Worship, Session 4: "Other People Make a Difference."

July 7.   CCEF 2015 Regional Conference: Anxiety, Session 2: "Practical Steps toward Change."

July 8.   CCEF 2015 Regional Conference: Anxiety, Session 4: "Where Do We Go from Here?"

July 9.   CCEF 2013 National Conference: Not Alone, General Session 1: "All Relationships Are Intentional."

July 10.	CCEF 2013 National Conference: Not Alone, Breakout Session: "How Can Talking about Yourself Help Someone Else?"
July 11.	CCEF 2008 National Conference: The Addict in Us All, General Session 2: "Escape to Reality."
July 12.	CCEF 2008 National Conference: "Escape to Reality."
July 13.	CCEF 2003 National Conference: Hope for the Suffering, Breakout Session: "Psalm 119: God and Your Hardships."
July 14.	Taken from *God's Grace in Your Suffering* (Wheaton, IL: Crossway, 2018), 15. Copyright ©2018. Used by permission of Crossway, a publishing ministry of Good News Publishers, Wheaton, IL 60187, www.crossway.org.
July 15.	"How the Bible Gets Personal," *Journal of Biblical Counseling* 29, no. 2 (2015): 3–4.
July 16.	*Speaking Truth in Love: Counsel in Community* (Greensboro, NC: New Growth Press, 2005), 99–101.
July 17.	*Facing Death with Hope: Living for What Lasts* (Greensboro, NC: New Growth Press, 2008), 9–10.
July 18.	*Facing Death with Hope*, 13, 18.
July 19.	*Breaking the Addictive Cycle: Deadly Obsessions or Simple Pleasures?* (Greensboro, NC: New Growth Press, 2010), 25–27.
July 20.	"Counsel and Counseling," *Journal of Biblical Counseling* 32, no. 1 (2018): 3.
July 21.	"What Can You Do When God Seems Far Away?" *Journal of Biblical Counseling* 30, no. 3 (2016): 2–3.
July 22.	"What Can You Do When God Seems Far Away?" 5.
July 23.	"Resisting Idols of the Heart and Vanity Fair," *Journal of Biblical Counseling* 27, no. 3 (2013): 37–38.
July 24.	"Resisting Idols of the Heart and Vanity Fair," 41.

July 25.	CCEF 2011 "Dynamics of Biblical Change" video course (filmed at Westminster Theological Seminary), Lecture 1.
July 26.	"Dynamics of Biblical Change," Lecture 2.
July 27.	"Dynamics of Biblical Change," Lecture 2.
July 28.	"Dynamics of Biblical Change," Lecture 2.
July 29.	"Dynamics of Biblical Change," Lecture 18.
July 30.	"Dynamics of Biblical Change," Lecture 3.
July 31.	"Dynamics of Biblical Change," Lecture 3.
August 1.	"Dynamics of Biblical Change," Lecture 4.
August 2.	"Dynamics of Biblical Change," Lecture 4.
August 3.	"Dynamics of Biblical Change," Lecture 5.
August 4.	"Dynamics of Biblical Change," Lecture 6.
August 5.	*Good and Angry: Redeeming Anger, Irritation, Complaining, and Bitterness* (Greensboro, NC: New Growth Press, 2016), 86–88.
August 6.	*Good and Angry*, 90–91.
August 7.	*Good and Angry*, 67, 69.
August 8.	"A Man's Identity," *Journal of Biblical Counseling* 34, no. 1 (2020): 80–81.
August 9.	"The Right Kind of Weakness," *Journal of Biblical Counseling* 33, no. 2 (2019): 4–5.
August 10.	"The Right Kind of Weakness," 3–4.
August 11.	"What Can You Do When God Seems Far Away?" *Journal of Biblical Counseling* 30, no. 3 (2016): 5–6.
August 12.	"Sex, Truth, and Scripture," *Journal of Biblical Counseling* 13, no. 3 (1995): 2–3.

August 13. CCEF 2016 Regional Conference: Everyday Worship: How God Brings the Bible to Life, Session 1: "What Makes Words Relevant?"

August 14. CCEF 2016 Regional Conference: Session 2: "Learning to Ask the Right Questions."

August 15. CCEF 2016 Regional Conference: Session 3: "Martin Luther's 3 Masters."

August 16. CCEF 2016 Regional Conference: Session 4: "Other People Make a Difference."

August 17. CCEF 2015 Regional Conference: Anxiety: How God Cares for Stressed People, General Session: "Six Ways to Help an Anxious Person."

August 18. "'Peace, Be Still:' Learning Psalm 131 by Heart," *Journal of Biblical Counseling* 18, no. 3 (2000): 2–3.

August 19. "'Peace, Be Still:' Learning Psalm 131 by Heart," 3–5.

August 20. CCEF 2007 National Conference: Running Scared, Breakout Session: "Gripping Fears."

August 21. "Don't Worry," *Journal of Biblical Counseling* 21, no. 2 (2003): 55, 59, 61, 63.

August 22. "Don't Worry," 64–65.

August 23. "How *Does* Sanctification Work? Part 2" *Journal of Biblical Counseling* 27, no. 2 (2013): 41–43, 48.

August 24. "How the Bible Gets Personal," *Journal of Biblical Counseling* 29, no. 2 (2015): 6–8.

August 25. "Why Do We Pray?" CCEF blog, January 13, 2017, https://www.ccef.org/why-do-we-pray/.

August 26. "Should We Really Call It a 'Quiet' Time?" CCEF blog, November 12, 2009, https://www.ccef.org/should-we-really-call-it-quiet-time/.

August 27. "Should We Really Call It a 'Quiet' Time?" https://www.ccef.org/should-we-really-call-it-quiet-time/.

August 28.   "Straight Talk," CCEF blog, March 28, 2016, https://www.ccef.org/straight-talk/.

August 29.   Taken from *Seeing with New Eyes* (Philipsburg, NJ: P&R Publishers, 2003), 121. ISBN 9780875526089. Used with permission from P&R Publishing Company, P.O. Box 817, Philipsburg, NJ, 08865.

August 30.   "Resisting Idols of the Heart and Vanity Fair," *Journal of Biblical Counseling* 27, no. 3 (2013): 42.

August 31.   "Resisting Idols of the Heart and Vanity Fair," 43–44.

September 1. *Safe and Sound: Standing Firm in Spiritual Battles* (Greensboro, NC: New Growth Press, 2019), 80–81.

September 2. Taken from *God's Grace in Your Suffering* (Wheaton, IL: Crossway, 2018), 115–16. Copyright ©2018. Used by permission of Crossway, a publishing ministry of Good News Publishers, Wheaton, IL 60187, www.crossway.org.

September 3. *I Just Want to Die: Replacing Suicidal Thoughts with Hope* (Greensboro, NC: New Growth Press, 2010), 20–21.

September 4. *Breaking the Addictive Cycle: Deadly Obsessions or Simple Pleasures?* (Greensboro, NC: New Growth Press, 2010), 14–15.

September 5. "How *Does* Sanctification Work?" Part 3, *Journal of Biblical Counseling* 31:1 (2017): 13–14.

September 6. "How *Does* Sanctification Work?" Part 3, 15–16.

September 7. "How *Does* Sanctification Work?" Part 3, 16.

September 8. "How *Does* Sanctification Work?" Part 3, 19–20.

September 9. "How *Does* Sanctification Work?" Part 3, 20–22.

September 10. "Getting Oriented," *Journal of Biblical Counseling* 30, no. 1 (2016): 6–7.

September 11. "An Invitation to Speak Up!" *Journal of Biblical Counseling* 29, no. 3 (2015): 5.

September 12. CCEF 2011 "Dynamics of Biblical Change" video course (filmed at Westminster Theological Seminary), Lecture 2.

September 13. "Dynamics of Biblical Change," Lecture 12.

September 14. "Dynamics of Biblical Change," Lecture 5.

September 15. "Dynamics of Biblical Change," Lecture 5.

September 16. "Dynamics of Biblical Change," Lecture 7.

September 17. "Dynamics of Biblical Change," Lecture 7.

September 18. "Dynamics of Biblical Change," Lecture 15.

September 19. "Dynamics of Biblical Change," Lecture 16.

September 20. "Dynamics of Biblical Change," Lecture 17.

September 21. "Dynamics of Biblical Change," Lecture 18.

September 22. "Dynamics of Biblical Change," Lecture 18.

September 23. "Dynamics of Biblical Change," Lectures 19 and 20.

September 24. *Safe and Sound: Standing Firm in Spiritual Battles* (Greensboro, NC: New Growth Press, 2019), 12–14.

September 25. *Safe and Sound*, 47–49.

September 26. *Controlling Anger: Responding Constructively When Life Goes Wrong* (Greensboro, NC: New Growth Press, 2012), 17–20.

September 27. *Controlling Anger*, 12–14.

September 28. "Anger Part 1: Understanding Anger," *Journal of Biblical Counseling* 14, no. 1 (1995): 52.

September 29. CCEF 2012 National Conference: Guilt & Shame, Breakout Session: "Low Self-Esteem."

September 30. CCEF 2009 National Conference: Sex Matters, General Session: "Jesus Our Redeemer."

October 1. CCEF 2014 National Conference: Loss: Finding Hope That Lasts When Life Falls Apart, General Session 1: "All Is Lost."

October 2. CCEF 2014 National Conference: "All Is Lost."

October 3. CCEF 2014 National Conference: "All Is Lost."

October 4. "An Open Letter to Those Frustrated by Their Progress in Sanctification," CCEF blog, June 5, 2017, https://www.ccef.org/on-sanctification-part-1/.

October 5. "How Can Christ Help Me Overcome My Sinful Past?" CCEF *Help and Hope* podcast, July 10, 2016, https://www.ccef.org/podcast/how-can-christ-help-me-overcome-my-sinful-past/.

October 6. CCEF 2012 National Conference: Guilt & Shame, General Session 3: "Guilt & Shame with Jesus."

October 7. "How *Does* Sanctification Work? Part 2," *Journal of Biblical Counseling* 27, no. 2 (2013): 45, 50.

October 8. "How *Does* Sanctification Work? Part 2," 45–47, 50.

October 9. "How *Does* Sanctification Work? Part 2," 47–48.

October 10. *When Cancer Interrupts* (Greensboro, NC: New Growth Press, 2015), 13–14.

October 11. *When Cancer Interrupts*, 10–11.

October 12. *Speaking Truth in Love: Counsel in Community* (Greensboro, NC: New Growth Press, 2005), 55–56.

October 13. *Speaking Truth in Love*, 58–59.

October 14. *Speaking Truth in Love*, 56–57, 61.

October 15. *I Just Want to Die: Replacing Suicidal Thoughts with Hope* (Greensboro, NC: New Growth Press, 2010), 3, 7–8.

October 16. CCEF 2011 "Dynamics of Biblical Change" video course (filmed at Westminster Theological Seminary), Lecture 1.

October 17. "Dynamics of Biblical Change," Lecture 3.

October 18. "Dynamics of Biblical Change," Lecture 9.

October 19. "Dynamics of Biblical Change," Lecture 16.

October 20. *Good and Angry: Redeeming Anger, Irritation, Complaining, and Bitterness* (Greensboro, NC: New Growth Press, 2016), 46, 54, 58.

October 21. *Good and Angry*, 54–55, 57, 59.

October 22. *Good and Angry*, 63–64.

October 23. *Good and Angry*, 80–82.

October 24. *Speaking Truth in Love*, 36.

October 25. *Speaking Truth in Love*, 43.

October 26. *Speaking Truth in Love*, 43–44.

October 27. *Speaking Truth in Love*, 44–45.

October 28. *Speaking Truth in Love*, 167–68.

October 29. "Dynamics of Biblical Change," Lecture 5.

October 30. "Dynamics of Biblical Change," Lecture 5.

October 31. "Dynamics of Biblical Change," Lecture 5.

November 1. CCEF 2011 "Dynamics of Biblical Change" video course (filmed at Westminster Theological Seminary), Lecture 5.

November 2. "Dynamics of Biblical Change," Lecture 19.

November 3 "What Do You Feel?" *Journal of Biblical Counseling* 10, no. 4 (1992): 58–60.

November 4. "Your Looks: What the Voices Say and the Images Portray," *Journal of Biblical Counseling* 15, no. 2 (1997): 39, 42–43.

November 5. "Don't Worry," *Journal of Biblical Counseling* 21, no. 2 (2003): 55, 57–58, 63–64.

November 6. "The Sufficiency of Scripture to Diagnose and Cure Souls," *Journal of Biblical Counseling* 23, no. 2 (2004): 4.

November 7. "The Sufficiency of Scripture to Diagnose and Cure Souls," 5–6, 11.

November 8. "The Sufficiency of Scripture to Diagnose and Cure Souls," 11–13.

November 9. "I Am Making All Things New," *Journal of Biblical Counseling* 24, no. 4 (2006): 2.

November 10. "I Am Making All Things New," 2–4.

November 11. "How *Does* Sanctification Work? Part 2" *Journal of Biblical Counseling* 27, no. 2 (2013): 37–39, 44.

November 12. CCEF 2005 National Conference: Redeeming Anger in a World Gone Mad, General Session 2: "Creation (A Just Anger) and Fall (A Corrupt Anger)."

November 13. CCEF 2005 National Conference: Redeeming Anger in a World Gone Mad, General Session 3: "Redemption—A Merciful Anger."

November 14. CCEF 2005 National Conference: Redeeming Anger in a World Gone Mad, General Session 4: "Sanctification: A Transforming Anger."

November 15. "Anger Part 2: Three Lies about Anger and the Transforming Truth," *Journal of Biblical Counseling* 14, no. 2 (1996): 13–14.

November 16. CCEF 2014 National Conference: Loss: Finding Hope That Lasts When Life Falls Apart, General Session 1: "All Is Lost."

November 17. *Safe and Sound: Standing Firm in Spiritual Battles* (Greensboro, NC: New Growth Press, 2019), 55–58.

November 18. *Recovering from Child Abuse: Healing and Hope for Victims* (Greensboro, NC: New Growth Press, 2008), 4–5, 7–8.

November 19. *Safe and Sound: Standing Firm in Spiritual Battles* (Greensboro, NC: New Growth Press, 2019), 23.

November 20. "How *Does* Sanctification Work? Part 1" *Journal of Biblical Counseling* 27, no. 1 (2013): 53–55.

November 21. "Dynamics of Biblical Change," Lecture 17.

November 22. "Dynamics of Biblical Change," Lecture 17.

November 23. Taken from *God's Grace in Your Suffering* by David Powlison, Copyright ©2018, pp. 27–28. Used by permission of Crossway, a publishing ministry of Good News Publishers, Wheaton, IL 60187, www.crossway.org.

November 24. "Dynamics of Biblical Change," Lecture 16.

November 25. "Thankfulness," CCEF blog, November 16, 2016, https://www.ccef.org/thankfulness/.

November 26. "How *Does* Sanctification Work? Part 1," *Journal of Biblical Counseling* 27, no. 1 (2013): 56–58.

November 27. "How *Does* Sanctification Work? Part 1," 65–66.

November 28. "Counsel and Counseling," *Journal of Biblical Counseling* 32, no. 1 (2018): 6.

November 29. "How the Bible Gets Personal," *Journal of Biblical Counseling* 29, no. 2 (2015): 2–3.

November 30. "Reading Scripture with David Powlison," CCEF *On the Go* podcast, April 11, 2018, https://www.ccef.org/podcast/reading-scripture/.

December 1. "Psalm 103," CCEF *On the Go* podcast, April 5, 2017, https://www.ccef.org/podcast/psalm-103-david-powlison/.

December 2. Taken from *Seeing with New Eyes*, pp. 48–49, ISBN 9780875526089. Used with permission from P&R Publishing Company, P.O. Box 817, Philipsburg, NJ, 08865.

December 3. "How *Does* Sanctification Work? Part 2" *Journal of Biblical Counseling* 27, no, 2 (2013), 35–36.

December 4. Personal journal entry, 1/1/1998, supplied by Nan Powlison.

December 5. "How *Does* Sanctification Work? Part 1," *Journal of Biblical Counseling* 27, no. 1 (2013): 49, 51–52.

December 6. *Speaking Truth in Love: Counsel in Community* (Greensboro, NC: New Growth Press, 2005), 65.

December 7. CCEF 2011 "Dynamics of Biblical Change" video course (filmed at Westminster Theological Seminary), Lecture 7.

December 8. "Dynamics of Biblical Change," Lecture 7.

December 9. "Dynamics of Biblical Change," Lecture 7.

December 10. *Good and Angry: Redeeming Anger, Irritation, Complaining, and Bitterness* (Greensboro, NC: New Growth Press, 2016), 39, 41–42.

December 11. *Good and Angry*, 121–22.

December 12. *Good and Angry*, 130.

December 13. "Dynamics of Biblical Change," Lecture 12.

December 14. "Dynamics of Biblical Change," Lecture 12.

December 15. *Controlling Anger: Responding Constructively When Life Goes Wrong* (Greensboro, NC: New Growth Press, 2012), 6–10.

December 16. "Dynamics of Biblical Change," Lecture 16.

December 17. "Innocent Pleasures," *Journal of Biblical Counseling* 23, no. 4 (2005): 22–23.

December 18. "Who Is God?" *Journal of Biblical Counseling* 17, no. 2 (1999): 14–15.

December 19. "Doing 'Wicked Good' Practical Theology," *Journal of Biblical Counseling* 24, no. 1 (2006): 2–3.

December 20. "Does the Shoe Fit?" *Journal of Biblical Counseling* 20, no. 3 (2002): 2–3.

December 21. Taken from *God's Grace in Your Suffering* by David Powlison, Copyright ©2018, pp. 82–83. Used by permission of Crossway, a publishing ministry of Good News Publishers, Wheaton, IL 60187, www.crossway.org.

December 22. "The God of All Comfort," *Journal of Biblical Counseling* 31, no. 3 (2017): 7–13.

December 23. "Dynamics of Biblical Change," Lecture 16.

December 24. "The Therapeutic Gospel," *Journal of Biblical Counseling* 25, no. 3 (2007): 3–4.

December 25. "Emmanuel Shall Come to You," CCEF blog, December 21, 2016, https://www.ccef.org/emmanuel-shall-come/.

December 26. "Dynamics of Biblical Change," Lecture 1.

December 27. *Recovering from Child Abuse: Healing and Hope for Victims* (Greensboro, NC: New Growth Press, 2008), 16–18, 20–21.

December 28. "'I'll Never Get over It'—Helped for the Aggrieved," *Journal of Biblical Counseling* 28, no. 1 (2014): 10–11.

December 29. "Innocent Pleasures," *Journal of Biblical Counseling* 23, no. 4 (2005): 22.

December 30. "Innocent Pleasures," 25.

December 31. Taken from *God's Grace in Your Suffering* by David Powlison, Copyright ©2018, pp. 78–79. Used by permission of Crossway, a publishing ministry of Good News Publishers, Wheaton, IL 60187, www.crossway.org.

David's Favorite Hymns

"Alas! and Did My Savior Bleed" by Isaac Watts (1707)

"Be Still, My Soul" by Katharina von Schlegel (1752)

"Be Thou My Vision" by Dallán Forgaill (6th century)

"Come Thou Fount of Every Blessing" by Robert Robinson (1757)

"Fairest Lord Jesus" (Anonymous)

"Great Is Thy Faithfulness" by Thomas Chisholm (1923)

"How Firm a Foundation" by John Rippon (1787)

"I Bind unto Myself Today" (St. Patrick's Hymn) by St. Patrick

"It Is Well with My Soul" by Horatio Spafford (1873)

"Joy to the World" by Isaac Watts (1719)

"Love Divine, All Loves Excelling" by Charles Wesley (1747)

"My Song Is Love Unknown" by Samuel Crossman (1664)

"None Other Lamb" by Christina Rossetti (1892)

"O Come, O Come, Emmanuel" (Anonymous, 9th-century Latin hymn)

"O, the Deep, Deep Love of Jesus" by Samuel Trevor Francis (1875)

"Rock of Ages" by Augustus Toplady (1776)

"Take My Life and Let It Be" by Frances R. Havergal (1874)

"Wake, Awake, for Night Is Flying" by Catherine Winkworth and Philipp Nicolai (1599)

"We Rest on Thee" by Edith G. Cherry (1895)

Index

"The introduction from Nan is a gift in itself. Then you get to settle into David's gentle and personal words about his personal God, each devotion being much more than mere education. Each one invites you to love God and respond to him."

Edward T. Welch, Faculty and counselor, Christian Counseling and Educational Foundation (CCEF); author of *A Small Book about Why We Hide*

"What a great book! Even with all his learning, David approaches Scripture like a child. So you will too when you read Scripture through David's eyes. The result of David's insights is hope. You'll get unstuck from your problems and look out at a wider world of God's love!"

Paul E. Miller, Author of *A Praying Life* and *J-Curve: Dying and Rising with Jesus in Everyday Life*

"Reading anything by the man who defined a generation of biblical counseling, the late counselor, theologian, author, and my dear friend, David Powlison, is a profound privilege. But reading words from his heart straight to yours, a brief conversation daily about your Lord with such a wise mentor? Few gifts will ever match it."

J. Alasdair Groves, Executive Director of the Christian Counseling and Educational Foundation (CCEF); coauthor of *Untangling Emotions*

"If I could have a few minutes of wise counsel every day from any man of my choosing, it would be David Powlison. Now, thanks to *Take Heart: Daily Devotions to Deepen Your Faith*, I can. So can you. We can still be helped, every day, by David's profound insights into the endless grace of Christ."

Ray Ortlund, Renewal Ministries, Nashville, TN; author of *The Death of Porn: Men of Integrity Building a World of Nobility*

"I am so grateful for this collection and so thankful that it allows me to enjoy daily wisdom from a man who was a tremendous blessing to me and a great gift to the church. I look forward to reading it day by day and year after year."

Tim Challies, Author of *Seasons of Sorrow*

"I was privileged to know David as professor, colleague, friend, and fellow traveler to the Celestial City. He arrived at the destination ahead of me, and I miss his voice and his wisdom. This beautiful devotional is a fresh mercy to all of us in the midst of David's absence, reminding us that 'through his faith, though he died, he still speaks' (Hebrews 11:4)."

Michael R. Emlet, Dean of Faculty and Counselor, CCEF; author of *Saints, Sufferers, and Sinners: Loving Others as God Loves Us*

"Like Oswald Chambers, David Powlison died too young. But also like Chambers, his wife and others have captured his wisdom for the ages. Powlison had a rare mind and heart, and these devotions beautifully capture his humility, originality, and profundity. Read and enjoy."

Os Guinness, Author of *The Call*

"Though David Powlison is greatly missed, he has left behind a considerable legacy. These daily devotions are full of wisdom, encouragement, and realism. They cover every human topic from fear to dependency to doubt, without ever slouching into either sentimentality or moralism. Each of them is gospel-driven. I plan to start my day with them, and I hope you will too."

William Edgar, Professor of Apologetics, Westminster Theological Seminary

"Oak trees of wisdom fill these acorn devotionals. David doesn't write *at* you—you sense he is sitting *with* you. His warmth simply radiates. These pages are likely to be in print a long time."

Steve Estes, Pastor; author of *A Better December*; coauthor of *When God Weeps*

"The combination of deep wisdom and practical application condensed into each day of *Take Heart* is mind blowing. Imagine sitting down over coffee and God's Word each day with one of the wisest, most caring, godly biblical counselors, and you will have a glimpse into this excellent work. It is one I will turn to year after year in my own personal devotions. Everyone who knew David Powlison or was blessed by his ministry will be blessed by this gift."

Curtis W. Solomon, PhD, Executive Director, The Biblical Counseling Coalition

"David Powlison had an inimitable ability to make Scripture come alive. In this posthumous work, David walks alongside us as both trusted friend and counselor, showing us the wonder of God's grace. I miss David's voice and presence, but I am thankful for opportunities like this where his encouragement and counsel can continue to be a part of my walk with the Lord. I trust it will be for you as well."

Jonathan D. Holmes, Pastor of Counseling, Parkside Church; executive director, Fieldstone Counseling

"David Powlison once again shows his natural way of shepherding people. His words breathe hope and comfort to your soul. *Take Heart* will remind you of God's unfailing commitment to you and your need to draw near to him."

Julie E. Lowe, MA, LPC, RPT-S, Faculty and Counselor, CCEF

"Whenever I had the privilege of speaking with my friend David Powlison, my faith was strengthened. Part of my sadness when David died was knowing that this side of heaven, I would never hear that voice again. Imagine my surprise and delight to learn that this daily devotional was being produced. Now I can hear from my friend again and be led afresh to the feet of our Savior."

Steve Viars, Senior Pastor, Faith Church, Lafayette, IN

"These short and meditative daily readings are presented like a brief word with David Powlison over coffee each day. As David always did, his words invite you to see how God connects you to the realities of your experiences by anchoring you to the truth of God's Word. As you read, your heart will be turned to the Lord for encouragement and your affections stirred so that you 'take heart' in the finished work of Christ."

T. Dale Johnson Jr., PhD, Executive Director, The Association of Certified Biblical Counselors (ACBC); associate professor of biblical counseling and director of counseling programs, Midwestern Baptist Theological Seminary

"David Powlison's heart was set afire listening to the promises of God in Scripture. In *Take Heart* we are invited to sit with David and discover what he learned through his own suffering and brokenness. His words are tender, the insights wise, and the impact for those who listen life-changing. Read and fall in love with the God who loves you!"

Bob Kramer, College roommate and longtime best friend of David; founder and fellow of Nexus Insights; cofounder and former CEO of NIC

"In these short devotional thoughts, old truths are expressed in fresh ways and new insights abound. With keen insights drawn from his years of counselling and personal warmth rooted in his love of the Lord, these devotions are always captivating, always compelling, and always faithful to Scripture. They will help us love Jesus more, and with that David would have been well-pleased."

Steve Midgley, Executive Director of Biblical Counselling UK; senior minister of Christ Church, Cambridge

"David was a beacon in the Biblical Counselling movement. His ability to dig deeply into the biblical text and come out with nuances was in my view unsurpassed, as was his empathy and patience with struggling believers. I always looked forward to his articles on counselling. They were a refreshing waft of Holy Spirit insight. I look forward to continuing to use these meditations."

Raju Abraham, MBBS; MRCP(IRE); FRCP(LON) Neuropsychiatrist; cofounder of the Association of Biblical Counsellors in the UK and India

"When you go through David Powlison's daily devotions in *Take Heart*, be prepared to be surprised, delighted, encouraged, disturbed, and enlightened. David speaks to our hearts and enables us to connect deep spiritual truths to everyday life. Very essential for us in the 21st century when people are seeking to interpret daily events and are getting confused."

Ashok Chacko, MD, Director, Biblical Counseling Trust of India, New Delhi

"To read through David Powlinson's devotions is to take a dip into a deep well of contentment, springing from the well of living waters.

David's ability to take a verse from Scripture and apply it to the reader's heart flows from his love of God's Word and its power to change lives. This volume is aptly titled *Take Heart*, for it will lift one's spirits in daily service for Christ."

Glenn N. Davies, Former Archbishop of Sydney

"In these devotionals, David Powlison invites us to cultivate an intimate communion with God and to anchor ourselves in his promises. He encourages us to examine, transparently and honestly, where our affections lie, while at the same time showing us that change is possible when the Holy Spirit sheds God's love into our hearts through the gospel. David leads us to contemplate the living Christ in a very beautiful way, inviting us to experience his resurrection power and giving us a glorious hope for this present life and the life to come."

Eduardo Saladin, Pastor of Sola Gratia Biblical Church, Dominican Republic; certified biblical counselor (ACBC); board member at CCEF

"David Powlison's decades of counseling practice, his skill as a theologian and biblical exegete, and his own experience as a Christian pilgrim all go into making these devotionals pure gold. With this volume David can continue to be the wise guide for you that he has been for so many others."

Tim Keller, Pastor Emeritus, Redeemer Presbyterian Church

"My friend, David Powlison, had deep and abiding trust in the love, presence, power, promises, and grace of his Lord. David was a master at mining the life-giving and life-changing wisdom of God's Word. As a seasoned counselor, David had a deep understanding of the hearts of people. These things together make David a supremely qualified devotional guide. This devotional collection of David's writings is a treasure. Get it and let your heart marinate in the gospel that sweetly flows from every page."

Paul David Tripp, Pastor; speaker; author of *New Morning Mercies: A Daily Gospel Devotional*

"We now have in this long-awaited book the most pristine gems of wisdom from David Powlison, perhaps the most renowned and respected biblical counselor of our age. Over the years, I have thrived on David's writings, and I'm so glad he is now speaking to a new generation of readers through *Take Heart*."

Joni Eareckson Tada, Joni and Friends International Disability Center

"What if you could wake up each morning, read God's Word, and have one of his beloved servants give you a morsel of wisdom to savor and to meditate on throughout the day? These short but wisdom-packed pages from the pen of David Powlison will edify and encourage you in your daily journey."

Justin Taylor, Managing Editor, *ESV Study Bible*; author; blogger

Christian Counseling & Educational Foundation

CCEF's mission is to restore Christ to

counseling and counseling to the church

by thinking biblically about the issues

of living in order to equip the church to

meet counseling-related needs.

For other resources like these,
please visit **ccef.org**